REMINISCENCE

Social & Creative Activities

WITH OLDER PEOPLE IN CARE

Sim

This book is dedicated to Carole Sutton, who helped me to 'know, understand, experience and give'.

Titles in the **Speechmark Editions** series:

Accent Method: A Rational Voice Therapy in Theory & Practice, Kirsten Thyme-Frøkjær & Børge Frøkjær-Jensen

Beyond Aphasia: Therapies for Living with Communication Disability, Carole Pound, Susie Parr, Jayne Lindsay & Celia Woolf

Challenging Behaviour in Dementia: A person-centred approach, Graham Stokes

Counselling with Reality Therapy, Robert E Wubbolding & John Brickell

Elder Abuse: Therapeutic Perspectives in Practice, Andrew Papadopoulos & Jenny la Fontaine

Essential Dementia Care Handbook, edited by Graham Stokes & Fiona Goudie

Family Therapy with Older Adults & their Families, Alison Marriott

Human Communication: A Linguistic Introduction, Graham Williamson

Manual of AAC Assessment, Arlene McCurtin & Geraldine Murray

Person-Centred Approaches to Dementia Care, Ian Morton

Reminiscence: Social & Creative Activities with Older People in Care, Roger Sim

Teamwork: A Guide to Successful Collaboration in Health & Social Care, Sue Hutchings, Judy Hall & Barbara Lovelady

REMINISCENCE

Social & Creative Activities

WITH OLDER PEOPLE IN CARE

Roger Sim

Speechmark

www.speechmark.net

First published in 2003 by
Speechmark Publishing Ltd, 70 Alston Drive, Bradwell Abbey,
Milton Keynes MK13 9HG, UK
Tel: +44 (0) 1908 326944   Fax: +44 (0) 1908 326960
www.speechmark.net

Reprinted 2000, 2003, 2006, 2008, 2010

002 3396/Printed in the United Kingdom by Hobbs

British Library Cataloguing in Publication Data
Sim, Roger
   Reminiscence: social & creative activities with older people in care.
   – (Speechmark editions)
   1. Reminiscing in old age – Therapeutic use 2. Social work with the aged
   3. Long-term care facilities – Recreational activities
   I. Title
   615.8'51'0846

ISBN 978 0 86388 493 1

Contents

About the Author

Roger Sim works as a freelance participatory arts and reminiscence facilitator with many years experience. He is currently a senior member of LIME (formerly Hospital Arts) located in the North West of England and has been responsible for projects involving older people and development of programmes of aural arts. Roger was co-founder and co-ordinator of the Salford-based Manchester Reminiscence Project, an arts organisation working with older people and staff in residential and healthcare, and co-ordinated *Spirit of the Valley*, Northamptonshire's Millennium Festival.

Trained as a community worker in Leicester and Manchester, Roger has been involved in numerous distinctive projects both within and outside of care. Among his most notable achievements is his book, *Reminiscence Social & Creative Activities with Older People in Care*, which was shortlisted for the prestigious Seebohm Trophy in 1998.

LIME (formerly Hospital Arts) acts as a channel between the arts world and the health world, enabling creative and positive outcomes. Emphasis is placed on consultative and collaborative artistic practice involving health service staff and those they serve. LIME considers that the arts have a key role to play in the health of the mind, body and spirit of individuals and their communities. Contact LIME at: www.limeart.org

Preface

L ast year as I was nearing what I supposed was the completion of this book, I had to spend a week as a patient on a hospital ward. While I lay on my bed with my notebook and my fruit I had an unexpected opportunity to reflect upon the implications of being 'in care'.

My senses were not impaired, but I did have to ask for help when I wanted to do anything that I could not do from my bed without curtains around me. The main emotional experience, apart from a sense of being at risk, was that of being totally reliant on others. This was not unpleasant initially and I could have got quite used to it, but as soon as I started to feel better I could barely tolerate the restraints necessarily placed upon me. I laid claim to a little red wheelchair which was used to take people to and fro, so that I could move around without having to ask for help. This little red wheelchair became a symbol of my independence of spirit. When the little red wheelchair was taken from me, which it was most of the time as it was the only one on the ward, I felt confined, frustrated and more than a little resentful.

A short way from me were two men, in their seventies, who every evening, as the sun went down, sat with each other and shared memories of times gone by. They needed no help to do this. They had no communication problems and were of similar age, background and culture. Their extensive and rambling discussions touched positively on many subjects and rarely expressed regret. The sharing and mutual support these men were able to give each other in this way helped them – they were as much in danger as at any time in their lives – to keep their spirits up and to cope with a difficult time. Although they had never met before, they had plenty in common and within a few days were the best of friends. These men didn't need help to reminisce, it came to them naturally and spontaneously. They gained pleasure, satisfaction and diversion from their storytelling. It was their little red wheelchair.

This book is for anyone who works with older people who need a little red wheelchair.

RS

Acknowledgements

It is not realistic to acknowledge all the people throughout the years who have contributed towards this book: hospital staff and patients, care home staff and residents, artists and reminiscence workers. I would like, though, to thank a few of those who have guided me along the way and to apologize to anyone I have left out – I'm thinking of you:

Dave 'n' Dave for being Dave 'n' Dave and getting me off my back-side in 1977; Dermot Healey for working with me to start the Manchester Reminiscence Project in the first place; Jane Bourne for working alongside me to keep it going and reminding me who is most important in this business; Christine Bull and Hospital Arts for funding me to do reminiscence work and trusting me to get on with it; staff and patients of Ladywell Hospital for putting up with me graciously between 1988 and 1996; Carol, who kept me kind of steady, helped considerably with the editing and without whom I would probably still be writing; Stephanie Martin and Winslow for being very, very patient.

To Ken Bates, Chris Agnew, Helen Davies, Claire Moore, John Woudberg, Peter Hughes, Brian Chapman, Georgie Morgan, Richard Coaten, Stuart Ashton, Langley Brown, Anna Todd, Liz Faunce, Helen Kitchen, Peter Senior, Sameena Hussein, Bert Santilly, Jack Sutton, Terry McGinty and all the other artists whose ideas I have 'borrowed' for this book, I am very grateful.

I want to thank and acknowledge especially Joan Poulson, Writer in Residence with the Manchester Reminiscence Project who complied and wrote material for *Window on Winwick, Ladywell Lives* and *Those*

Were Dream Days with, respectively, people in Winwick Hospital, Warrington, Ladywell Hospital, Salford and the Platt Day Hospital, Manchester Royal Infirmary, between 1991 and 1996. I have liberally quoted from contributors throughout this book and thank them all.

I wish to acknowledge artists Carol Davies, Carole Miles, Maggie Warren, Richard Conlon and residential care staff for allowing me to draw on their experiences and quote from reports submitted during residencies set up by myself on behalf of Wesminster Healthcare PLC and Arts for Health during 1994/5; also the residents of Westminster House, Cubbington who contributed to *Westminster Tales* for Richard Conlon.

Thank you to Mary and Harold Middleton who, with their friends, enjoyed reminiscing and gave me ideas for the 'themes' section.

Lastly, and especially, thank you and salutations to Jean Parker in Burton House, Withington Hospital, whose faith in me and in older people pointed me in the right direction.

The band has been playing some lovely old tunes
They drift through the bottles and the fallen balloons
So I hope you'll understand, when I take you by the hand
I just want to make you feel you
Can sit down and dance with me

We've been here for hours and we're both wondering why
We're watching the dancers and the evening go by
So I know you'll understand when I take you by the hand
I just want to make you feel you
Can sit down and dance with me.

(Courtesy of the Bungalow Boogaloo Band © 1995)

Introduction

Still here

Old age, something which happens to others, not to me.

Or so we think when young. Where do the years go?

I am a child at school, running home for tea, I am a girl going to dances, having a first date, my first boyfriend, laughing and giggling with friends knowing the latest pop songs, the latest fashions, my life exciting before me. Where has it all gone?

I look in the mirror and wonder who this old woman is. This envelope of flesh has deteriorated. I no longer have a trim figure and slim ankles. An ageing body is not a pretty sight.

Inside though — inside I am still me — the little girl, the bride. The mother of sons is still there. I can still be delighted by sunsets, by music and poetry.

I can still be interested in life though many of the people most dear to me have gone.

Please don't judge by outward appearances ... the essential me is still here.

(Dorothy Walling, *Ladywell Lives*)

I

Over the past couple of decades, in elderly people's residential and nursing homes, on hospital wards, in day centres, clubs and societies, 'doing' reminiscence has become a popular and widespread activity. Recall sessions and a host of associated activities are perceived as an appropriate and effective way of bringing pleasure and stimulation, meaning and purpose into the lives of older people who, for whatever reasons, and in varying degrees are in need of professional help and care. An explosion of interest in what old people have to say has made itself apparent in an astonishing variety of forms and has caught the imagination of thousands of people.

Reminiscence has provided the impetus and the context for an unprecedented degree of creative and imaginative stimulation amongst older people, including those of the fourth age, the elderly and frail, whose interests are frequently ignored. When used sensitively and appropriately in care settings, as something to do and as a context for doing things, reminiscence, and associated social and creative activity, enhances the quality of interaction between young and old and graces the experience of 'care', not only for those who are being cared for, but also for those who do the caring. Reminiscence acts as a foundation for communication and new friendships, for artistic endeavour and expression of individuality, for leisure and pleasure, for therapeutic activity and for education.

The concept of 'reminiscence' as it has unfolded in the last two decades no longer simply concerns 'remembering' but rather represents a value system and a way of working that aspires to bring the best from professional care itself. Reminiscence has come to represent an approach to the organization of social and creative activities in hospitals, old people's homes and other places where older people live, meet and socialize in groups. It has come to mean not only talking about times gone by, but also doing things together and doing things that have meaning and relevance to those involved. In this book I describe this broad diversity of activity as 'reminiscence work'.

The term 'reminiscence work' implies a whole range of interactive, creative and expressive activities that have a basis in the interests and past experiences of the people who participate in them. This spectrum of activity includes not only social groups and interactive sessions where people talk about their pasts, but also arts-based creative projects, oral history projects and activities that link with the surrounding community. It embraces the work of the care assistant who is trying to get people talking to each other, the social and activity programmes of the specially employed activity organizer or director, the carefully directed skills of the therapist and the more, and less, specialized activities of professional reminiscence workers, artists and performers.

Despite justified enthusiasm for reminiscence work, we must beware of taking claims made for its effectiveness too much for granted. Positive benefits are not attained as a simple matter of cause and effect but as a consequence of the quality and depth of attention given to the spiritual and emotional needs of those involved. Reminiscence is not a dose of medicine to be handed out at regular intervals to make older people feel better. If it is simply considered as yet another process or as the only thing old people are interested in doing, then we are not understanding the true potential. If when we try to organize appropriate activities we are really only making thoughtless assumptions about people's interests and limitations, we are not taking advantage of an exciting opportunity to increase our ability to understand those we care for. Reminiscence-based activities are a *context for involvement* with people on a personal and individual level.

When I first started working with old people in hospital I had, I can see now, a limited view of what reminiscence was and could be. I had some kind of perception that old people were something to do with black and white films, had experienced the Second World War and didn't like pop music. I was stereotyping people. I saw reminiscence inherently in terms of entertainment that was familiar to people. I struggled to find music and stimuli which that generation would recognize in order to make my work relevant to them. In my attempt to be appropriate I made gross assumptions and set up what was in fact a one-way process. I provided a stimulus and they reacted (or not). Although I was working with old people, they were in reality all different ages — chronologically and in terms of their own maturity and development.

I had not recognized then that the material required for my sessions was already there in the hearts and minds of the group participants. The art was in being able to inspire and stimulate recall by creating an atmosphere that encouraged and enabled people to share their experiences with me and with each other. Attempts to give a voice to those who are not heard, the invisible people hidden away in hospitals and old people's homes, will fail if we do not listen and respond to what those voices have to say to us. If what is expressed is not heard we are in danger of giving confirmation to those, including many old people themselves, who consider that the elderly live and belong to the past, locked into their memories with little or nothing to offer to younger generations, or indeed to the process of their own lives.

> All too often, elderly people do not have a voice. Decisions are made on their behalf. It may be said that they are unable to participate or that they won't want to. It has been clear to me that they do want to and are willing to try all kinds of new things. (Carol Davies, Artist in Residence, the Rhyl Nursing Home)

The arts, in a wide variety of guises, passive, interactive and creative, act as an ideal complementary companion to reminiscence work both as a means of stimulating activity and as a medium for expression of emotional and imaginative experience. As therapy, as decoration and as entertainment, the arts have long had a place in our hospitals and old people's homes, but now, more than ever before, not only do the arts offer possibilities for enriching the lives of participants, but the memories and stories of ordinary people who have had extraordinary lives are beginning to be perceived as able to enrich and transform the arts themselves. Artists, of all kinds, have found the care setting a fulfilling and stimulating environment to work in, finding older people willing and intriguing companions on a journey of exploration and discovery.

The arts have become, in some areas, and to one degree or another, an integral element of care provision. Established organizations especially promote creative endeavour by artists among people working, living and undergoing treatment in healthcare and, to a lesser extent, residential settings. Health and social services provision represents an increasingly significant source of funding and arena for creative arts activity.

I feel that art, as well as activities, has a vital role to play in these settings. If it wasn't appropriate then nothing would have happened over the last six months. That all kinds of things happened and developed was due to the residents. They responded in a very positive way. They all had creative abilities and a lot to contribute. (Carol Davies, Artist in Residence, the Rhyl Nursing Home)

Although the involvement of professional arts and reminiscence people is a welcome development for both caring institutions and the arts, it is a fact that in most residential and care settings the quality of experience of residents, patients and clients remains, appropriately, within the domain of the care staff, as always, mostly hard pressed and undervalued. It is these people who I hope will find useful ideas in these pages. This is not an academic book, full of tables, footnotes and cross-references. It is not a recipe book, there is no blueprint for action as such, although there are suggested avenues for exploration. I acknowledge that every situation, group and individual is different and encourage you to adapt useful ideas to suit your own circumstances and interests. There is no formula. When I nervously tried my first few reminiscence sessions, armed with pictures and suggested questions, my security blanket, I had still to realize that the only real obstacle to success was my own fear of failing. The way forward was to be marked by trial and error — and still is. I trust, though, that what I have to say will be of help to those of you who are either involved, or planning to be involved, in creating opportunities for older people whose options are, for physical, psychological or environmental reasons, more circumscribed than they have to be.

I have tried to summarize, simply but thoughtfully, what I have learnt and observed during several years working with older people, artists and care staff in long-term care contexts. There have sometimes been spectacular results, but more usually the simple satisfaction of knowing that some meaningful and enjoyable contact has been made with those who, too often, have little to do but wait. I have been lucky and privileged, not only to explore the fascinating world of long-term care, but also to have tasted the flavours of years before I was born in such a way that I feel, at times, as if I have been there. The capacity that older people, often in difficult situations, have for sharing, for humour, for endurance and for adventure, astonishes me still. As do those staff, who, often against the odds, still believe in what they do and still warmly care.

Read this book, read others, think about it all, discuss ideas with colleagues and clients — then (and you may already have done this) take a deep breath and 'Have A Go, Joe'.

What's in a name?

I had to decide how to refer to older people in care as a group, while trying to make it clear that people are all individuals and must not be lumped together in terms of their situation. At the same time, conventions change as to how groups are named — a name deemed acceptable in some circumstances becomes unacceptable in others. It is the subjective connotation we attach to a word that gives it a negative or positive meaning. I consider that the words we use, excluding those that are clearly derogatory, categorize people in the sense that they describe a relationship to another. In formal terms of their relationship to a hospital, a person is a patient; in an old people's home, a resident; in a club, a member; in a group, a participant; in a shop, a customer. This is not a description of the individual but describes an obligation, a 'contract', on the part of one to the other. The shop agrees to serve the customer, the hospital is committed to caring for the patient and so on with whatever commitments are contracted or customary. The name used describes the relationship and whatever that relationship implies. In the end it is the way that we are treated that is of most importance — not how we are referred to — as long as the language used is appropriate and not intentionally or inadvertently insulting.

Let me tell you of a hospital group who met especially to discuss how they should be officially described. The word 'geriatric' was universally loathed, with its dehumanizing connotations (people cannot be geriatrics any more than children can be paediatrics). 'Client' made one person think of prostitutes, while the term 'elder', generally considered to imply respect, was not a familiar term (though it is used in some situations and may yet catch on generally). 'User' was rather suspect, but 'senior citizen' was popular. 'Patient' (in a hospital setting) did not cause anyone a problem. There was a general mirthful consensus that 'old buggers' was an appropriate and apt description of those in the group.

After some further discussion, it was finally pointed out to me that it was we, the 'young whippersnappers', who were afraid of using the word 'old' and it was seriously agreed that this was what they were — 'old people', and proud of it. Old is not only the opposite of new, with a connotation of worn out and useless; it can refer equally to something that is respected, treasured and cherished, that has stood the test of time. Old is the opposite of young, but no value judgement need be implied by this: old can imply tradition and experience, longevity and meaning whilst young can imply inexperience and immaturity.

In this book I refer to older people interchangeably, and for variety, as clients, patients and residents, simply for convenience in this context. I use the term 'staff' when referring generally to nurses, care assistants and others whose job is to look after people in hospital and in care.

Looking forward to looking back

In earlier centuries, becoming aged would, for most people, be something to be held in dread. Unless one had private means or a secure family, old age was a sure route to the punitive workhouse and the onset of inevitable crippling pain and disability. Advances in medicine generally, the advent of geriatric specialities in the 1940s and wider availability of healthcare and welfare services have increased not only the length of time that people are active and mobile, but also the numbers of people living or spending time in institutional or 'care' settings. Professional carers have also become more concerned with the overall well-being of those in their care. A training manual for care assistants illustrates this when it instructs: 'You have to relate to people — to understand their psychological, emotional and social needs, to help keep mind and body active ... caring happens in all sorts of ways. It's an ongoing process — stimulating, chatting, listening sympathetically, nursing, reassuring, helping.'

Until recent years it was generally considered that to reminisce was not a 'good thing' and that looking back, thinking and talking about times gone by, led to unhealthy introspection, a lack of confidence in and unawareness of the present. The tendency was to associate reminiscence with abnormal ageing and mental ill health. From the 1960s onwards, a number of trends started to come together until, by the 1980s, there was not only acceptance that there is a value to reminiscing, but a very enthusiastic embracing of reminiscence and related activities by those who work in hospitals, old people's homes, community and day centres — anywhere that older people meet in groups. Reminiscence has been incorporated into the work of occupational therapists, speech and language therapists, physiotherapists, psychologists, nurses, auxiliaries, care assistants, social workers, community workers, teachers, adult education organizers, librarians, museum staff, disability organizations, voluntary organizations, art galleries, artists, musicians, dancers, writers, teachers, drama groups and a myriad of hobby therapists, activities organizers and others with exotic titles whose concern, in one way or another, is the welfare of older people.

The 1980s saw not only reminiscence group or recall session appear formally on timetables of activities in homes and hospitals, but also the growth of a number of organizations set up especially to promote this work with conferences, training programmes and even a specialist magazine. A watershed in England was the publication by Help the Aged in 1981 of the *Recall* series of tape/slide programmes devised by the Reminiscence Aids Project led by the architect, Mick Kemp. This package, which is becoming aged itself, but still useful, consists of a set of images, sounds and reminiscences with suggested avenues for exploration and example questions to ask. It is based on different decades and relates these to different stages of life, the earlier part of the century reflecting childhood, the 1930s and 1940s illustrating working life, child raising and so on.

At a time of great concern about the effects of institutionalization and the idea of caring for the whole person, this was the first commercially produced resource pack made available in the UK to thousands of professional carers seeking solutions to problems of boredom and apathy amongst both staff and residents in homes and long-stay hospitals. Since the excitement caused by *Recall* there has been a variety of informed publications about reminiscence and development of a few resource packs such as Winslow's *Nostalgia* series. A Northern Ireland recall pack *Do You Mind The Time?* (1984) was produced by

Faith Gibson who, with the publication of *Using Reminiscence: a training pack* in 1989, distilled good practice and academic respectability to give credence and informed support to the practical use of reminiscence with older people and its significance in the context of residential care. In Britain the value of reminiscence work has been endorsed by the National Health Service, social service departments, local authorities, regional arts boards and major charities such as Help the Aged and Age Concern.

Specialist reminiscence-based arts organizations link the creative understanding of professional artists of many kinds — painters, musicians, drama workers, writers and others — to the needs and interests of older people. Creative arts practitioners all over the world have contributed greatly to the development of a role for the arts in the 'community' and have broadened the perspective of reminiscence work from being a 'therapeutic' tool to being a context for the overall improvement of the quality of experience of all kinds of people. In England, for example, the integration of arts-based reminiscence work into the care context has been pioneered by the work of organizations such as Age Exchange in London and Hospital Arts' Manchester Reminiscence Project, whose roots lie in the arts, the former developing from a theatre company and the latter from a hospital-based team of visual and performing artists. Organizations like these consider the arts, in a variety of forms, as having a vital nurturing, stimulating and expressive role to play in older people's lives. They have demonstrated through practice that artists can have a fundamental role to play in care settings, and that reminiscence can provide a useful and accessible point of contact between artist and audience, acting as meaningful context for all kinds of social, creative and interactive occasions.

Another significant strand of development comes from the work of the Oral History Society promoting an interest in the contemporary past and working class history through the words of 'ordinary' people. Based on an understanding that history is not so much about dates and battles as about the experience of real people, research and projects with schools, colleges and special interest groups throughout Britain have established an extensive resource of oral historical material.

Robert Butler

An outline of the development of reminiscence work must include reference to the seminal work of American geriatrician Robert Butler, whose theories of life review are often used to justify the use of reminiscence as a therapeutic tool and as a response to the direct psychological needs of older people.

Butler postulated that people nearing the end of their lives become involved in a process of looking back at their experiences in order to identify and come to terms with past events that are unresolved. Such events might include significant loss, guilt and reactions to grieving as well as a need to make sense of things. Butler suggested that the life review process is a healthy psychological preparation for death and is part of the natural process of human development. It is argued that reminiscing, by encouraging people to explore their past experiences, encourages life review and helps older people come to terms with impending death and to adapt to the frailty of great age.

Research, and there has not been much, does not seem particularly enamoured of the idea that life review is a universal process, or indeed to confirm that reminiscence itself effectively fulfils some of the claims made of it. It does confirm, though, that reminiscence can provide a valid context for interaction and communication that is of very evident benefit to people in hospital and residential care. There is need for further research into reminiscence work, which is, in fact, an assortment of disparate activities carried out by a variety of people with differing degrees of expertise in all kinds of contexts.

I conclude that psychological research and greater understanding of the overall needs of individuals, awareness of the effects of institutionalization associated with policies to open up closed institutions to the wider community, an ethical commitment to the right to a good quality of life with subsequent changes in nursing and caring practice, a strong voluntary sector and arts world interest in working in special settings and an academic interest in working class oral history have all converged to create a new multidisciplinary area of expertise and cultural activity: reminiscence work.

Reminiscence

- Reminiscence is not about the past.
- Reminiscence is something we do here and now — slap bang in the present.
- Reminiscence is something most of us, but not all of us, do at some time or other, some of us more often than others.
- Reminiscence makes us happy.
- Reminiscence makes us sad.
- Some people hate reminiscing.
- Reminiscence is not just for the old.
- Reminiscence is not about being old.

Consider the following:

Do you ever walk past a building and smell something — something from the past, something that reminds you of … what?

When you feel a little lonely, do you take a stroll to that special place where you used to go when you were little?

Every now and then, do you have to treat and reassure yourself and tuck into pilchards on toast, toffees, lemonade powder, rice pudding (please add your own example)?

Do you still eat things you used to eat as a child? Cook some things the way they *should* be cooked (as mother would do)? Always put the milk in the tea first (or last)?

Have you ever gone back to where you were born or used to live or work to have a look?

That song — every time you hear it …?

Do you think there is more to you than the job you do or the role you fulfil — an inner you who hasn't changed that much over the years? Do you ever wish this 'you' would get a little (or a lot) more attention?

Perhaps you have a box, a drawer, a trunk, a room (or a house) full of all those little old things and photographs you have picked up as you travel through your life?

Do you enjoy doing those quizzes ... amazing what you learn over the years, isn't it?

Do you like to go on your holidays to the same old familiar kinds of places?

Do you like to watch old films/TV programmes?

Do you like to continue those old traditions?

If you have children, have you told them the stories you were told, the little bits of wisdom passed to you by your parents?

Do you ever browse through your photograph albums?

Answering these questions positively indicates that most of us, regardless of age, will to some degree try to retain a sense of continuity in our lives by treasuring and revisiting something that reminds us of how things, and we, used to be. This is because, if we are well, we are not only the person we appear to be at this time, we are a patchwork of all the experiences we have ever had, of all the things we have ever felt. We can enrich our lives by reviving within ourselves feelings that we associate with a particular moment or aspect of our past. We may do this via entertainment and the arts, such as listening to music, dancing or reading; by retaining contacts with people and places we have loved, or perhaps through a special interest in preserving some aspect of heritage, tradition or our own personal history.

Many of us occasionally, or frequently, seek solace and respite in the experiences and cultural trappings that come from our past, perhaps from a time when things were simpler and happier, or from a time of drama and obstacles that we endured and overcame, that we coped with — important times in our lives that have helped us become who we are today. At times and, if we are troubled, often, we may think of or dwell on something that we so much wish had been different. If only we had not spoken that way, lost touch with that person, made those mistakes — if only those things had not happened. We may be disturbed by thinking these things and we will push them away, bury them back in the mists of time with regret and sadness. Sometimes they will stay with us, haunting our dreams and disturbing our lives.

During an ordinary day we will be reminded by something — a snatch of music, a casual reference, a smell, scene, taste or texture, even just a thought — of another time and another place. There may be a strong urge to communicate and articulate this, especially in a situation that encourages and approves. We may prefer to keep our memories to ourselves, to smile or feel sad, laugh or cry or quietly wonder as we mull over our inner thoughts. We may not even be quite sure whether this is a pleasurable experience or a distressing one. We may be *unable* to share these inner moments.

Reminiscence is probably a universal cultural phenomenon, a common human activity. Older people pass cultural information to younger people, the experienced warn the innocent, what was informs what is. Tradition and storytelling, the basis of education, pass down the generations the understanding of things that have been — not necessarily the exact dates and details, but the human story, often embellished and mythologized, representing a rich store that shows us the wonder that is the experience of people — all of us the same, yet all of us completely different. This story tells us a little of how things were before ourselves and brings the past alive in a way that no formal history lesson can do.

Reminiscence is an emotional experience that often, but not always, helps many of us to reinforce ourselves and strengthen our ability to cope. The communication and sharing of that emotional experience can help us and, importantly, help others to understand a little of who we really are. Sensitive exploration of that emotional experience can enable others to help us when we are experiencing difficulty. For those lucky enough to be surrounded by friends, family and neighbours, the opportunity to share recollections may be at hand, but for those who for one reason or another are remote from others, through great age, disability, illness, mental frailty, social isolation or institutionalization, opportunities to reminisce may be severely curtailed and will need to be deliberately created.

Reminiscence can be fun, and the potential and value of reminiscing purely as a leisure activity must not be underrated. It is healthy to enjoy oneself. Leisure activities, which can be hard work, help give meaning and purpose to our lives. Recreation, or more properly *re-creation,* allows us to refresh and to identify ourselves in a variety of ways. The role of 'patient' or 'resident', indeed of 'old person', can be very demanding and everyone deserves a little rest from this job. A well organized programme of age-appropriate and individualized social and/or arts-based activities should offer a chance to engage with something other than our immediate preoccupations.

Reminiscence offers an opportunity for professional carers legitimately to relate to their clients as people, not merely as objects of care. Reminiscing with those you care for educates you about them and allows you to encounter the other person more completely:

The reminiscence work gave opportunities to share past experiences of work and home life as well as reflect on memories and past pleasures. It also enabled me to see the whole person. (Carol Davies, Artist in Residence, the Rhyl Nursing Home)

Zen and the art of being in care

The experiences we have in our lives are the foundation of who we are now, of how we react now, and how we feel about ourselves. The experience of change in our lives is how we recognize growth and how we recognize decline — in fact, how we recognize the very nature of life itself. Without memory of change there would be no history and no culture. There would be no sense of continuity, no awareness of our place in time, of the totality of ourselves: the person we were is interwoven with the person we are now.

When I look into the mirror the person I see in front of me is so different from the person that I would have seen years ago, yet somehow I know that this is still me. If I were *not* the same person, I would not know that I had changed. Yet I am many people all rolled into one: the child, the adult, the parent; a success at some things and a failure at others; an inner self and an outer self. I may be a talented gardener but a terrible cook, able to act with confidence in some aspects of my life while feeling insecure in others. I may be seen by others as competent while feeling that I am not and express myself amidst friends and family in a way that I would never wish to be exposed to colleagues or strangers. We are the sum of all the various aspects of our selves, old and new, public and private, marked, informed and matured by psychological, emotional, physical and spiritual experiences.

We do not remake our identity every morning from scratch. We start each day with our own unique reality interpreted and reacted to through a filter that comprises our personality, our physical senses, our emotional experiences (past and present), our cultural background and our expectations. Our personalities, while staying remarkably constant throughout our lives, unfold as we adapt and learn and as we forget, or try to forget, much that is not of value and retain that which offers us meaning and a sense of coherence. Also, our physical senses, rarely perfect, may be impaired, our emotions unintegrated, our cultural view simple or complex and our expectations positive or negative.

A move from independence to a care setting is a time of crisis associated with the passing of independent living, severe illness, sudden disability, loss and grief. Morbidity itself, the acute or chronic experience of decline in old age — having to acknowledge we are no longer able to look after ourselves properly, knowing that death may not be far away — is a time of crisis.

The way we value ourselves and in consequence the expectations we have of old age will affect our ability to deal with and retain a sense of continuity of self during crisis. Some feel trapped and 'finished' and plunge into despondency and introspection. Others react with gratitude and compliance. Still others retain a positive outlook, realizing they have yet another challenge in life to face. Some may react with philosophical calm and endurance. Our culture and our spiritual beliefs will influence our experience of care and the perception we have of it, whether or not we consider dependence through age or disability to be a bad thing. Our ability to question and challenge decisions made on our behalf will depend not only on our current physical and mental condition but also on whether our upbringing and education have given us the ability and self-confidence to articulate our concerns effectively. The choices we are able to make will also be defined by financial circumstances. Whether we feel at home and understood will depend on the congruity of care to our class, race, religion or nationality — whether values, attitudes and, indeed, language are understood or shared by those around us.

Also, most changes in our lives are gradual. When change is sudden, we become stressed, we can become traumatized and, unless becoming ill, we strive to 'deal with things' within the framework we have that is our current perception of ourselves. In order to cope, to understand and to respond effectively in a time of crisis, we draw on our many experiences — our inner selves — seeking the insight we need. We also look for understanding and emotional support to strengthen or guide us from spiritual and cultural sources, from the medical and caring professions, from family, friends and others, from the present and from the past. Reminiscing can help to revive aspects of our inner selves that help us cope by allowing us to draw on our reserves, interact with others as a more 'complete' personality, challenge stereotypical assumptions, assert our individuality and perhaps, just possibly help us to find meaning where there may seem to be little. It can help us, for a moment, to regain some control over what is going on. It gives us a chance to say 'I'm here — this is me' in a situation where doctrine, economics or design may be striving to make us feel invisible.

When we first meet someone new, we tend to look for ground on which to find common reference so that we can communicate. We often start by finding out where people come from or what they do for a living or a hobby. We hope to find a point of shared understanding that will help us identify with that person in some way. This can often be harder than it seems as all of us make assumptions about people based on first impressions which may be wrong. An old person who is traumatized by going into care may bury his or her personality in order to cope with feeling worthless and uninteresting. To make sense of our apparently being treated like an object, we may become like an object, passive and non-responsive. Or we may react with anger and suspicion. Life can become a depressing and frustrating experience of loneliness, even despair, with limited or no opportunity for pleasure, self-expression or social interaction.

Hospital and residential care will naturally focus on a person's basic physical needs, sometimes unwittingly encouraging dependence and compliance in order to facilitate the care process. This can lead older people to see themselves, and the carers to see the clients, as a problem to be solved, as a damaged item to be fixed and eventually as a physical shell to be maintained. A task-oriented view of caring gives low priority to other than basic needs, and it is increasingly common for permission to be required for staff to interact personally and emotionally with clients. Reminiscence work gives permission by validating and justifying such interaction. Participation in reminiscence sessions can raise staff awareness of individual personalities and increase levels of interpersonal communication and understanding.

I was able to offer the residents quality time which is available from no other source in such a situation. The organization of care mitigates against choice and real human relationships; I hope I was able to overcome this to some extent. I feel that the people I worked with were being, in some way, validated as individuals as they never normally are in such a situation. Perhaps this was the real product of the project.
(Richard Conlon, Artist in Residence, Cubbington)

The Fourth Age

DISCRIMINATION ON THE BASIS of skin colour, religious belief, origin, class, gender, sexuality and disability has a history that reaches far and deep into antiquity. In recent times, great movements have arisen to combat injustice, eventually leading to historical changes such as the abolition of slavery or universal suffrage. However, a perception that there is discrimination on the basis of chronological age — 'ageism' — is a relatively new idea and has only been an issue for discussion in the last few years

Discrimination expresses itself subtly in the way that people treat and respond to each other, consciously or not, and this can often be seen in professional care sectors, not only with regard to the allocation of resources, but also directly in staff behaviour and institutional practices. The 'welfarization' of older and disabled people in receipt of care and support can lead to demeaning attitudes from the providers of services which cultivate a recipient's perception that they are receiving charity. There can sometimes be a very distinct 'us and them' experience in care settings, exaggerating the differences between people rather than highlighting those aspects of ourselves that we hold in common.

Our tendency to stereotype those reaching great age is also reflected in the use of terms such as 'the elderly' or 'geriatrics', as if we were trying to put old people, who may not even be the same age as each other, into a category that, for the moment, comfortably excludes ourselves. We therefore do not have to behave as we normally would to people 'like us' and 'they' are kept separate and distinct. Stereotypes can range from what has been called 'the tranquillity myth' — little white-haired grannies spinning out their days in contemplation — to the 'inevitability myth' — tragic, disabled and confused figures living in a twilight world of despair and chronic ill health.

It is not helpful to anyone unconsciously to coalesce the word 'old' with the word 'problem' and we should not confuse old age with illness. Old age may be accompanied by problems but is not inherently a problem itself. The majority of old people are able to lead independent lives and the proportion needing total care is relatively small, although of course this proportion increases with age. A life cycle framework avoids this confusion. For the more academically minded, it is called a status construct and is summarized as follows:

The First Age: the age of childhood and socialization;
The Second Age: the age of paid work and family raising;
The Third Age: the age of active independent life beyond work and parenting;
The Fourth Age: the age of eventual dependence.

To use this way of looking at people's circumstance does not put any 'value' on chronological age. Someone, a politician or musician for example, may be in the second age when they are 70, whilst someone else may be in the third age at 50, having retired and their children being grown and independent.

Changing roles

In a broad sense, society tends to value us primarily for the role we play rather than for who we are. Recognition of our worth is often demonstrated by, for example, payment for work, respect for a parent or deference to social status. There can be a great sense of worthlessness at the loss or involuntary change of role: unemployment, retirement, end of child rearing, hospitalization, acquiring a disability and reaching frail advanced age can all cause withdrawal, depression, anger and frustration.

As we age, our inclination and ability to 'adapt' to new situations tend to lessen, and our motivation to satisfy our needs may diminish. To a certain extent this limitation is imposed on us by the expectations of others and, having at one time been one of the others, also by our-selves. We may believe that, because we are old, we are more limited than we actually are and society, by the low value it places on older people's achievements, reinforces a negative perception of our signifi-cance and worth. We begin to believe we are a burden.

Going into care, older people may become more dependent on others than they need to be and staff sometimes reinforce this by 'help-ing' too much. A change to an unfamiliar social and physical environ-ment makes it difficult enough to use coping strategies that have been learnt over the years in order to retain our sense of self and ability to take independent action without our frailty being exaggerated by the behaviour of others. The older person who is perfectly capable of mak-ing a cup of tea may be forbidden from undertaking the simplest of activities, which reinforces a sense of dependence and infirmity.

During our lives we develop strategies that help us to cope with and adjust to loss and change — the departure or death of those who are important to us — and changes in our own strengths and abilities. These strategies are distinctive and personal to each individual. They may be reinforced, for example, through the church, family and friends, or through creative and artistic endeavour. We may find suc-cour in music, through our pets, in nature, by helping others or by spending time alone. In times of difficulty, individuals must be allowed and helped to draw on their life experiences in order to respond to and deal with what they are going through. In practical terms, this will ini-tially require the immediate treatment of illness, implying also the removal of barriers to that treatment. We do not easily sort ourselves out when we feel very ill. After that, with particular relevance to long-term care, this involves the provision of friendly environments, not only aids to independent activity but also the creation of environments that are enhancing and nurturing, that help people succeed, that are meaningful. This means opportunities for making choices, for educa-tion and for stimulation, expression and interaction in a context where people feel comprehended, respected and valued. This implies that ini-tiatives that are based on the life experience of individuals — reminis-cence work — must operate in an individualized and flexible frame-work that takes into account the things that have real meaning to those involved. It also puts into doubt the effectiveness of reminiscence and activity programmes that do not take individuality into account.

The quality of the experience

Underpinning the development of the ideas behind reminiscence has been general acceptance that we all, when unable to look after ourselves, have a right to lead as good a quality of life as is realistically possible and that the caring professions have a responsibility to do their best to enable us to do so. Ill health is not simply a direct result of disease or injury. Physical health is a component of mental health and our mental, physical and emotional health or ill health influences our whole state of well-being. The role of the healer is to pay attention, not only to our physical ailments, but to our condition as a whole — all is interactive.

Individuals have varied and multiple needs, including those beyond the physical. People whose opportunities are restricted by great age, disability, frailty or the circumstances in which they live may be unable to meet some or many of their own emotional needs without considered help and special provision. Unmet emotional needs have a negative effect on our physical well-being and our ability to cope and it is important that the caring process be sensitive and responsive to the overall life style of older people living or participating in care. It must be acknowledged that the quality of care is measured by the quality of experience a person has while receiving that care.

While it is perhaps not realistic for institutional care services to provide the 'total care' sometimes expected of them, we must make every effort to ensure that care practice does not contribute to ill health and cause avoidable emotional impoverishment. Try discussing the following questions and reflect upon some fundamental causes of involuntary disengagement, loneliness and unhappiness:

Do your clients have a chance to talk to a variety of people, in any depth, about things other than their physical needs?

We all need contact with and attention from other human beings that confirm our sense of whole identity and allow us to feel wanted and cherished. When we are ill, lonely or frightened we may need increased emotional help and support. If the only attention we receive is based on what is wrong with us and not what is right with us, we begin to see ourselves only in terms of our difficulties. It is easy for hard-pressed care staff to deal only with 'problems'. This may lead people to exaggerate distress in order to receive attention.

Do your clients have approved opportunity to express strong emotions?
We all need to express our thoughts and feelings, to share these with others. In our culture we are not expected to express ourselves very distinctly and in the context of residential care the expression of strong emotion or exploration of the subtler aspects of what is happening to us, and around us, is rarely encouraged. At worst, the opportunity to express is repressed, sometimes quite brutally. The internalization of emotion and of intellectual activity with no effective outlet can lead to withdrawal and depression. When this repression is extreme it can cause severe physical or psychiatric illness.

Do staff know much about their clients as individuals?
If you are to respond to someone as a whole person then you need to get to know that person. It is frightening to be surrounded only by strangers. Getting to know people can only happen by interacting with them on a variety of levels. Some people, including staff, need help to devise a context in which to interact.

Are relationships between staff and clients friendly, polite and respectful?
Anticipation of rudeness or disrespect in the behaviour that we expect from others can make us angry, resentful, low in self-esteem and unco-operative. We may consider ourselves not *worthy* of respect if we exhibit behaviour that reinforces a low opinion of ourselves.

Is the environment in which clients live pleasant and agreeable?
Our sense of well-being is directly affected by the environment in which we spend time. If our surroundings are stressful, unwelcoming, alienating, impersonal or unwholesome, this will negatively affect our mood and our behaviour. If we live in an environment that is relatively stress-free, pleasant, friendly and nurturing, this will make us feel better. We all have to experience stressful environments, but it helps us cope with this if we are able to enjoy pleasant and soothing alter-

natives. Continuous exposure to a stressful environment can make us very ill.

Is there somewhere for clients to go to reflect, to spend time alone?
Most of us at times, and some people frequently, need a place we can go to sit quietly to 'centre' ourselves, to steady ourselves quietly in order to face the challenges that face us. We must not assume that because a person enjoys company they never need to be alone (and the other way round). This is particularly important for people who live communally.

Are there opportunities for a diversity of relevant cultural activity?
We are all different and we all have our respective forms of recreation, that is, of 're-creating'. We confirm our sense of self by engaging in a variety of activities that reflect our character and our cultural background. This may be the occasional drink with friends and/or the chance to worship in a way that is meaningful to us. It may be following football and/or engaging in political debate. It may be reflected in our way of dress, our traditions, the way we mark out the passing of time. For as long as possible during our old age we should be able to enjoy the customary and everyday activities that give us pleasure, a sense of purpose, a sense of self-respect and a sense of personal significance.

Is there a choice, or at least a good diverse selection, of music available?
Music directly affects and reflects our emotional state. The choices we make of music we wish to hear represent a statement of our individuality and/or our group identity. It can be intolerable to be surrounded by sound that is unpleasant to us and have no control over it. Music is a very very powerful force in our lives and can be used for good or ill.

Do clients ever see animals, children, flowers; hear running water; feel the rain; smell perfumes; watch the sun go down?
We all need sensual stimulation and to experience beauty and pleasure. The world is full of interesting, heart-warming and beautiful natural phenomena. We should not be deprived of the opportunity to enjoy these things, they make life worthwhile.

The quality of experience lies with the processes of care and the way that care is given is a measure of its effectiveness.

A sense of belonging

We have a sense of belonging to a 'time'; we have a *generational* identity. This is usually developed early in our lives and is especially noticeable during our youth, when we very much identify with our peers, but is also apparent in later life. For most of us, the association with others of a similar age has a profound effect on the way we interpret and express ourselves — on likes and dislikes, political views, tastes in music and so on — and therefore on behaviour and the way the world is perceived. We like food prepared in particular ways or consider a certain way of behaving to be proper or respectful that differs from the customs of people who are older or younger than ourselves.

When communicating with those of the same culture, class and generation, we often talk in a kind of shorthand. Mention the name of a place, a person or a special date and we all know what or who we are referring to. There are many unspoken associations made. For example, if I mention the names John, Paul and George to a member of my generation I will almost certainly elicit immediate recognition, but not if I say the same to an 80-year-old or an eight-year-old.

This shared recognition can be very reassuring and often a context for spontaneous reminiscence and mutual acceptance. It can be very satisfying for individuals to feel they belong to a group that has a common identity of generation. Nevertheless, the fact that people identify themselves as belonging to the same generation certainly does not mean that they are all the same. There are many other aspects to our personalities that enable us to identify with or separate us from others: background, race, class, nationality, occupation, education, religion, sexuality, gender as well as taste in music, political views, intelligence, an inclination to being practical or intellectual, being 'incomers', immigrants, emigrants, parents or childless, and so on. Personal experiences we have had during our lives may also distance us from our peer group: for example, experiences during the war, mental illness, trauma, great calamity and great achievement. People of similar age have many differences.

Generational identification, while representing a powerful and, in our context, significant component of group identity, must always be acknowledged as only one aspect amongst many of our personalities. Also, while generational identity can strengthen and bond a group, it is totally inappropriate to allow it to reject people from different parts of the country, other countries or other ethnic and class backgrounds. By its nature, a clique leaves those excluded alienated or mystified.

Many people feel rather proud of having reached great age, and projects based on shared generational experiences can be very enjoyable and invigorating. We should remind ourselves, though, that a group of 'old' people may consist of individuals whose chronological age differs by as much as 30 years, so they may not be of the same generation. If you do decide to bond the group through identification based on generation, encourage them to reach out to other age groups and to share their experience of life with others.

Speculating about informality

In some ways people brought up before the Second World War can tend to be less direct than later generations. Before the permissiveness of the 1960s, people were not so forthright about sex or personal emotions. People perhaps expressed themselves in other ways and certainly men and women related differently.

You may perceive yourself as a professional person, but to the old person you may just be a young thing, deserving, of course, of respect yourself, but equally being expected to show respect to your elders. Many older people, for example, find it rather insulting to be called by their forenames or nicknames by people whom they do not know very well, or who are younger. The use of the title Mr, Mrs or Miss is regarded as good manners and the giving of permission for the use of a more intimate name can be seen as a kind of gift, an offering of friendship and equality.

Be careful not to abbreviate or use names that are not how that person likes to be called. Christina may hate being called Chris, Fred may always have been called Frederick and Mr Smith may only have been called Alf by his wife (Alfred to you). Always find out what people like to be called. Do not assume that, because *you* have permission to refer to someone in an intimate way, *I* have, when I do not know them so well.

We live in a time when the pseudo-informal is a fine art: the president wears a baseball cap, the car salesman calls you by your first name (how dare he!). Those who come from earlier generations have different social norms. What to you represents friendly informality can be interpreted as patronizing or disrespectful by others.

Of men and women

Anyone who works with older people will tell you that working with a group of men can be a different experience from working with a group of women, or indeed with a mixed group. This is a generalization, and of course all of us will be able to identify many exceptions, but often you will find that women seem more amenable to organized social interaction than men. It is sometimes the case that men find it harder to be gregarious, less able to function in a group and more prone to being inactive.

Men, at least those of the generation currently in care, tend to acknowledge their public identities in relation to their line of work and are much more bound up with what they do than who they are. A man's identity is often totally interwoven with his work. You can see this illustrated by the suffering and apathy that can arise when a man becomes unemployed or retires. Many men find this loss of occupational role very hard to cope with. It can be a good idea to encourage men who have low self-esteem and trouble with communal activity by asking for their help to achieve something specific, and allow the social dimension to develop naturally as they relax and feel able to make a more spontaneous contribution.

Another potential issue to be sensitive to is a male client's perception of his relationship to the carers. Most care staff are women and some men of this generation do not feel at ease in female company. They are used to fulfilling a dominant role in relation to women and will perhaps resent being asked 'intimate' questions or told what to do by a young 'girl'. Having spent most of one's life in a predominantly male-oriented workplace, relating to others impersonally on a 'technical' level, can, on occasion, cause difficulty with adaptation in a predominantly female-oriented care setting. You will find sometimes that male reminiscence workers elicit more response from older men. It is as if they can talk the same emotional language. Women, whose work, particularly in the past, has been seen as relatively peripheral, may have had to discover themselves in other ways.

In an admittedly stereotypical framework, a man may well have been at work all day relating to others impersonally, whilst a woman at home with the family may have had the opportunity to interact socially and emotionally with others — particularly other women — and therefore is in fact much more at ease socially. In the workplace, women may have had to develop a strong sense of self to counteract perceptions of their 'place'.

For many people brought up before the Second World War, behaviour acceptable while interacting with those of one's own sex is very different from that acceptable in mixed company. You will notice sometimes, in a mixed group, that people will behave differently — most obviously becoming more concerned about the suitability of their appearance — and it becomes very important that people are helped to retain their dignity as much as possible. It can be embarrassing for a man to be unshaven or a woman to be without make-up when mixing socially. A man may not feel dressed properly unless in a tie and a woman if not wearing stockings. In some situations a hat and gloves are essential.

Do not make assumptions about what may be appropriate or you run the risk of making someone uncomfortable because they are not living up to *your* expectations of what is right for them. Just pay attention, get to know people and be aware of the way people react in different situations.

A place for all

We must not tolerate behaviour that is directly abusive, for example, in response to someone's race, gender or sexuality. Not only does this kind of behaviour demean the abused, it demeans the abuser.

Dubious opinions based on prejudice and intolerance can be discussed with some people, but dealing with this issue becomes less clear when people have a view or use language based on attitudes that were generally acceptable decades ago but are not acceptable any more. If the offence they are causing can be explained to them and no insult is intended, perhaps all can be worked out amicably, but this can be difficult when people are mentally frail or confused.

And what if it is intentional? Is it too late to influence the attitudes of someone if they are no longer able to debate on equal terms? Have we the right or the obligation to try? How much do we tolerate, or challenge, the views of frail older people before becoming patronizing ourselves? It is important in this situation to be clear as to whether someone actually understands the implications of what they are saying: are they meaning to insult or using an expression naively in total innocence? Sometimes it can be a symptom of an illness that people are unable to express themselves within acceptable social conventions. At other times, aggression and abuse may be a reaction to frustration and anger, or prejudice and fear.

In a context where older people are being encouraged to express themselves and their views you can find yourself in an uncomfortably ambiguous situation if those views represent discrimination and intolerance, as with a person whose reminiscences are clearly anti-Semitic or racist. Do we, should we, censor this? I can only draw your attention to these issues; there is not an appropriate solution for every situation. They can become complex and you must be clear about whose sensibilities are actually being offended (yours?) but it is important to devise policies on how you and co-workers should deal with prejudice and intolerant views in practice. Everyone has a right to feel that they belong where they are.

Institutional environments

Despite changes and improvements in recent decades, many centres of care are still housed in old workhouse accommodation or 'asylums' that were devised when political attitudes to old age, illness and disability were very different from those today. Some of the old buildings appear grim and austere, with high windows and institutional atmospheres that still echo a past that had more to do with incarceration than with healing.

Owing in part to ambiguous care in the community legislation and also as a consequence of relatively more enlightened attitudes to care and higher customer expectation, the old asylums with their containing walls and infinite corridors will gradually disappear, many dark Victorian buildings being replaced with shiny new provision.

While I endorse wholeheartedly any progress that offers an environment of care that is more luxurious, warm and encouraging of independent living, it does seem to me that newer purpose-built environments can be as alienating as older, visually grimmer environments. I
have worked in hospitals and homes that were built in the nineteenth
century that have a wonderful homely atmosphere. I have also
encountered superbly built, plush and comfortable modern accommodation that is so alienating that residents are afraid to put a glass of
water on the table. I have worked on old hospital wards full of lively
evidence of the occupiers' identities and contrasted this with luxurious
surroundings that were inhospitable and enervating.

It is my experience that, sometimes, a home or hospital ward will
be run with such an exaggerated fear of criticism that the appearance
of order and cleanliness takes priority over the needs and interests of
the residents. Of course, older people's residential accommodation
must be well looked after and should be inspected often and unexpectedly — there have been too many examples of cruel abuse and dis-
gusting conditions not to make this crucial. Of course it must be safe
and hygienic, but, after this, other standards are very much to do with
management policy.

There is something vital missing in those places where everything
is consistently put away — not a newspaper or a pack of cards in sight;
those places where nothing is ever put on a wall for display — not a
postcard or family photograph to show who lives there; where cookery
is not allowed, not for safety reasons but in case a kitchen surface gets
dirty or is scratched. I was particularly outraged by the place where
calls were made for a scruffy visitor to stop taking a very noisy disabled person outside in case it 'gave the wrong impression' to potential customers. The nurturing effect of the environment within which
one lives is brought about, not only by the aesthetic and practical
aspects of that environment, but also by the way in which the occupants, individually or as a group, make an impact on it. In our own
homes many of us make our mark by surrounding ourselves with our
own choice of colours, textures, artwork and memorabilia.

It seems to me that sometimes homes and hospitals have replaced
the atmosphere of the workhouse with the atmosphere of the hotel.
This is certainly an improvement but, while a 'corporate image' may

be suitable for a business or even an acute hospital, I suggest it is inappropriate when it causes alienation by being fundamentally out of tune with the individuality and culture of the occupants.

Our home should reflect our identities and what happens within it. A hotel or an airport lounge will not do this; these are places of transitory occupation. Residential provision is an older person's home and the ambience should as much as is possible reinforce this fact.

A lady on one of the wards asked me several times if I would like a cup of tea. Each time I said that I was going to wait but she eventually took matters into her own hands and went to the staff kitchen where she started to fill the kettle. A nurse saw her and told her to leave. "This is my home you know," said the lady, "and I'd like to offer a friend a cup of tea."
(Joan Poulson, *Window on Winwick*)

Residential provision should aim to create opportunities for

- privacy: to be alone with our thoughts and our feelings;
- togetherness: to socialize, to be with friends;
- lively times: to play, have fun and make a noise;
- peaceful times: to rest, recuperate and meditate;
- hospitality: to welcome visitors, to offer (even if we cannot make) refreshment;
- work: a place where we can create and achieve.

There should be access to

- plants and animals;
- water;
- trees, gardens and weather;
- children;
- friendly, but respectful, contact from others;
- protection from bumptious 'do gooders';
- our own choice of clothes: to feel dressed in the way we consider suits us in the colours we like, in the materials that make us feel good;

- sensual experiences: bathing, hairdressing and shaving should be pleasant and soothing;
- (assisted) liberty: a chance to go to the pub, to the shops, to church — not as a therapeutic exercise, but because one wants to;
- safety and security, with as little restriction as possible;
- a variety of atmospheres.

In the way our homes contain items that have associations for us, so reminiscence work can bring these things back into view, not professionally provided, but placed as part of living, enthusiastic activity. The art group can decorate with friezes, paintings and ceramics. The arts 'studio' itself can become a place that is full of interest, with smells and textures of all kinds. The place where the music happens can be accessible, with instruments available, tapes to play, somewhere to sit and listen. There could be things to play with, to look at, to interact with; places to take visitors, to wander into, that hold beauty, interest, surprises; a little of ourselves, a little chaos, a little natural disorder.

To bring about true and innovative change in the institutional environment we need to integrate the skills of care staff with those of artists and architects. Education of staff, managers and policy makers should address these issues in depth and begin to help them acquire the necessary skills to accept and understand this. Is it really out of the question to: take a risk, knock down or build walls, use space differently than it has been for years, change the routines or think creatively?

Time to talk

Reminiscence is not something that can be confined just to reminiscence sessions. We are aiming to create a 'culture' that generally encourages positive human interaction. Spontaneous communication should be recognised and responded to. Staff can be encouraged to chat informally while carrying out tasks such as bathing, dressing and toileting clients, still showing respect for the dignity, privacy and customs of individuals. Mealtimes should be a sociable occasion. However, 'chatting' while engaged in everyday tasks should not be a substitute for more formal activities.

A unit is under stress when staff consistently do not 'have time'. The culture becomes hostile to casual contact and spontaneous interaction. This is common but not good practice. A regime of care that is overly task-oriented can mean that a staff member trying to relate personally to clients feels under pressure from managers, from other staff, themselves and even the clients to be 'on the go' all of the time. This can mean that time is not perceived as being available for conversation, for going out and for enjoying each other's company. Staff will naturally respond first to those in greatest need of immediate physical relief. This can mean that a client wishing to attract attention may have to demonstrate distress or immediate physical need in order to obtain the attention that they crave.

On a subtler level, the pressure to get on with 'the job', often aggravated by traditionally inadequate staffing levels and thoughtless prioritizing, can lead to intense frustration amongst staff. They know that they care but have little time to express their caring, perhaps feeling guilty if they stop to talk. If they do try to introduce more creative and sociable elements into a resident's day, they can find they are challenged by managers who either do not understand what it is all about or even may be rather scared of facing the emotional realities inherent in a truly caring activity. If we do not know someone, we are less likely to feel for them, so avoiding personal emotional risk.

Normally, though, it is sheer pressure of work that leads to a persistent sense of there not being 'enough time' for what are perceived as peripheral activities. Managers need to demonstrate that high priority is given to responding to the emotional needs of clients via staffing patterns, allocation of resources, provision of staff training and their own interpersonal behaviour. If the pressure you or other staff are under never allows time for spontaneous contact, you should try and have this discussed and acknowledged. Do what you can to try to influence those who have the authority to make changes in priorities. Do not pretend that things are not as they really are.

Managers can ensure they back up the efforts of staff by:

- making sure that timetables are organized properly;
- discussing issues associated with the emotional life of clients;

- making sure there is a budget or adequate resources;
- arranging appropriate working space;
- making sure the activities programme is endowed with some authority;
- meeting regularly to discuss progress seriously, and acting on information received;
- arranging for all staff to participate in training;
- helping and supporting — not just tolerating;
- cultivating an atmosphere of respect and consideration in all directions;
- acting as a consistent and realistic model of good practice and expecting the same effort from others.

Residential care that is really to be 'home' must be responsive to the true needs of the people that live there.

The Benefits of Reminiscence Work

REMINISCENCE OFFERS a context for meaningful interaction and is a starting point for building relationships and mutual communication. The process of reminiscing is not just the act of remembering, but also the act of communicating and sharing in a context of sensitive attention by others. It is the quality of the interaction that matters most and you should concentrate on the person, not on the past.

The kinds of benefits attributed to reminiscence are not exclusive to reminiscence, and occur in situations where there is a high level of interaction between staff and clients. Reminiscence can act as a fundamental driving force to bring about this interaction, the general culture and environment of care combining to create an atmosphere that is not unkind to those of advanced years. It is helpful, though, in a situation where you will have to argue the case for running sessions, using valuable staff time and therefore costing money, to be clear about what benefits can be gained for the participants.

These may summarized into four main categories:

1 *Reminiscence can maintain, or raise self-esteem and confidence*: focusing on the things the person is most sure of; reversing roles so that the person reminiscing becomes the expert; allowing sharing of wisdom and experience; and confirming a person's individuality and encouraging them to express it.

2 *Reminiscence can have a therapeutic effect*: providing an opportunity for emotional expression and mental stimulation; encouraging positive communication, activity and social interaction; in cer-

tain contexts, helping come to terms with unresolved conflicts and emotions; acting as a bridge to the present and helping with orientation; being pleasurable and interesting.

3   *Reminiscence can be educational*: creating a context for interaction between young and old; helping the carer understand the cared for; and increasing our understanding of the past, and therefore the present.

4   *Reminiscence can be enjoyable*: encouraging conversation and discussion; acting as a context for a range of other interesting activities; encouraging people to get to know each other better, and do things together.

Reminiscence focuses on *individual experience*, creating the opportunity for an individual to express feelings, intellectual capacity, sense of humour and knowledge, and also to receive from others a positive valuing of the self. For someone to experience this confirmation and benefit from it, they must be aware of it through the behaviour of others. Reminiscence also focuses on *collective experience*, encouraging individuals to share the common experiences of a generation, of a community, with each other and with younger people. For the individuals within a group to experience this confirmation and benefit from it, they must know that they are part of what is going on and that their contribution is welcome and seen as important.

Reminiscence and the art of caring

Reminiscence work is not only a technique, it is a way of looking at care, of seeing and understanding those you care for. Sensitively organized programmes help staff and patient or resident to respect each other as they encounter each other as individual personalities. Sessions become more special moments for all involved. Staff can become more motivated and gain more enjoyment and satisfaction from their work.

The staff could see the benefits of the residents joining in the project, achieving something of their own. Their added interest made the residents feel special and often staff would say "How about asking X to join in too?" Everyone is very proud of what we have achieved, residents, their families and staff.

(Barbara White, Activities Organizer, Ringshill Nursing Home)

In practice, reminiscence work can be considered as taking a number of overlapping forms.

A means of discussing aspects of the past in a co-ordinated and organized way
This is likely to include straightforward reminiscence sessions: looking at photographs, handling objects, perhaps watching videos, slide shows, listening to music and so on directly to encourage recall. This process may be developed by further activity, for example, taking people to their old place of work, to museums or to the park where they can encounter stimuli that trigger memories and emotional reactions. Sessions will usually be formal, participants selected and progress monitored and evaluated. Do this with fairly small groups to encourage intimate discussion and interaction.

A basis for creating a less clinical and semi-familiar style of homely environment
In this case, interaction will occur informally as people are fed, bathed or toileted, ideally backed by a management policy that explicitly allows staff to spend time getting to know the clients. Reminiscence sessions are likely to be informal, perhaps a mixture of chat, music and tea drinking, and will be perceived as predominantly social. The aims will be to cheer people up, get them talking and to make them feel more at home. Old photographs may be used to decorate the walls, old films shown on the video, old music played in the background. Rather than going to the museum, trips out will be to the pub, the country or the seaside. Activities will probably be organized with relatively large groups and will not be seen as a clinical exercise.

A foundation for creating something
People will be helped to use and adapt their existing skills, or learn new skills, to produce directly something of value now: making things, composing music, painting memories, writing poems, stories or reminiscences. Where people are less able or less willing to do things for themselves, they can be helped to contribute their knowledge and understanding to a project organized by an enabler or facilitator, perhaps an artist. People may be encouraged or helped by a writer to

recount their memories for a book. A visual artist may draw on people's memories to create a work of art or a musician ask people to choose what music to play.

A means of reducing isolation and institutionalization
People living and working in care settings can often feel isolated from the rest of society and take on a narrow view of daily life that becomes petty and institutionalized, at its worst leading to aggression and ill treatment. An interest in the past can be used as motivation for bringing the outside world in, encouraging non-medical, non-clinical and non-institutional influences into a closed environment. This could include, for example, the person from the library who comes to give talks, the Arts Council, the local school or volunteers. Working together on a reminiscence project gives a reason and a framework for interaction. Equally, a project can be used to channel energy out into the surrounding community.

A general context for deepening understanding
The aim of sessions may well be primarily to encourage staff to talk to clients. This may include working as above, but may also include, for example, construction of biographical accounts that help staff to understand better the people for whom they care. A display of memorabilia, or visits to museums and so on may be seen as a way to stimulate interest by staff in the past lives and experience of individual clients and this kind of project can be especially valuable for those young staff who often have a very limited knowledge of a way of life that preceded satellite TV, supermarkets and Big Mac.

Reminiscence work demonstrates to people that they are of value and of interest to others — not simply in need of care and help. In an environment that tends to dehumanize, a good level and quality of reminiscence-based activity can help those in care to assert their individual and generational identity. Symbolically, reminiscence work can reverse roles between carer and cared for. The younger carer is no longer the 'expert', the older person can take control and remind you and themselves of their individuality, of their personality and the 'wholeness' that is represented by all their experience of life.

In reminiscence work the younger person *needs* the older person in order to proceed. In a small but significant way, a degree of power is offered to the powerless. The reminiscer is in control of what they tell you, able to embellish, fantasize, even lie, and to withdraw co-operation.

Relevant to the concept of raising self-esteem is the idea of the 'exchange relationship'. This is the wisdom that 'it is better to give than to receive'. We may like to accept gifts, but most of us also need to give, to present those we love and like with tokens of our esteem, our respect and our affection.

There is often a stigma attached to having to accept help without being able to give something in return. Even if you are entitled to receive, at the end of a lifetime spent giving to your country, your employer and your family, it can lead to a state of dependency and can seriously lower self-esteem. We all need opportunities for giving — perhaps to return something to those who are 'giving' to us — and therefore to retain some sense of self-worth and value.

If we are honest with ourselves, it can be extremely frustrating if some-one starts to reminisce 'at' us when we are trying to do something else. If someone starts to relate the same old story time after time while you are trying to clean the cupboards or deal with a telephone call it is pos-sible, and understandable, to be overly or unintentionally dismissive. If someone tries to tell you something and you really do have some-thing else to do that is more important, explain this and return to them when you have more time. Try not to ignore people, especially if attempts to make contact with you are a consequence of reminiscence work. If you do, you may well be wasting time and effort, rather than using it constructively.

Although reminiscence can improve an individual's experience of the present, their ability to engage in recall will be affected by con-cerns in their life now. Reminiscence becomes not only a technique for encouraging people to talk about themselves because it is good for them but a starting point for the creation of contexts of care that embrace good practice by helping staff to address the issues that con-cern people.

Someone who is preoccupied by an impending operation, a visit from a relative, some financial difficulty, or perhaps grief, guilt, depression or anxiety may need action taken before they are able to relax enough to enjoy recalling matters that might seem irrelevant in the circumstances.

In an environment where there is bad practice — for example, where staff are rude to residents, or where people are generally understimulated — the good effect of an hour or two of reminiscence sessions is soon dissipated. It is clear in some situations that the primary need is not for life review or recall as such but to have someone to talk to seriously, someone to offer reassurance and acknowledgement of individual personalities.

Remember that an older person in care is not just someone with an illness or a clinical problem, but also, for example, a son or daughter, a mother or younger brother; a philosopher, a priest, a traveller, a thinker, an entertainer, a storyteller, a wise person or a fool. Unless serious illness alters our personality, we rise to the challenge of ageing as the kind of person we are. Reminiscence activities in a supportive environment can bring those whole, real people to the fore.

So here we have 'reminiscence', all things to all people by the sound of it!

- a stimulating/therapeutic semi-clinical activity; in formal groups or one-to-one sessions;
- a basis for social activity and interaction; less formal or completely informal reminiscence;
- a basis for creative/productive activity;
- a channel from the outside in and inside out;
- an educational process for staff.

I spy strangers: a nearly true story

In that first vision you see the superficial: the ill, the old, the decrepit. The room is full of strangers. You enter the room and one or two heads look up, but, not recognizing you, turn away. As usual you are not for them. No member of staff is apparent to greet you, so you warily find an unoccupied place, just to get your bearings. The chair seems to be covered in something sticky. You can smell disinfectant.

Nervously you rise and go from one person to another, trying to make some initial contact, a pack of photographs, unopened, under your arm. "I've come to talk to you about the old days, I wonder if you'd like to join me for a chat?" "Not me, dear. Not today." Finally, you manage to get a little group by the window interested and tentatively start to ask some probing questions: "What is your name?" (Always a good one for starters!) You cannot quite catch the answer.

It seems very noisy so, bravely, you go and switch off the television: no-one is watching. Someone yells! Is that because you switched it off? A friendly-looking character clutches your arm and asks whether you can take them to the toilet. You seek out a busy someone in a uniform. "Oh, she always wants to go to the toilet; someone will see to her." You relay back the information. "Can't you take me?" Well, no, I'm not allowed to, not insured (I wouldn't know how). You hear a scream from the other side of the ward, and a phone is ringing and ringing.

The tea trolley! This cheers everyone up, and cups of tepid tea are passed around. The trolley rolls off. But they didn't give me one! "Didn't you want a cup of tea, dear?" You'll manage.

Being the persevering type, you endeavour to remember the names of some of your little group and you are gently asking the person you think said her name was Mrs Greaves where it was she was born. She is explaining how she moved here to be nearer to her son, but he doesn't come to see her much. In comes a member of staff (at last, some moral support) — perhaps she'll tell you some more names or at least whether the man sitting next to the fish tank is deaf or just not interested.

"Don't know why you bother — you'll not get anything out of them. They don't know what day it is! They'll forget you as soon as you've gone, so I don't see any point!" Without saying a word more she pulls a wheelchair away from the table, startling the occupant. In comes another member of staff, who thinks reminiscence is a good thing. "The poor dears don't do anything. You are good coming here, though they won't get anything out of it." The staff stand talking about the patients.

As you turn to ask another question, a voice loudly says, "No point in talking to Mary, she'll tell you a load of nonsense. Talk to Fred — he's our songbird. Go on, Fred, sing your song for this nice person who's come all this way to see you." Fred happily starts to sing a beautiful song. You've never heard it before. Fred forgets the rest of the words. While this is happening, three of your group start to wander off, until the staff firmly usher them back into their seats. One gets angry and pushes the staff away. They take her away.

It's quiet at last. You turn to Mary once more — and she is fast asleep. You start to talk to Fred and he smiles broadly. Well, Fred, when you sang that song, it sounded like you'd had some professional experience. Fred, slowly, but with clarity, starts to tell you how he used to be involved with amateur dramatics ... You hear the sound of chattering voices: "We've brought some more for you" — 15 people and four staff are watching you. The patients look bemused, confused and one or two look a little frightened. You feel bemused, confused and a little frightened.

You start to go round the new group, introducing yourself, as you should, asking who each person is and where they are from, while Edna helps put knives and forks noisily onto hard Formica tops. You have nearly had a word with everyone when staff suddenly reappear and everyone goes to dinner.

The pack of photographs remains unopened.

You look around, thinking how you really would like a cup of tea now, and could use the toilet. But there is no-one except a tired-looking person dishing out what looks like mashed potato and smells like school dinners.

Picking up your bag, you feel a little angry and low in self-esteem. Edna waves at you from the dinner table. You begin to feel a little better. You write up a few notes in your diary: 'Mary sounded like a local; I'm sure she must know lots about the area. Perhaps I could find the rest of the words to Fred's song, and I must ask him where he used to perform. I should find out when the staff have their break and see if I can join them — might get a cup of tea and get to know them a little better. I could explain what I'm doing here! What about that dayroom — couldn't we make a bit more space in there?'

The tired-looking person, now dishing out what looks suspiciously like custard, calls out to you: "Thank you, dear, you've worked very hard. There's a cup of tea for you in the other room." Well, all right, you are gasping and you'd better tell someone you are leaving. In the other room, a couple of people are eating sandwiches.

"You know," says one, "I've never seen Mary like that before. She's taken a real shine to you." And the other one says, "Yeah, they like to see a new face. Fred was really cheerful; usually a bit down, that one. We were a bit short today. Three people off, but next week we'll make sure there is some room in the dayroom for you. Help yourself to tea, that's what we do — we don't stand on ceremony here!" You smile gratefully and shyly.

The door opens and a head pops round and says, "Settling in? Good" and disappears. The head returns for a moment: "We must have a chat. Thursday?" and is gone in a flash. The first one who spoke leans over. "They never told us you were coming, but I am pleased — what did you say your name was?"

Note in diary: first session — 'Think it went rather well. Must remember to bring lunch with me next week.'

Principles of Practice

As part of our project we talked about the past and memories. The residents opened up in amazing ways. Talking about memories, one resident said, "They are like a tide – they come back, they roll back to the background and then they come flooding back." Another resident who was normally very quiet would not allow the care assistant to put her in the other lounge when she knew Maggie, the artist, was here. A number of residents who were physically hindered by arthritis, for example, participated in sessions and derived great benefit and pleasure from their efforts. Everyone was made to feel that they had something they could contribute.

(Barbara White, Activities Organizer, Ringshill Nursing Home)

Reminiscence may occur spontaneously, or as a result of encouragement and stimulation; privately, one-to-one or in groups; informally or formally; in 'recall' sessions, in 'creative' sessions, or in 'social' sessions.

Groups and sessions

The aim of reminiscence sessions (and many other activities) is usually primarily to create opportunities for interaction:

- amongst clients,
- between staff and clients,
- between clients and others,
- between the 'venue' and the wider community.

In order for this to occur, you must create an overall environment that:

- allows communication,
- stimulates communication, and
- encourages communication.

A reminiscence session or group should aim to be:

- an opportunity for socializing,
- an emotional and/or stimulating experience,
- a context for purposeful activity,
- enjoyable and meaningful.

This is brought about by:

- good practice when communicating with clients;
- allowing yourself, and being allowed, time to spend with clients;
- creating conducive atmospheres;
- having something meaningful and interesting to talk about;
- helping clients with communication difficulties to communicate;
- being able to respond positively to spontaneous communication;
- imaginatively developing possibilities, trying things out, developing your skills;
- the involvement of a variety of staff, including management, in activity programmes; and
- having time to prepare and review.

I think the residents gained satisfaction from being engaged in purposeful physical and mental activity; enjoyment in working with a group and a sense of achievement in what they produced. They enjoyed the attention of staff and visitors who took an interest in the work. Some residents became stars for the photographers who visited the project.
(Maggie Warren, Artist in Residence, Ringshill Nursing Home)

Informal and formal groups

A reminiscence group may be set up as an informal or a formal meeting. An *informal* session will appear casual, possibly evolving over refreshments, and will probably be open to whoever is interested, or even everyone who happens to be in the room, including passing staff and visitors. People may choose to sit in their habitual places in the lounge or the day room, although you might prefer to find a special place to gather.

The 'reminiscence worker' will attempt to involve people in conversation, debate and discussion which should, despite an informal atmosphere, be serious and thoughtful as often as light and entertaining. If a group is considered informal, this does not mean that no effort and attention is given to guiding the session. You will need to make sure that participants can hear and see each other, that the room feels comfortable and conducive to talk, that individuals are helped to contribute if need be, and that stimulating 'prompts' and subjects are introduced to encourage contributions from as wide a cross-section of people as possible. It may not suit everybody to recall their memories in such a public way and you will need to observe closely what is happening in the group and tailor your own contribution to help the session be enjoyable, meaningful and stimulating.

A *formal*, or focused, group should be planned and held somewhere where people can concentrate. The participants may, particularly in the early stages, need help in focusing on a specific subject or, indeed, in broadening their perspective and reaching deeper memories. It is probably best, particularly if people are not used to this kind of session or do not know each other, initially to encourage them to share information about themselves and their background. As it all becomes a bit more familiar, they can start to explore issues in a little more depth. The sessions will need to be thoughtfully and sensitively guided and you should be prepared to explore the emotional content of memories more deeply than in an informal group. The group should consist of a restricted number of people who have agreed, or chosen, to meet at regular intervals over a specific period of time.

Generally, most groups actually fall somewhere in between focused and casual, and a group get-together is likely to include elements of both. It can feel quite comfortable to have a quite sharply focused discussion preceded and/or followed by some light-hearted chat; one does not exclude the other. Whichever kind of group you aim to develop, and they can be equally rewarding, consideration of the quality and process of group activity is important.

Setting up a group

How used to getting involved and being interactive are the potential members of your planned group? In a place where active interaction between clients, and between staff and clients, is a common occurrence you will probably find 'getting started' can be introduced fairly quickly. If your clients are normally understimulated, very frail or stressed, you may have to be particularly flexible and take into account day-to-day differences in mood, capability and motivation. In this case you will find it harder to motivate people and will have to spend longer building people's confidence.

What is the purpose of setting up the group? The aim of reminiscence groups is nearly always to do something together in order to encourage interpersonal interaction. Reminiscence in groups has what we might call a 'social' dimension, and for many people this will be the most obvious and attainable reason for doing reminiscence work. A group set up for social purposes has a great deal to offer participants.

Often people living in homes and hospitals are isolated partly because they have problems relating to others. This may be because of sensory impairment or difficulty with communication caused by illness or disability. They may have lost, perhaps because of depression, the incentive to relate to others, or may simply have spent a long time alone. There may be very little going on around them that is comprehensible or stimulating, and there may be few social occasions at which there is an opportunity to interact with others. We can be comfortable *alone* surrounded by our memories and possessions in a familiar environment, but to be *lonely* in an inhospitable and strange environment can cause serious dislocation and disorientation.

When trying to encourage social interaction amongst your clients, you will have to think hard about how things are set up and how you proceed. Bear in mind that not everybody finds it easy in groups, and of course, some people are not interested at all in socializing. Certain people will confidently have a go at all kinds of things, others need gentle encouragement and reassurance (itself an opportunity for some attention). My experience is that most, but not all, people do like to get together with others sometimes, though it will depend on how they feel. Some people positively thrive on being in company.

If there are specific therapeutic aims for individuals, you will have to think quite carefully about who participates in which group and what it is they are going to be doing. You should liaise with appropriate therapists and clinicians to ensure you have an agreed care plan. You need to be sure what aims you have for an individual and work out together how you are going to arrange things to achieve these. It is important to explain clearly what it is you are asking of people, especially if the activity is new to them. To say 'reminiscence group' may sound rather intimidating or even incomprehensible.

Decide whether existing groups are in fact suitable for that particular person's needs: for example, someone with communication difficulties may not, initially, be comfortable in a group where conversation is fast and furious; someone who needs to practise writing after suffering a stroke may not get the opportunity in a group which is planning a tea dance, and so on.

Seating arrangements
You will need to think about how people are to sit. If you see two people struggling to communicate, you may have to rearrange their seating to help them interact, perhaps so they can work on something together. There can be no perfect plan as to how you are going to 'seat' members of the group, although seating arrangements are significant and affect the flow of discussion and roles taken within the group: *people sitting opposite tend to communicate most; people sitting side-by-side tend to communicate least.*

The obvious arrangement is a circle, since each person has the maximum number of people sitting opposite and no-one is precisely side-by-side. If people are grouped around a table, there are positions which will affect behaviour. For example, the person who can see most people, is sitting most centrally or who is alone on one side of the table is likely to emerge as most dominant or as the leader. Positions will often be chosen with instinctive recognition by the most dominant or shy.

You may need to arrange seating to maximize communication from all participating in the session. If you want to look into this in more depth, it is recommended that you read some specialized books or go on one of the many training sessions available that cover 'group-work'. Also bear in mind arrangements that have worked for the next time the group meets.

Size

The main thing to consider when deciding the size of a group is whether there will be enough opportunity for all the participants to contribute. If the people in the group are going to need a lot of individual attention from you, the group should be smaller.

A group that is too large will not, within limited time, offer the opportunity for exploration of any depth with everyone involved and some people may feel neglected as you will be unable to give them enough attention. Large groups will tend to break into smaller groups and you may find yourself actually running two or more little groups at the same time. If you can handle this, it can be quite an effective way of working with large groups of people, especially if the different groups are able to 'get on with it' while you are dealing with someone else.

Groups for formal reminiscence work should normally be kept fairly small – six to eight people is plenty. Aim for quality not quantity.

Selecting participants

A decision you will need to make, and it may be worth discussing this with colleagues, is whether or not individuals should be selected for reminiscence sessions, and how that selection is to be made.

In a residential home you may have people that tend to 'hang around' together and are friends, and it may be appropriate to work with them, adapting yourself to what is already a 'natural' group. In a hospital or nursing home, where people may need quite a lot of personal attention, or where you have specific interest in involving people with special needs, you may want to select people who you consider would benefit from involvement in formal or social activity. There are advantages and disadvantages both ways.

Someone with severe communication problems may be encouraged amongst a group of people who chat easily, or they may feel intimidated. Lively people may become inhibited by people suffering from depression or, on the contrary, they may be able to help lift their spirits a little. There may be individuals who have a positive or a negative effect on one another.

It can be difficult to deal with people with different abilities all at the same time and it can help to have specific groups for people with distinct needs or interests. A 'special needs' group that is quite small and intimate may be a sensible idea for those who have particular difficulties that need close attention and a lot of help. After a while, they might move on to a more general group. Having said that, some people can get great pleasure just from being part of a group — just listening and watching — and it may be inappropriate to separate people. Think about it, discuss issues with other people involved, and your clients, and decide for yourself.

If you are going to explore reminiscence with people in some depth and with some continuity then a group must ideally be allowed to bond and settle. Once you have decided on 'membership', try to stay with that for a while. If someone new does join the group, be aware of what it could feel like to be new for that person and take steps to help them start to feel part of what is going on. Make sure they are introduced and welcomed. The arrival of a new participant can be a good opportunity to get the group to assert who they all are and what they have been doing. Try and get the group to look after the newcomer until they are settled. Bear in mind that a newcomer joining an existing group will have an effect on the group dynamics.

Thinking about the physical environment
When setting up sessions, you need to look carefully at the place in which you are going to hold them. Although initially you may find it easier to work where your clients habitually gather, there are distinct advantages to making a special place for reminiscence. For some people, to go out, that is to get away from where they usually spend the day, can in itself be a refreshing change that helps to take minds off daily problems for a while.

Ideally, in the interest of your group and good relations generally, you should meet somewhere away from the everyday distractions that surround us: ringing phones, clattering trolleys, disruptive people, kitchens and noisy comings and goings. If you can, find a reasonably quiet, but not necessarily closed, room that is preferably airy and light, where you can settle down without too much disturbance and everyone can concentrate on what is going on. *Too big a space can inhibit intimate conversation; too small a space can feel cramped and pressured.*

The room used for the sessions was the conservatory. It was very pleasant, light and comfortable for the residents. As it was open on one side to the small dining room and corridor it could have been a problem. As it turned out, even though visitors and staff sometimes called in to have a look around, it wasn't too disruptive. I felt it gave an 'open' feeling which prevented individuals from feeling 'shut in' the session.
(Carol Davies, Artist in Residence, the Rhyl Nursing Home)

Try and arrange the layout of the room so that people feel able to leave. A sensation of 'being trapped' can be very unpleasant.

Residents may have associations with certain spaces, so take this into account. If, for example, you meet in the place where people eat, they may be inclined to have food on their minds and start to get hungry as soon as they arrive. If the group meets in the side room where people go when they are bereaved or receive bad news, this may not help create a positive atmosphere. Confusion can arise if you share a room with the hairdressers. It may be that you have little choice, so just be aware.

Even if you decide it best to work with people where they usually sit, you may find, by gentle use of diplomacy, that you can stretch the boundaries of the places people may habitually be inclined to spend their time. For example, a mixed group could meet in an area that tends only to be used by women. The room that no-one ever uses may become more hospitable if you take all those old walking frames out first. Be careful if space is usually used by other residents who are not in this particular group — they may feel excluded and may even become disruptive.

Making a special place
Differentiated space is quite important. By this I mean trying to make it unlike any other so that it is special. Consider hanging pictures on the wall, such as photographs of trips out or of local scenes — pictures that

mean something to the users — a variety of books to read or browse through and some nice curtains, plants and comfortable furniture.

Although lack of appropriate space seemed to be the biggest problem, we came up with a solution that had big advantages. We moved most of the chairs from a small lounge area and brought in two firm tables for the residents to work at. There was also a row of armchairs for those who preferred to watch. This area was near the main entrance, so a lot of people had to pass by and became involved. The tables, besides providing a work surface, gave the activity its own special setting. It did take a long time to set up and dismantle this area each week but it was well worth it. (Maggie Warren, Artist in Residence, Ringshill Nursing Home)

I know space is at a premium and it is possible to set up something temporarily, but it is better to develop somewhere as a quiet room, as a study or library, a club room or maybe even an art studio. Try and avoid the space you do have being commandeered by, for example, other professionals for meetings. It should, if possible, be space that is for the patients, for the residents. In one old people's home the 'reminiscence' room had as its centrepiece a rather ugly filing cabinet. The only solution until the managers were finally persuaded to move it was to cover it with a chintz table cloth and stick a plant on top. It looked a bit odd, but a little less out of place. In a hospital room the doctors met for their lunch and had to be embarrassed out of the habit of leaving half-eaten food and sweet wrappers on the floor! It the space is to be shared by others, make it clear to them that they must leave it as they found it, and why. (If they are a bit obstreperous, gently but firmly remind them that your group represent the most important people in the building!)

If you cannot find a room, make a reminiscence corner, with some screens. I know of a hospital ward where the patients' dayroom has a variety of memorabilia on display, a stained glass window and some special paintings designed by the reminiscence club, and is crowned by a signed picture from the Queen Mother given in response to a birthday card sent to her by the club members. It is still the same old dayroom; it just feels more interesting and distinctive than it used to.

Think about the atmosphere of your place. Does it feel welcoming? Is it friendly and interesting? Even people who do not appear to respond to much may subtly respond to a good atmosphere, as in a conservatory, pub/bar, an old-fashioned room or a kitchen. It can be lively or quiet, bright or soft, snazzy or pastel; it should not be formal and sterile.

Think about fabrics, colour, textures, artwork, photographs, mirrors, lighting, stained glass (introduces ever-changing colour), wallpaper, friezes, pottery, ornaments and so on. Remember, if people are using wheelchairs the height of surfaces, displays, pictures and so on will have to be taken into consideration. You do not need to try and create a replica of a 1930s or 1950s room, just aim to create a welcoming atmosphere of normality and friendliness, a room where the users can make an impact. Care of your clients' immediate environment illustrates the care you are offering to them. *Our environment is something we interact with and influence, not merely something we sit passively inside!*

Making a special time
It is important to allocate a special time for reminiscence sessions, whether they are informal or formal. When considering staff priorities, if something is not timetabled in, the chances are it will be left out when other time pressures build up. If the emotional lives of your clients are considered very important, and they should be, then sessions and activities should be treated as very important and staff time allocated, not just for the sessions themselves, but for preparation, discussion and evaluation. Time should be set aside on a regular basis; this shows everyone that this is a significant activity, allowing participants, who can sometimes feel they are bothering staff who have better things to do, to consider this, as one resident succinctly put it, "time for us".

The commitment of time also demonstrates that there is official support from management for staff efforts to improve quality of life. Too often, staff are expected to deal with issues related to the emotional well-being of those in their care 'on the side'. Physical care, of course, has initial priority, but can we really say we are caring for someone if they are well fed and watered, warm and sheltered but unnecessarily neglected emotionally?

All activity programmes must be taken seriously and to say that 'we do it anyway' does not encourage staff to get involved directly with those in their care. It allows for too many opportunities to divert energy to other tasks. Allow time to talk and listen when people reminisce spontaneously. Plan time for groups and sessions into a timetable. Be prepared to negotiate for, and justify, space and time for reminiscence work.

When to hold a group will depend on what else is going on. It can be very disruptive if people have to leave a session for a clinic or to go to the hairdressers. A session just before visiting time may not get the best from those keeping an eye on the clock and some people may get anxious if they believe their visitor may not be able to find them. Trying to lead a session while tables are being laid or doctors are sweeping through can be very frustrating. We were presenting a film show in a long-stay psychiatric hospital and it was going extremely well. Suddenly everyone got up and left. It was 3 o'clock — tea time. Once, when we unintentionally clashed with hymn singing, only one person turned up.

It is simply a matter of planning. Try negotiating with those who are providing other services so that different activities do not clash. Sometimes, for example with the hairdressers, it can be a good idea to work in harmony with them so that people arrive at the club looking their very best. If the physiotherapists seem continually to turn up to take someone from the group, do not just grumble — discuss your difficulties with them. It is most likely a planning problem, not personal rivalry, so it can be resolved with a little goodwill and flexibility on both sides. Remember, your sessions are important as well!

That hour leading up to lunchtime (about 11 to 12) can be just right for those who cannot concentrate for too long, while for others the 'golden hour' of 2 to 3pm is perfect. If you are actively trying to involve relatives and friends, an evening social session may be more suitable, and can be a pleasantly relaxing time after a hard day. Do bear in mind that straight after eating is often not such a good time: it is quite natural to feel a little sleepy after a meal.

Try to persuade the inexorable tea trolley to wait for an appropriate moment to make its arrival. Tea time, or the equivalent, is an important event and should be respected, but that trolley does not have to make its appearance regardless of any other factor. Plan, if possible, to have a break at a natural place in the session: refreshment at the beginning to welcome everyone in, a break in the middle (all this remembering can be hard work) or at the end to mark the last phase. Tea drinking (or other choice) is, in England anyway, traditionally a social time: *use* the break rather than just dish out the drinks.

Always ask whether tea or coffee is required with milk and/or sugar — even if you know the answer. With this small gesture, and it is a good habit to cultivate, you are demonstrating that there is a decision to be made and that you are not making assumptions about people's needs. How do you know whether, after years and years, someone may have decided to give up sugar? You don't and you must ask. There should always be alternatives available — fruit juice, milk and mineral water are all easily obtained. A drop of beer or a sherry may be most well received. Always check that this is compatible with any medication or other treatment first. (One lady I know always surreptitiously has a drop of whiskey in her tea. It is done with a wink from understanding staff and she needs no sleeping pills.) *A refreshment break is an opportunity to relax and chat, to make contact with people.*

Starting and finishing
Once a starting and finishing time is agreed, try not to change it without good reason and gradually staff and clients will get used to the fact that this is a 'special' time. Devise a system for arriving and departing. Are you to collect everyone or is there help you can arrange? It can drastically shorten a session if you have to spend half an hour finding out if everyone is ready and half an hour getting everyone back to where they have to go.

It was very time consuming accompanying individuals to and from sessions, especially if I was working alone. I think it is important that roles are defined in this area. The session ran from 2pm to 4pm. It was necessary to start collecting people soon after 1pm ... it took until nearly 5pm to return people to their rooms. (Carol Davies, Artist in Residence, the Rhyl Nursing Home)

It is a good idea to try and arrange to have someone or something to keep people occupied if they are waiting for everyone else to arrive:

some music, perhaps, or magazines to browse. It can work very well if the first part of the session is a sociable, informal refreshment time welcoming people as they arrive with tea and biscuits and so on. This can make the wait while everyone arrives a pleasant part of the day.

It is a friendly touch to greet each group member individually as they arrive, asking their name if you do not know it and introducing yourself as appropriate. If there is a newcomer to the group, ensure that they are introduced to everyone. Only use their forename if this is customary in your group and if you are sure you have their permission. A few moments' personal attention for everyone is polite and respectful. I usually shake hands. If someone arrives late, make sure they are welcomed by name and explain where things are up to in the session. Repeat any particular information that has been given to everyone else.

Plan the end of your session so that you all stop together in a satisfying manner with an opportunity to discuss what has happened or catch up on the latest gossip. Refreshments, a chat or a song or two at the end of a demanding hour of remembering can make the session feel complete and accomplished. It can be disorienting for everyone if people are taken away singly as you frantically try to sum up, or have to finish in mid-flow. Allow plenty of time to round up the session. This gives everyone a chance to finish what they are doing and to reflect. You may like to allow some time for relaxation to help people unwind. Ask for people's reactions to what they have been doing, thank them, acknowledge their contributions and tell them what is happening next, and next week (even if you know they may forget).

Then get together with a colleague for a brief appraisal and make a note of things to get sorted out before next time, such as 'Sit Alice on the other side next to Fred, find a tape of Spanish music, and make sure there are some paper towels for cleaning hands. Don't sit George next to the radiator, remember to bring back Agnes' photographs and think of something for Nelly to do. Avril said she used to go tobogganing — can we take that further?'

Working in blocks
Plan finite blocks of sessions, eight to 12 sessions at a time. This allows you to stop and review progress. You can continue if all is going well, but you also have the opportunity to adjust things, introduce new

ideas or try something different. Working in finite blocks also helps if you have to work with too many people for the time you have available. Form small groups and work with each group for a fixed length of time. Then work with another group. This is a practical way of making sure everyone gets something.

Review

It is important to review progress at regular intervals and to discuss developments with your group and your colleagues. Get into the habit at the end of each session of allowing some time to assess what has happened and make a few notes. You may have noticed a particularly unusual or animated reaction to a particular stimulus or piece of information that may help others respond better to someone's needs. At the end of a block it may be appropriate to have a full discussion with everyone concerned and produce a report.

Allow yourself to be open-minded and honestly self-critical. Seek the opinions of others. Often there is not a right and wrong way that things should happen but we can all take steps to influence things for the better. There is rarely a 'perfect' session and always something to learn. I have seen the most experienced group workers struggling because people were sitting in the wrong place, or because the lighting or temperature was wrong.

Look for the good things that happen as well. You may think you had difficulty getting someone to talk when in fact another staff member would tell you that it was a breakthrough that the person stayed in the session at all. Mary hardly said a word in sessions, just sat contemplative and serene, occasionally allowing us a wry smile. I became used to her reserved behaviour and she was always welcome in the group. It only became apparent after discussions with her regular care staff that in the evenings, when certain staff that Mary considered friends arrived for work, she began to open up. The staff commented how animated and chatty she became on the day the reminiscence group met. Her family noticed as well.

When people say 'no'

It can sometimes be quite a subtle process to ask people whether they would like to join in with something new to them. Often they will say 'no'. This can be a habitual reaction, perhaps one that they have had throughout their life, or it may indicate insecurity about their own abilities and capacity to cope in the present. There may be genuine lack of interest in what you are offering; a misunderstanding about what is on offer; a negativity brought on by previous experience of activities or genuine voluntary or involuntary disengagement. They may be unwell, or have other unresolved problems on their minds. All these possibilities need to be considered before you accept that a simple 'no' means exactly what it says.

First of all, you must ensure that people actually understand what it is you are asking of them, and what kind of commitment you are talking about. As I have already stressed, there must be a clear option to pull out at any time and it is important that everyone potentially involved is helped to understand what the group is for and why they are being asked to join.

If a negative reaction is due to lack of confidence and self-esteem, you may have to clearly devise a project so as to start very simply. For example, start off with a simple social gathering and focus on fairly accessible topics. Steer the group very gently, with their approval, towards something with a more practical or sophisticated aim. If people are unsure about what you are asking them to get involved in, it can reassure them that they are not committing themselves to something they will not enjoy if you suggest they come along just for ten minutes and they will then be free to leave (and remember to offer them the opportunity!). Ask people to give it a try, making it clear that there is no obligation to stay if they do not want to.

An act of non-co-operation may in fact be a positive action. In a situation where most decisions are made on someone's behalf, or if they are unable for whatever reason to express or communicate needs and preferences, resistance to voluntary activities may be a way of asserting independence of spirit. Some gentle coaxing is acceptable, but always allow the ultimate right of non-participation. If you yourself cultivate an attitude that is encouraging and willing to give new things a try, this will positively affect your clients' reactions.

Remember: making a positive decision to participate is part of the process. You must never ever force, even by default, someone to participate in any kind of social, recreational or other activity. There is no point. It may look good to have numbers on your list but if someone does not genuinely want to be there they will get nothing from the session and possibly make difficulties for you and others involved. Perhaps they would like to do something else. *Do not assume that what you organize has to appeal to everyone and do not confuse your own interests with those of other people. Ask again another time — they may have changed their mind.*

Memories as a painful reminder of what is lost

Staff can sometimes be a little fearful of getting too involved with the emotional lives of those in their care and may believe that the possibility of upsetting residents makes it all too risky. There is a lot of discussion these days about 'rights and risk' and this applies as much to emotional risk as to physical risk. As long as great attention is paid to supporting people, they must be offered the opportunity to choose whether to take emotional risks, and it is, amongst other things, the role of reminiscence work to offer this opportunity. It is often surprising for people new to reminiscence work to realize that, as long as one takes a little care and is sensitive to people's feelings, people rarely get seriously upset. Older people have often come to terms with the past a lot more effectively than you might expect. If you do touch on unacceptable subjects, people who are able will probably shut off and withdraw from the unwelcome stimulus. This is OK as long as you allow them the right to withdraw and do not try and dig deeper 'for their own good'. Many people will resolve feelings and protect themselves from any unwanted emotional effects of recall for themselves and, unless you are a trained therapist or counsellor, you should not attempt to disturb people's control of their own emotional exploration. You should be as sensitive as you can to non-verbal signals and respect these. If someone does get upset, do not make a fuss. Someone who has burst into tears in public may, as much as anything, be embarrassed by their loss of control. Men, conditioned not to cry, are likely to feel particularly vulnerable and exposed.

It is not always such a bad thing if someone cries: a good cry can be a chance to release some bottled up emotions and can be very good for us. Staff must respond with support and kindness, offering consolation when appropriate. Ask, gently, whether they would like to go somewhere else. The person may wish to leave the group or may not. If they do, ensure there is someone to stay with them if wanted, or at least to keep an eye on them. As soon as you are able, check whether they wish to talk about things with you quietly. Sometimes their peers can offer support with a level of empathy and understanding not available from younger people.

If someone frequently and easily gets upset, you should try to find out what it actually is that is causing them a problem. Is the difficulty caused by the content of the sessions or are other issues concerning them? They may be suffering from anxiety or be in a lot of pain. It may be a consequence of medication or of illness. If no obvious reason for distress can be found and dealt with, it may be best if an alternative activity is suggested that does not look back over the years but is still interesting and stimulating.

At times, the relief or catharsis provided by a few tears can be rather enjoyable. I remember two ladies crying on and off all through the session. I felt a bit worried. As they left they happily asked me when we were going to do this again because they had enjoyed themselves so much! In one of my earlier sessions, a song we were singing brought one lady to tears. The staff responded as if to an emergency! The group was stopped and with a sense of urgency she was removed from the group and taken back to sit by her bed. I went to see her later and she was most aggrieved at missing out on the rest of the music session. *Reminiscence, by bringing to our consciousness people, places and moments, that, except in our hearts, are gone for ever, is likely to touch some tender places.*

Leading sessions

A good session leader will:

- identify subjects that people can relate to or already have an interest in;
- encourage participants to explore their experience, including emotional experience;
- listen to those who have something to say and be sensitive and responsive to non-verbal communication;
- offer, with care, sensory experiences that may bring back memories; and

59

● identify and help those who need help to participate and contribute.

It can work well if you are able to run groups in pairs, with a session leader and a helper. These roles are interchangeable and, within the same session, or week to week, the 'leadership' may pass between people. On a practical level, this will mean that if someone needs to 'leave the room' they are not put in the embarrassing position of stopping the group to ask you publicly for your help. If one of you has to deal with someone for any reason, the other can keep the group going, causing minimal disruption.

If you are able to run a group with a colleague regularly, you could find that the two of you build a close rapport and work together effectively and intuitively. You must be careful, though, not to digress into too much conversation between the two of you and never talk about the group as if they are not there. While the group is running, your attention must always be turned towards the individuals in the group.

It is possible to do sessions on your own. Many of us have to and some prefer this, fearing potential embarrassment or interference (an unhelpful 'helper' can be a big problem) but a degree of positive mutual support can allow you to maintain a good level of quality response throughout the session without losing people's attention or leaving you frantically wondering what to do next. You can also reflect on each other's performance. It can be quite demanding to run a group on your own and two heads are usually better than one.

The role of a session leader is to: stimulate, encourage, enable and motivate. Imagine yourself as the conductor of an orchestra, the chair of a meeting or the host of a party. The leader acts as, or provides, a stimulus — this may be by asking questions or using a 'reminiscence aid' — and then guides the response of the group so that everyone can comment or contribute as they wish, gently encouraging responses and then enabling responses to be expressed, elaborated upon and shared.

The role of the helper is to support the session leader by ensuring everyone is able to participate, offering reassurance, possibly making sure someone is heard, or is clear about what is being discussed. The helper can sit with people who have special difficulties, explaining and helping them join in. They should participate and contribute, but should not take over, unless it is agreed that they will do so.

Remember that, in a session lasting an hour or so, you will need to try and ensure that everyone gets a reasonable amount of attention. When working with people who are very frail or have special needs, organize sessions for small groups of three or four so that you can give full attention to the needs of each individual.

Listening and hearing
Most people, in order to express themselves confidently, need reassurance and confirmation that they are being understood and being heard. We know when someone is not really listening to what we are saying by the way they respond to us. Communication, like water and electricity, has to have somewhere to receive it or it does not flow.

Try to listen and *show* that you have heard what is said. If someone makes a contribution to the conversation, take it into account as you proceed. Do not ignore any contribution. Doing this can take a great deal of conscious effort, especially when working with groups where some members are talking confidently and someone less assertive tries to say something. If a contribution is out of context, acknowledge that it is very interesting and gently guide things back to the subject the group was discussing. Unless this is inappropriate, come back to it later. Attempt to involve everyone in the group in some way, and do not let yourself become dominated by those with plenty to say at the expense of others. You must pay attention to what is happening in the group and adjust your own responses to this.

Be aware of non-verbal cues. They can help you be effectively in tune with what is going on. If someone leans forward, they may have something to say — and why is that person smiling to themselves? Take care because, while body language and non-verbal signals can be helpful, they should only be interpreted as a possible indication of what is happening. For example, if someone turns away it can indicate they are not receptive to what is being said or they may be feeling *very* receptive and it is a little too much. Crossed arms may indicate someone is preparing for a challenge or they may be shutting you out. But are they protecting themselves from the message or the messenger?

When communicating, most of us are sensitive to the non-verbal and verbal 'cues' that tell us that the listener is interested and it is all right to continue talking. The skills needed to demonstrate that we are listening are accessible to almost everyone, although they come easier to some than others. We more or less do this intuitively when we are in a receptive mode during a conversation. The difference in a reminiscence session is that you may have to emphasize your responses so that they are clear and unambiguous. Your acknowledgements should be quite overt: nodding and encouraging, turning towards the person contributing, smiling or frowning to acknowledge the emotional impact of what is being said. This may sound a little false, but you are demonstrating clearly that you are paying attention. It becomes more natural with a little practice and if tried with confidence.

The trouble with awareness of body language is that, when you start thinking about it, you can become too self-conscious. As soon as I try to be aware of levels of eye contact I do not know where I am supposed to look and my eyeballs start rolling all over the place. Am I looking at people encouragingly? Or am I staring at them? Oops, I just looked away and now I'm scratching my head, my nostrils just flared … perhaps my pupils are too small and, oh no, my foot's going up and down, which means I want to be somewhere else, doesn't it? And so on.

I find the best way of dealing with this is to consider just occasionally how you are reacting and if necessary adjust your responses. For example, if I find my attention is wandering and I am not concentrating, I change my position as if I were extremely interested: leaning forward slightly, open-armed, relaxed and focusing on the person talking. Within a few moments, I usually find I really am paying greater attention. We can alter our subconscious reactions by deliberately changing our posture.

Before a session try and get yourself into a frame of mind that is relaxed and receptive. If you are too preoccupied with yourself or other issues, you will not be able to give the attention that your clients need and you will find people less willing to communicate with you. The cultivation of attitudes familiar in counselling theory can increase the effectiveness of positive listening.

Genuineness, authenticity or self-congruence involves responding to people not as a 'patient' or 'old person', that is, in terms of their role, but naturally and spontaneously, as you would to a good friend. You should not be guarded and when appropriate should be open and communicative about yourself.

I was startled recently when, during a getting to know you conversation with Violet, she suddenly said, "Well, that's enough about me. What about you? Where are you from and what do you do for a living? Why aren't you at work?"

Non-possessive warmth is the ability to demonstrate non-critical acceptance of another, with words and in non-verbal responses. You are clearly showing acceptance of the person with your tone of voice, facial expression and eye contact. You aim to help someone feel safe and confident.

Normally, it is important not to give signals that indicate you disapprove of, disbelieve or are uninterested in what someone is saying. This is particularly important if someone is sharing emotionally difficult and disturbing information. You should aim to accept and not judge. An example might be if someone has been involved with activities you consider immoral.

Empathy is the ability and a willingness to put yourself in another's place, to be able to enter into another's subjective world and identify with what is happening, or has happened, to them.

If, for example, someone is telling you about a childhood experience that was embarrassing, you should be willing to get sufficiently in tune with that person's view of the world to have a sense of how they felt then, and what they are feeling as they tell you. This can give an individual a sometimes intensely reassuring experience that they are not alone and are being understood and accepted.

Working with people whose senses are impaired or who are uncertain and lacking in confidence will involve not only hearing what someone has communicated but unambiguously *demonstrating* that you have heard, by the following means:

Using repetition: without sounding like a parrot, occasionally repeat or sum up what someone has said, or the group has concluded, to reinforce that you have understood.

Remembering: it happens to us all, but try not to ask a question that you have already had the answer to. Try to incorporate information you have been given into later conversations. Remember, and confirm that you have remembered, in subsequent sessions.

Responding: do not ignore any contribution, although you may wish to ask someone to bring the subject up again at another time. Make sure you give them the opportunity.

Taking action: examples of acting on information someone has shared with you may be something like finding a photograph or an article in a magazine that relates to a place they told you about. This very positively shows that you heard what was said.

You should aim to demonstrate, ideally, not only that you listened at the time, but that you were interested enough to follow this up. Reminiscence work should allow someone to feel that they matter, that they can still influence events and that the life they have lived has interest and meaning. *Good practice involves hearing and responding.*

Pacing yourself

Remind yourself that your residents may take a few moments to gather their thoughts and answer a question or respond to a stimulus. They may have difficulty speaking, and reactions may be slow. It is easy, too easy, in order to get things done (and we all do it at times) to put words into people's mouths, make assumptions about what they are going to say or speak on someone's behalf. We can even be a little afraid of a silence in conversation. Try to pace what you are doing at a speed that suits participants. Be patient and do not feel you need to fill every silence quickly with the sound of your own voice:

● allow time for people to answer questions;

- respond or act on to what is said or communicated;
- demonstrate, verbally and non-verbally, that you have heard;
- help and prompt only when appropriate;
- do not ignore any contribution;
- involve everyone.

Asking questions

You will need to ask questions in such a way that they encourage a response, and one way to approach this is to consider whether questions are 'open' or 'closed'. People planning to run groups sometimes get a little nervous about this, but it is quite straightforward. Essentially, an open question encourages an elaborated or extended answer while a closed question demands a 'yes'/'no' 'or don't know' answer. "Were you a good cook, Molly?" is a closed question, while "What did you like to cook, Molly?" is an open question. "Are you well?" is a closed question, while "How are you feeling today?" is an open question. It can be rather inhibiting to get too concerned about what is an open question and what is closed: do not become too pre-occupied with this.

I find the following framework more use in helping me to decide what kind of questions to ask. I think of questions, when I think of them at all, as evoking recall in three categories: 'Who I am' memories, 'What I did' memories and 'What it was like' memories. 'Who I am' and 'What I did' memories, which are similar, may encourage a fundamental assertion of individuality, whilst 'What it was like' memories can open the discussion and encourage more interaction and contribution from the group as a whole, still allowing for plenty of personal references.

For example, George tells you he was a bus driver for 20 years (*who I am*). You can help him develop his story (if need be!) by asking something like "How far did you drive in a day George?" (*what I did*), eventually leading on to "What were the roads like in 1937, I wonder?" (*what it was like*). I am not suggesting you go around being too conscious of this, and many responses do not fall neatly into a category, but sometimes, if you find someone's *what I did* memories are limiting the debate, try gently moving on to a discussion about *what it was like*.

Perhaps Molly is getting a little stuck on the details of her holiday at the seaside (*what I did*) so try broadening the discussion by asking, "How did people travel to holiday destinations in the 1950s?"(*what it was like*). Any series of responses is likely to include all three:

Where are you from Fred? ... Did you have any sisters? ... You were from a large family, weren't you? ... Worked in a shop I seem to remember? (*who I am*)

What was your job in the shop, Fred? ... You were the manager? ... Sounds like a job with responsibilities! ... How did it feel to be in charge of all those people? (*what I did*)

I suppose a shop worker in those days didn't earn too much ... You know, I've noticed in photographs that people who worked in shops never seemed to wear hats, when everyone else did. Does anyone have any idea why? (*what it was like*)

Oh, you used to be a hat maker Muriel? ... (*who I am*) I have no idea what it involves to make a hat (*what I did*)

I hear you, Doris, I'll have a word in a moment but we are just hearing about Muriel making hats ... Now, Doris, what's this about 'The Sun has got it's Hat On?'

The first subject people talk about easily will often be themselves, but with a new group, or new member of a group, do not be too intimate and do not ask questions that might be seen as overpersonal until the group or individual is feeling settled and secure.

Your delivery
Reminiscence work in groups is accessible to most thoughtful people, but do not expect to know how to run everything smoothly when you have not had much experience. You will learn as you go along and develop your skills and confidence. Do not try too hard.

Think about your own delivery. Try to ignore any embarrassment or shyness you may feel and aim to develop an attitude that says you are going to make an effort to do this effectively. This may involve letting yourself speak clearly and assertively sometimes and quietly and sensitively at other times. Try to be fairly expansive, especially if you feel a little unsure, and you will find it gets easier and you will get better at it. It is important to remember that, as with any other skill, the more you do it, the better you will get.

Listen to others. It is important that you are open to criticism that is offered helpfully, and willing to be honest with yourself about how you are working. It is a good idea to invite a colleague into your group to observe and offer feedback afterwards. This will increase your expertise. You will also gradually develop a stock of information in your head about your clients and about the past that you can draw on as prompts and as triggers.

Do you enjoy the company of others? If you are basically interested in people and the small details of people's lives, as well as concerned with the real well-being of your clients, you are likely to enjoy reminiscence work. You can work in the way that suits your personality: if you are a quiet, reserved person, organize quiet, intimate groups. If you are a natural entertainer, perhaps you should consider something a bit more lively where these skills can begin to shine. Getting involved with clients in this way can enhance your experience of your work, your enjoyment, your morale and hence your capacity to do a good job: less sickness, less depression, less shyness, better social skills. You could become more assertive, more knowledgeable: working with your clients is good for you!

There is a sense, although this may sound rather mystical, where you will get a response comparable to the amount of energy you are putting into the room. Fill the room with your consciousness; it will exhaust you, but will pay off. Ask any musician or teacher — they know what I mean.

Bringing something special

It can be a good idea to have something else for the group. This can be particularly useful where you have a group that is predominantly geared to individual activity and you would like to cause some group interaction.

Examples might include doing some relaxation to music as you near the end of an art or reminiscence session. Perhaps you could have a 'thought for the day' or a poem to read that allows you to rally everyone round to listen together. Bring in some object or information of interest, such as special fruit, sweets, flowers, newspaper cuttings, photographs and so on. Be imaginative. This way you allow the individuals in your group to begin to have some semblance of shared experience.

Dealing with disruptive behaviour
There may be times when you find that the behaviour of a member of the group is disruptive and affects the enjoyment of others. If this is only an occasional event or is temporary then it will not matter too much, but if unacceptable conduct tends to carry on you will have to decide how best to deal with it. You will need to consider *why* someone is causing you problems.

It is important to find out whether this is normal behaviour (for that person) or if it has changed recently. Are they having particular problems in all situations, certain specific situations (in which case you can identify common factors) or only in your sessions? There may be causes — illness or depression, reaction to new medication, problems in their personal life or with adjustment to residential care — that can be addressed.

There are a variety of ways in which an individual may intentionally, although not necessarily consciously or voluntarily, disrupt activities. This may be a cry for help and attention that can be satisfied. A need for attention can cause demanding behaviour in situations where there is an opportunity to gain a response, such as in the reminiscence session. An individual may try to dominate the session, insisting through their behaviour that you pay a lot of attention directly to them and making demands of you when you try to listen to others. This is likely to be an indication of insecurity or loneliness.

Someone may be dismissive of another's attempts to reminisce, tending to be insulting and critical. It may be that they are, or think they are, more capable than other members of the group and become frustrated at the level of discussion. Equally, they may feel less educated than others and be concerned to keep the subjects on familiar ground. If someone feels inadequate and fears they may 'do it wrong', they can overcompensate for this by trying too hard.

There may be someone who frequently gets upset which, in itself, is not necessarily a significant problem unless it affects everyone else. This may well be a symptom of illness; for example, the effects of a stroke can make it difficult for someone to control the balance of their emotional responses. The reminiscence itself may be causing distress, and someone who is disturbed by their memories but wants to be part of what is going on may try to divert things to avoid reminiscing. The emotional content of the reminiscence can be uncomfortable or even too much for some people. A different, less intense or more practical group may enable someone to participate at an emotional level that suits them.

Another consideration is whether other members of the group are causing the problem. Sometimes there can be conflicts and resentments that have built up that you are not aware of. There may be issues to do with race, class, gender and status or, quite possibly, interpersonal conflict stirred by other events. Mary was always making dismissive comments and getting agitated whenever Mabel tried to contribute to the session. This got to the point of causing so much aggravation in the group and distress to Mabel that something had to be sorted out. An atmosphere was beginning to affect everyone. During a private discussion with Mary, an educated and well brought-up woman, it turned out that she had known Mabel in the past. Mabel had been in service, whilst Mary had employed servants. Mary was having some difficulty, but was willing to acknowledge this, with accepting and listening to the viewpoint of someone from a different class.

If someone is restless and comes and goes from the group, this may be all right, but if they are too disruptive then you may have to decide to exclude them from the group, or limit their involvement. It is quite possible that the agitated person should become involved in a more energetic activity, where movement and physical expression are acceptable.

A group of interacting human beings function on many levels at the same time and can represent a fascinating, intricate labyrinth. There are no 'instant solutions' to these kinds of difficulties, but there are a number of things you could consider trying that may help someone become less disruptive:

- giving them a job to do, such as clicking the slides on, or passing round photographs;
- asking them to look after someone else, such as someone who is frailer or new to the group (as long as this will not cause problems for the other person);
- running your session so that people take turns to contribute, this allows you to make it clear that you are giving fair attention to everyone;
- having a helper sit with that person to give them special attention and help them participate in the group effectively;
- changing seating arrangements so that they are not able to affect another, or so you can give special attention;
- talking quietly to them on a one-to-one basis: some people may be very responsive to this and after this may settle into the group more easily;
- setting up special groups where you can give a lot of personal attention, or where people can work independently at a level and pace that suits them.

Sometimes people will wish to entertain, or chat, when a more serious discussion is under way. There should be no problem in having groups with different emphasis: a group that goes quite deeply into personal experiences and another that is more light and sociable. It may simply be a matter of making sure the person has the opportunity to undertake the kind of activity that suits them.

Look very carefully at situations where you are experiencing apparently inexplicable disruption and consider honestly whether there are aspects of your own behaviour that are causing or aggravating this. Is it possible you have your own mental image of how the group should be and that someone's behaviour is not fitting in with your preconceptions? You may be trying to control someone so that they 'fit in'. If you are unconsciously threatened or annoyed, you may send signals that influence their behaviour. Perhaps you do not like someone? Perhaps they are not easily liked — we cannot expect everyone to be 'nice' just so our reminiscence groups run smoothly.

A certain amount of disruption and conflict is to be expected in the intensely communal experience of care; it is human nature. It is my experience that disturbing people seem to be at their best in the mornings — but then again, so am I, so it may be that together we can put more creative effort into the session. Try having a quiet talk and discussing the problem with the person concerned. There may be good reason for their behaviour, or they may simply not be aware of how their activities are affecting others. You can ask for their help in helping to resolve things to everyone's satisfaction.

Key points

1 Always remind yourself that a group of older people may be diverse in age, culture, class, race, tastes, intelligence, wisdom, maturity and capabilities. Just because you are old does not make you the same as another person of the same age. We are all individuals. There is no description of an older person other than in terms of years. Even then, some of us are middle-aged in youth and youthful in old age.

2 Do not get enmeshed with the memorabilia and the facts and figures of history. They may be interesting, but are only a means to an end. You do not need to be an expert on the past.

3 Do not expect memories to be factually accurate: memory is notoriously inaccurate. Some people, at any age, may have very precise recall of events, names and dates, whilst others remember in a more impressionistic way. Some memories will be clear and crisp and others faint and hard to grasp.

4 If memories get a bit muddled, gently try to unravel these, but leave the last word to the person involved. Change the subject if need be, but try not to lead people into situations where they are likely to fail. Expect and enjoy a degree of exaggeration and imagination, whether deliberate or unconscious. In the end, it is their life and experiences we are recalling and they are the only authorities.

5 Reminiscence can trigger a wide variety of emotions and people can swing from laughter to tears, and back again, very quickly. Expect some pain, but try to elicit emotional resolution. A person may benefit from expressing emotions such as sadness and anger, but you should not thoughtlessly provoke people to guilt, regret, grief or fear unless you really know what you are doing and are able to help them resolve this. *This is no place for amateur psy-*

chotherapy. Aim to create opportunities for people to have experiences of pleasure, interaction, emotion, understanding, interest, stimulation, consideration, respect, dignity, choices and sensations.

6 Many people do not like to reminisce and find it irrelevant and meaningless. For them it is. Respect this view. They do not wish to look back. Some find it painful and depressing and are threatened by the comparison of who they were with how they are now. There may be much unresolved pain and conflict from past events that a person does not wish to face or share publicly. Disengagement from the past may have a protective function.

7 Some people do not like or do not function well in groups: some of us are loners, rather claustrophobic or downright unsociable. They may absolutely hate jolly social occasions surrounded by lots of people. They may prefer serious groups or not to be in a group at all. That is all right. Get to know them.

8 People have off days, or may be affected by things outside your control, such as medication and private frustrations. Understand this. Meaningful dates such as Christmas, anniversaries or birthdays can be times of great sadness, indicating a need for reflection rather than celebration. Go gently.

9 Do not use an activity as a baby-sitter — you are deluding yourself and wasting time and effort.

10 Pitch your work at different levels and allow your own expertise to develop. There is not a system of techniques, but your skill will develop with practice. Work in a way that suits your own personality, but take a risk now and then. Remind yourself that you are working on behalf of these people, and that giving in to your own fears or timidity will deprive them of the possibility of some pleasure or satisfaction.

11 There is no need for everyone to be doing. In a friendly, sociable atmosphere where some people are 'making', others may be happy to sit and watch and perhaps chat. If someone is not directly participating in the activity, do try to ensure they are not left out socially. You may find that, after they have sat back and watched what is going on, they decide to have a go. Make sure everyone understands that it is all right not to participate and that they will still be welcome. It may be that there are other ways they

can join in, or you may redefine your group to include them. If you want everyone in the group to participate, suggest a different activity for next time. Whatever you decide is most appropriate, make it clear what the situation is. One client who was excluded from a group because it was thought she would not enjoy it believed she was being punished for bad behaviour.

12 Daydreaming or private reminiscing is important and of value, certainly not to be discouraged. It can, by its nature, be inaccessible to others and may be difficult for people to articulate. For some this may be their only way of remembering and we have to judge the effectiveness of our work through non-verbal signs such as smiling, brightness of the eyes or even just staying in the room.

13 Make a fuss over people now and then; compliment them on their new cardigan or their smart tie — all those little things that make people feel welcome and identified. Do not overdo so-called 'stroking', or it will seem like flattery.

14 Introduce as many opportunities for people to contribute and make choices as you can and do not let staff answer all the questions. Guide a group, but do not feel you have to have absolute control.

Trouble with colleagues

Regrettably colleagues may sometimes cause problems. They may, with the best of intentions, join in enthusiastically and answer all the questions, or start reminiscing, so that you have to choose between ignoring them and ignoring a resident. And then there are those who deliberately set out to make things difficult, to disrupt your attempts to run a social programme with unnecessary interruptions, negative comments, even mockery. Perhaps they are resentful of the fact that you are apparently able to sit down and enjoy yourself, when there is work to be done. Perhaps they fear being asked to organize groups and run sessions themselves. Perhaps they cannot cope with perceiving those they are caring for as individuals and can only do their job (the way they do it) by ignoring personalities. They may simply be cynical, disillusioned people, in which case your best option is to ignore them: if you fail to respond to their provocation, they may go away.

There are a number of things that you can do to help you resolve, and survive, serious difficulty with colleagues, which happens more often than it should:

1 Remind yourself that the client's well-being has priority and that reminiscence work is as serious an element of care as any other.
2 Try to be as sure as possible of what you are trying to do and why it is of value. This can help you feel stronger and confident, able to respond to uninformed criticism.
3 Discuss with your colleagues, formally and informally, what you are trying to do and as much as is practical involve them in aspects of what you are doing. Encourage a positive contribution — many people appreciate being asked for help, though they may grumble.
4 If staff disrupt purposefully, for example interrupting by bringing in tea regardless of what is happening, walking around jangling keys, or even just running your efforts down, *deal with it immediately*. Unless you do so, this kind of disruption will get harder to stop. Aim to help your colleagues feel proud of the atmosphere your home, ward or centre is trying to create.
5 Make sure that you have clear, practical support from your manager, and, if possible, that the whole unit is aware of your role.

Staff generally were interested though not supportive. Perhaps a more across-the-board introduction to the project next time, so that six months into it you don't find yourself telling people what you are doing there.
(Richard Conlon, Artist in Residence, Cubbington)

Generally, staff disruption of reminiscence work is unintentional. They may be applying the same old routine they always have or may simply be unaware of the difficulties they are causing. Understanding the problem is the first step to solving the problem. *It is important that staff not involved should be aware of what the reminiscence work is trying to achieve. A brusque attitude from someone may undo much hard work.*

Supervision

Responding to the emotional expression of people is a demanding and subjective undertaking and you may find it personally helpful to identify a person who is sometimes called a supervisor. This is definitely not someone who tells you what to do.

'Supervision' should be an opportunity for you to explore your way of working and your feelings about what happens with someone who can sensitively help you to develop and improve your awareness of what you are doing and resolve any difficulties you are having. A supervision session should be with someone who has no authority over you and understands the nature of your work. You arrange to meet at regular intervals to explore, not only your fears and worries, but also your triumphs and successes.

Evaluation

At the end of every project it is important to reflect upon and learn from the experience. This exercise should be carried out formally and can be helpful when planning future work, writing reports and fund raising. I have found it useful to ask the following questions:

● Was there enough time to achieve what you had hoped? Did you have to spend more time than you consider acceptable working in your own time?
● Were you able to find appropriate space for what you wanted to do? Is there anything you could do to make it better?
● Did you have adequate materials? Did you need anything you could not get hold of?
● Did you have adequate support and encouragement from managers and colleagues?
● If other staff were involved, was this helpful?
● Were clients 'enabled' to work with you effectively; are there ways you consider the project/timetable could have been organized differently to facilitate clients' involvement?
● What do you think clients gained from working with you? Are there changes you would make to improve the nature of the clients' involvement?
● Were you able to involve anyone from outside in the project?

- Were you and the participants happy with the product?
- Were the ideas you had at the beginning appropriate or did you have to adapt them and, if so, how?
- What did you learn from this project?

You may want, or be obliged, to set up an exercise that allows you, or someone else, to measure the effects of reminiscence work on individual members of a group. You may, particularly if you have clinical aims, wish to evaluate someone's progress over a series of sessions and you will have to observe their behaviour both within and out of the sessions, while taking into account other things that might be happening to that person, then comparing their behaviour before and after. You can only really do this properly if you have clear, achievable aims for individuals that you measure progress against. You may wish, however, to observe the effectiveness of different input to compare someone's reaction to one kind of activity and another. This can be a good idea if people's individual aptitudes and likes and dislikes are noted on a care plan to improve future provision.

Evaluation of reminiscence work is fraught with difficulties as so much of what happens is subtle and subjective. There is a place and a need for some deep analysis, carried out by people with research expertise, but I personally have doubts about the true value of half-hearted evaluation carried out to fulfil clinical criteria. It would be better to put the energy into the work in hand. Generally, subjective review and discussion with the participants, complemented by commonsense observation, is adequate for most practical purposes.

Confidentiality

You must make it clear to people what you intend to do with information that they give you. If you are going to use this in public in some way, you must get their permission and, if they are unable to agree to this, it may be appropriate that you contact relatives. This applies equally to photographs that may be taken. Most times people are more than happy to see their names and recollections on display or in print, and the fact that they have voluntarily offered information means they agree to its being in the public domain. But check first!

Do not mislead older people when approaching them to discuss intimate details of their lives. There must be no sense that you are using them for your own purposes and the nature of the relationship must be clear and unambiguous. Do not promise to do things that you will not or cannot do and, unless as a consequence of your professional role, do not get so deeply involved that you find yourself in conflict with members of someone's family.

Normally, I would say that sensitive information not offered explicitly and openly should be treated as confidential, but if you discover, for example, that someone is suffering some kind of abuse, you will have to share this information. You should, however, tell your client that you feel you have to tell someone.

Working one-to-one

There can be distinct benefits gained from working with individuals outside the group setting and this may be particularly appropriate with people who are very frail, are suffering from anxiety or depression, or have communication difficulties.

To work with an individual can be time-consuming but immensely satisfying for both of you, allowing you to communicate at a depth and with an intimacy that would possibly not be appropriate or possible in a group setting. You can build a special rapport and a profound level of trust and understanding and will be able to recognize the individuality of people who perhaps are usually isolated in more communal sessions. You can adapt style, pace and frequency of contact especially to that person's needs.

Attentiveness that is especially aimed at helping someone resolve grief or adapt to present difficulties may be effective and practical projects involving the collection of reminiscences may be successful with individuals who feel more able to talk freely when you give them exclusive personal attention.

Reminiscence Resources

RESOURCES FOR REMINISCENCE work fall into three categories:

1   Reminiscence resources that you purchase, find, borrow or make yourself and use directly to stimulate conversation and recall.
2   Community resources that you can work with, draw on, places you can visit.
3   People who are able to work with you, work for you or advise you.

Reminiscence resources

Reminiscence resources have three functions:

1   As triggers and stimuli that you can use to encourage a response. This may involve passing round photographs or objects, watching a slide show or video, listening to tapes, viewing an exhibition and so on.
2   To help you feel more confident, especially in the early days. They provide you with something to talk about and with information about the past to draw on as prompts and aids to memory.
3   As a resource for the enhancement of your own projects. A pack of hand round photographs can be put into an exhibition or framed for the walls; a film can act as a context for a more elaborate cinema event; memorabilia can act as props in a dramatic reconstruction.

A variety of packs of photographs, slides, games, music and books and other resources are available from commercial companies such as Winslow and Nottingham Rehab in the UK (see appendix). They catalogue a broad selection of purpose-made reminiscence resources. These can be a useful asset for any collection. However, do think carefully before you rush off and buy hundreds of pounds' worth of packs and resources. Borrow some and try them out and only purchase materials that are going to be helpful and that you are going to use regularly.

There are a variety of individuals and organizations who have made up collections or exhibitions that you may be able to borrow, often at no or minimal charge. Examples include Age Exchange in London, The Red Carpet Service to Older Adults at the Topeka (Kansas) Public Library or Elder Resources in Delaware County, Pennsylvania. It is not practical, though, to name all of these as they change over time and vary greatly in nature in different districts and countries. Probably the best way to find out what is available is through your local librarian or by asking colleagues in the same area of work.

It may be well worth considering getting together with other people and starting a resource library between you – after all, you cannot use the same item every week. Among a few of you, you could purchase a wider variety of material and make sure it gets used, and not, as too often happens, end up forgotten in a cupboard somewhere.

Points of good practice when using reminiscence resources

- Do not bombard people with too much material.
- Content should be appropriate to age, background and culture.
- Content should be within people's experience.
- Images should be clear.
- The texture or smell of an object can be as stimulating as its appearance.
- Allow time for a response; you may have to prompt, but give people a chance to collect their thoughts.
- Listen to people and take your lead from them.
- Do not try to stick exclusively to a subject; the aim is to stimulate, not to limit.

Making your own collection of reminiscence aids
This is not something to do in a few days. Over a period of time, collect a variety of information, images, objects and music from any source you come across. Much that you would like to have is going to be rather costly, but keep your eyes open at garage and jumble sales, car boot sales and flea markets, and ask family, friends and colleagues. Tape relevant radio and television programmes (taking care, naturally, not to break copyright laws). Keep the collection broad. Literally anything about the locality, about aspects of everyday life, national and local events and personalities may be of interest to someone either directly or as information you, and other staff, can draw upon and learn from.

Once you have clear in your mind the sort of things you are looking for and people are aware that you are collecting, you could be surprised at what you will come across and the things people will offer you. Try putting a box in your place of work and asking *everyone* to collect things such as newspaper and magazine cuttings, old calendars, photographs, music, tapes and records, objects and reminiscences. People will donate once they realize what you are collecting for, although these days you should not expect anything too rare or valuable. There are collections of local reminiscences and 'nostalgia' publications available that can add to the sum of your collection and your knowledge. Libraries and bookshops will certainly have books on local history.

If you are going to put out an appeal for material, perhaps through the local paper or local radio, you may get a better response by asking for specific items, items for a particular purpose or relating to a theme, rather than just asking generally for donations. People are not always aware that the bits and pieces in the shed or the attic may be of use and interest to someone.

Classify things you collect into themes such as local life, transport, pets, popular music and so on and, as you use your collection, start to note down information that comes from your group and put it with the resource, ideally neatly typed so it is legible. This in itself acts as a resource for the future for you and others. If you are devising a collection of any size, you are likely to want to catalogue the collection as it grows. This is best done as you go along, or you end up with a monumental task that you may well not get round to doing. This is particularly important if you expect to lend out the collection, as you will need to keep track of who has what and try to keep your packs complete.

Looking at photographs

A picture needs to be interesting in itself and must, especially if people's vision is impaired, be crisp and clear. Although old photographs will often fascinate people, they are not interesting just because they are old but because of the glow of identification they evoke and the often amusing comparison with how things are now.

When showing a picture, as the prompter, you need to look and see what there is to talk about within the photograph and draw attention to aspects that will help encourage discussion. You are looking for 'triggers' within the picture that may evoke recognition, association, comparison, opinion and comment. If, for example, your picture is of an old market scene, you should identify whether it is really the local market or a 'typical' scene. Does it in fact look like your clients' local market? If it is, is it recognizable as such? If an image of the actual scene is rather poor, perhaps you could accompany this with a clearer image from elsewhere. What is sold in this particular market: perhaps clothes, fruit and vegetables, crockery or all these things? What is actually happening in the photograph? Are people queuing; is someone being served; is a delivery being made? You use the content of photographs to initiate discussion that relates directly to experience. In our 'market' example, you may want to ask people where they went to market. What day was market day? Were there different markets selling different wares? What were they called? In some areas, some people may have gone to livestock, fish or rag markets. What happened when it rained or got dark? Were market traders friendly and what did people think of their 'patter'? You can personalize the recall by asking how people got there, how they got the shopping home, how often they went. And so on. Are there smells, colours and sounds people associate with market day? Sometimes markets have unusual names, such as the Flat Iron Market in Salford, so called because of its shape, not because of what was sold. How does today's market — if such a thing still exists — compare with those of the past? Have they changed much? Are there advantages to market shopping or do people prefer the supermarket? Perhaps it is time to plan a visit to a local market? What else was happening around the time the photograph was taken — happening to the individual and happening broadly in the wide world?

Another example might involve a picture of a local church. "Do you know where this is?" (a closed question) would probably elicit "Yes" or "No". A rather better approach might be something like: "I think this is a picture of a local church; have you any suggestions as to where it could be?" (an open question). To take it further, you can start to discuss, if appropriate, which hymns people liked to sing; was anyone in a choir; did they attend Sunday School; were they in any processions; how did they get to church? And so on. What different styles of sacred building are people aware of?

NB If discussion of this kind leads to expression of personal religious beliefs, you must take care not to exclude those with differing religious convictions and traditions. Our spiritual beliefs, whether instilled during childhood or evolved over many years, become fundamental building blocks of our personalities — certainly worthy of discussion and comparison but not of judgement. It is not appropriate to evangelize in a reminiscence session.

Think about what there is to draw attention to in a photograph and what related discussion points this could introduce. Visual recognition and recall may not be as sharp as you think, and recognition of, say, the town centre may have to be encouraged via a clear focal point such as a church or building of note. Look as well for indications of when the photograph was taken in styles of transport, road markings, clothes, hairstyles and prices.

If you are trying to evoke a direct emotional association, you may get more reaction from a picture of a dog or children playing than from a typical empty street scene. A picture does not in fact have to be old at all to suggest a topic for conversation. You may find you get better responses to pictures that are generally evocative rather than a direct image of a particular scene. For example, a picture of ducks may suggest many visits to the park, a steam train may stimulate memories of travel. Do not feel you must only use photographs: great pleasure can be obtained by looking at paintings and drawings.

Remind yourself that the pictures are only aids to memory and a stimulus for discussion and conversation. Avoid a 'have you seen my holiday snaps' scenario where you bore everyone for an hour with a selection of badly taken and, to them, irrelevant pictures.

Hand-held photographs
The use of these is often the starting point for reminiscence. They provide very direct stimulation as long as the individuals understand the content of the photograph and are able to see them properly. I would recommend using hand-held photographs for small groups and one-to-one work as long as the photographs are clear and have relevance to the participants.

There is a significant drawback to using hand-held photographs, which is that only one, or perhaps two can look at them at a time. This may be all right, but, even if your group is small, you may find that, while one person is looking, others could be waiting unattended or looking at a different photograph. Be aware that this could lead to a situation where members of the group are talking at cross-purposes and that attention may wander. One way round this would be to have larger photographs, but this would be costly.

When photocopying photographs, you are in danger of inadvertently breaking copyright laws (depending upon the age of the photograph) and in any case this does not usually produce a result that is particularly attractive. The photocopier will try to turn the greys in the photograph into black and white, and it will not look very clear. There are special screens that you place over the photograph when copying and which give a better result, or you can colour photocopy a black and white photograph to get a very good result, but this is expensive. A good computer set-up can produce a very high quality scan but, to get the best result of all, you should seek the help of a photographer who can copy photographs for you. If you can bring yourself to do it, you can cut up books, using the photographs for your own purposes.

When mounting a picture on card, it will look much more professional and last much longer if you trim it neatly; mount it on black paper; trim the edges to leave a neat black border about 1/4 inch (6 mm) wide; stick it onto a thin piece of card, leaving just a slightly larger margin at the bottom than the top; cover it with thin plastic, put it in a plastic envelope or, if you can afford it, get it laminated, so that it will take rough handling.

Slides/transparencies
I like slide shows. Slides, or transparencies as they are also called, when projected onto a screen, allow more people to see the image clearly. This is ideal with large groups. Everyone sees the same image at the same time and you can linger on an image that causes discussion and move on quickly when it does not.

The 'carousel' type of projector is efficient and easy to use but works out quite costly. You can load up your carousel well in advance. There is also a kind of box projector, looking a bit like a television, which can also have the facility to play cassettes in conjunction with the pictures and you can 'pulse' the tapes so that the carousel moves round in time with a narrative, sound effects or music. It is easy to do this for yourself with the correct equipment.

Of course, you must darken the room somewhat (some people do not like this, so be careful) but most people feel at ease in low light and will perhaps be more willing to speak. There are 'daylight' projection screens available, which are not really suitable for bright light, but are effective in subdued light. (Before setting up your slide show, make sure it is not *impossible* to darken the room. Don't laugh, I've done it … more than once.)

Go through the slides slowly and do not show too many in one session. For a good show where there is plenty of discussion, you will probably not need to show more than 20–30 slides, and quite possibly fewer. Show the slides, asking prepared questions and pointing out areas of interest. Encourage contributions from the audience. If this is quite large, you will need to arrange to have helpers scattered amongst the audience so that quieter people have someone to talk to. Not everybody is capable of talking confidently in a large group.

Television and Video
Watch out for interesting things coming up on television — not just old films, but documentaries about all kinds of subjects, such as wildlife, science, gardening, sport and so on. Some excellent

social/historical programmes are made, often incorporating the views and reminiscences of older people, and there are always plenty of nostalgic and biographical programmes, particularly during special anniversaries. There are many programmes on television that may be of interest to you and your clients and it is worth scanning the listings, together, every week and either making sure people have the opportunity to choose to watch these programmes, or videoing them so that you can watch them together. As with many other choices to be made in group living, a certain amount of negotiation may be needed.

Video shops, may, amidst the explicit modern releases, have a limited range of material that could be useful, and public libraries often hold collections. There are a few specifically reminiscence videos around (see appendix), but not many. Commercially available nostalgia videos perhaps containing collections of newsreel film from specific years, may be useful.

After watching a video or television discuss what you have seen. Remind yourself that your objective is to stimulate and communicate. If you are going to stop and start a video to make points, choose sensible stopping points or the whole experience can become rather confusing. I do not like working with television very much, but it has a place. We all know that television can be abused to baby-sit people in care and have seen sleepy people left to sit in front of a flickering screen. No-one is watching, and no-one is talking about what they see. Having the television on can create the illusion that our clients are entertained and occupied, when in fact they are not.

In an ideal world, residents in all homes and hospitals would have the opportunity to make selections and choose what they are going to watch on television. To make this possible you would need to ensure that people know what is on, understand what the programme is about and have control over the television.

Film
Real, or do I mean reel, film is rare these days, but if you can get hold of some, it can be very atmospheric: the flickering screen and the old projector whirring round create a comforting and familiar context for recall. A similar, but ersatz and less reminiscent, effect can be obtained

by using a large video screen. Find out what your clients like and see if you can find some appropriate material. Ask about musicals, cowboys, comedies, romances, historical dramas and thrillers. The film stars of yesteryear are often held very dearly in people's hearts.

Do not assume that a film has to be old to be meaningful. Some modern films address issues of interest to older people. Looking at those that are set in an earlier decade, it can be pleasurable to compare the film maker's idea of an era with the recollections of people who lived through it. Going to the pictures represents a whole event in itself and a good subject for reminiscence. How about some ice-cream and pop corn? Everyone got their ticket?

Film from archives
Some cities and localities have film archives that keep, restore and preserve old film, much of which will be local footage — some amateur, some professionally shot. They may produce videos that you can hire or buy but, if not, they may still be interested in helping you. It is always worth asking.

In common with, but perhaps more so than, old photographs, most local and newsreel film is usually of special events, such as parades, visits by celebrities, politicians or royalty, national occasions and so on. If these events are familiar or typical, they can be of great interest, but you may have to look hard for film clips of everyday life. As described elsewhere, it is recall of common everyday events that tends to be most effective in enabling shared group reminiscence: 'what it was like'. Film is likely to suggest ideas for reminiscence rather than explicitly depict them. You will also have to look hard, perhaps wading through hours of film, to find the pieces that have quality, both of film and filming, that is good enough to be easily watched, where there are clear identifiable triggers and where the film is interesting enough to hold people's attention.

The possibilities inherent in the use of archive film have not yet been explored in depth and this represents an area where you could try hard to seek out material that has direct relevance to your client group and their specific background. Then you will be able to astonish everybody with 'live' footage from the past. As time goes by, there will obviously be a lot more material available, and there are going to be some very exciting projects using the moving image put together in the future, I am sure.

The moving image can sometimes leave little room for people to use imagination and fantasy, seeming but in fact failing to capture the moment in its entirety. On the other hand, with the right content, the excitement of seeing the past in the flesh as it were, can be a dynamic and emotional experience.

A variety of sensations

Looking at things is not the only way to experience them. We have other senses to help us to enjoy and be aware of the world we are in. We rarely pay enough attention to developing our awareness of sounds of subtlety and beauty. Try drawing people's attention to the birds, the wind and the rain, to children playing and workers whistling while they work. We do not hear properly what is around us: how about taking that person whose sight is impaired to a place of beauty, just to sit and listen?

It may be that not much can be done about unpleasant ambient noise, but it is worth considering if you can. At least be aware of the effect that noise from the surroundings can have on someone who cannot escape it. The clatter of everyday life may be reassuring or may be disturbing. Shut your eyes for two minutes and listen. What does it sound like in your workplace? Is it quiet or noisy? If quiet, is there a restful silence or an oppressive one? If noisy, do you hear a friendly bustle or an irritating cacophony? I have been saddened by institutional sounds: cutlery being banged loudly and brusquely onto hard table tops; keys provocatively jangled as if to make some point; the phone that rings and rings but is never for you. Often some of the noise created in institutional settings can be avoided. Are the television and the radio on at the same time (it has been known)? If you have the radio on, is it really most appropriate to have the latest pop hits blasted out all day long? Some of the speech programmes can be very interesting: have you considered plays, interviews, magazine programmes and so on?

If you regularly use a record player or tape recorder, have a good selection of records, tapes or CDs for people to choose from. Are you sure it should be Max Bygraves or Mitch Miller? Perhaps a little Cole Porter, Mozart or *My Fair Lady* would make a refreshing change? It is change that brings variety and relief. If you never play music, put some on; if you always play music, turn it off! Any restaurant owner knows that music can create subtle and influential atmospheres, but please, for me, beware of muzak, music that has no meaning or quality to it. As with anything else, use music, but in moderation, not as wallpaper. (I was once working in an old people's home that had just one record that was left to play all day, repeating endlessly, repeating endlessly, repeating endlessly ...)

Touching things reminds us of their reality and their power, of our own reality and sensuality: holding hands; feeling textures, cool, warm, rough, smooth, hard and soft; stroking cats and dogs; clay feels wonderful, so soothing and cool; try touching trees, the earth; reach for the sky! Awareness of the 'feel' of things is an often under-rated sense and one can become sensually deprived by a lack of opportunity to touch and be touched. If someone has severe difficulty getting out or up from a chair, they may hardly be able to touch anything — literally to *feel* anything. If what surrounds them is put away for 'safety' or is not allowed for use in case it gets a few fingerprints on it, they may feel unable to explore their surroundings. Especially if sight is poor as well, being cut off can cause disengagement and isolation.

Handling a familiar object can be a very direct aid to recall. The texture, the weight, the colour and the smell of an object will often elicit a response from someone who cannot take much notice of pictures and discussion. I have been quite fascinated, when a visiting performer is dressed up nicely for a show, to see how much pleasure some people get from touching the material of their clothes. Many people are very aware of the different textures of materials. Silk, calico, velvet, wool, fur, lace — all can be very sensual and evocative. (How about a 'guess the fabric' quiz?)

Do not forget about all the materials and objects around us, especially natural ones, such as shells, stones and wood, that can give pleasure. It would also be a good project for a local school or college to design and produce sculptures that are meant to stimulate a tactile rather than a visual response.

I feel there is a lot to be gained in terms of sensory stimulation through handling and working with art materials – colour, texture and the varying qualities of different papers, fabrics, ribbons, sequins, clay and so on are appealing even for those with confused thought processes.
(Carol Davies, Artist in Residence, the Rhyl Nursing Home)

Touching other people can be reassuring, as long as it is acceptable to each party. The occasional hug or stroked hand can demonstrate warmth and caring. Reflexology, aromatherapy and remedial massage can all involve 'acceptable' and pleasurable touching as well as being therapeutic in other ways. So can dancing. I always try to shake hands with people I have not seen for a while, even though it does not come naturally to me. It reminds us very directly that we are physical entities and can be in contact with each other.

Smell is perhaps our least acknowledged sense and the smells of this world can be unexpectedly suggestive of times gone by. They can have very powerful associations. For example, the odour of seaweed or of pipe tobacco could be very evocative, as well as being pleasurable and sensual in themselves — although these particular examples may not be pleasant odours for everybody! The smell of bleach immediately transports me back to the swimming pools of my childhood, or is it to my mother cleaning the kitchen? The association gives me a good feeling, even though I cannot quite place it. I also find the distinctive smell of old wood panels rather pleasing.

Reminiscent smells can be created directly, for example the mouth-watering smell of baking bread or the appealing odour of percolating coffee. Other sources can be collected and handed round: spices, herbs, foods — especially fruit — perfumes, incense, soaps, flowers and so on. Many household goods, such as wax polish, carbolic soap, mothballs and coal, have distinctive smells. It is even possible to get bottled smells such as 'laundry' and some aromatherapy oils, such as lavender and fennel, could be familiar. Try talking to people about the smells they associate with good times.

Of course, our sense of smell and sense of taste are almost the same thing. Although older people's taste buds are not always what they were, and some people are very conservative about what they eat, after a diet of prepared and easy-to-digest food, all of us would sometimes, whatever our tastes, appreciate something less institutional: good fresh food; long-forgotten home-cooked food (like mother used to make); strong, spicy food; fancy food; food cooked with alcohol, with cream, with care and finesse; fresh fruit pies, home-made pickles, chutneys and sauces, jams and cakes; home-made bread or crumpets with butter and fresh coffee.

The exploration of food can be great fun, but do take care to take into account any special dietary requirements, including cultural ones. Try tasting exotic, unusual fruit, traditional foods from different parts of the country, or making up people's favourite recipes.

Although not strictly senses, there are sensual experiences that can contribute to awareness of our wholeness as human beings, represented by such activities as praying, singing, dreaming, fantasizing, gambling, daring, winning, succeeding, taking risks, caring, leading, giving, loving, sharing and, of course, remembering. No doubt you can think of more.

Be very aware that contrived stimulation of the senses may have a negative effect. Some people absolutely hate to be touched and people's tolerance of sensory stimulation, particularly if they are ill, can vary greatly. Certain music and foods, particularly, can bring back undesirable memories in a context where you are not expecting this.

There is a well-known example of men who cannot bear to eat rice because of experiences they had in prisoner-of-war camps. A song innocently sung may be a too poignant reminder of a person who has died. If people overreact to stimulation, ease off and gently reintroduce the activity until you find an acceptable and enjoyable level of toleration.

Community Resources

It is well worth forming a working relationship with the local library, museum and public art gallery. All three, to a certain extent, have an obligation to reach out into their local communities and should welcome the opportunity to liaise with people like yourself who can help them make contact with a proportion of the population that usually does not have easy access to the services and facilities they offer. It is best, unless there is an obvious point of contact such as an education officer or local history officer, to get in touch with the head librarian or curator and discuss with them what you are trying to do. Helping you will not cost them much, if anything — they may already have packs for schools lying idle in the summer, exhibitions that have done the rounds now packed away, events and promotions for which they are only too keen to increase the audience. One museum I am aware of will lay on a guided private tour and plenty of refreshments.

Libraries are not just for borrowing books but are a network of public information and resources. Most cities, larger towns and districts will have a specialist local history department, if not a local history library. You may gain access to maps, directories, photographic collections, packs of slides, local history publications, cassettes and videos. The library may be able, usually at a small cost, to reproduce local photographs and documents. Some enlightened libraries administrate a reminiscence collection especially devised for people using recall in their work, and would certainly welcome your custom. A few places have taken this further by having a member of staff whose role is especially to promote this kind of work.

There may be displays and exhibitions both to borrow and to visit. Some libraries these days hold concerts and events that you can go to, or they may even be able to come to you. There are experts on all kinds of subjects to be found working in the library service who may give talks and slide shows, although there is likely to be a waiting list.

Museums, and sometimes art galleries, may offer similar outreach services with staff able to give talks and co-ordinate visits. If they do not, why not suggest it? Many museums have collections available for schools and it is a small step from that to having collections made available to hospitals and old people's homes. Perhaps the basement is full of treasures? Do not forget the specialist museums and the heritage centres. There are many places that aim to recreate the themes of yesteryear, often with original buildings and actors dressed in period costume. They should hardly refuse an approach from the people that provided them with their livelihood (and if they do — and they sometimes do — make a fuss).

I suggest that you do not only go in to see what is available but that you get together with the cultural providers and work with them to see what could be made available. You will be surprised at what may be possible. A joint project can encourage everyone to be adventurous, as the following examples illustrate.

The patients and staff from the day hospital were invited over by students from the art gallery to look through and discuss the collection of all kinds of works of art: abstract and figurative, classical and modern. Most of the visitors had never been in an art gallery in their lives and were in a little awe of it, but a friendly welcome and attentive approach by the students soon dispelled any fears that people had. Based on the choices made over a number of visits, a special exhibition was organized displaying the works of art chosen by the visitors, accompanied by their philosophical meandering on the meaning of each piece.

The Lancastrian textile mill that is now a heritage centre asked us to contact a variety of local homes in the area to find out the names of retired mill workers who were then personally invited to join us for a special trip to see displays of weaving, doffing, spinning and more. Welcomed by volunteers who were (only just) younger retired mill workers themselves, the visiting group, with much laughter and tears, shared their memories in a private occupational language that arose from their common trade. It was wonderful to watch excited faces, stimulated and invigorated by the smells and sounds of their lifetime's work, lighting up with recognition and powerful emotion.

Before you plan visits to any centres, *check on the accessibility*. It can be very disappointing to arrive for a day out and find that you cannot get into most or all of the building, into the tea-room or that the toilets are up a narrow flight of stairs.

People

Schools

What an underrated resource schools are! Bursting at the seams with optimistic and lively young people and enthusiastic teachers, all keen to get involved in social projects and their local community ... well perhaps not, but ...

For many years, homes and hospitals have welcomed schools that offer carol singing at Christmas and have perhaps gone over for a school play or concert, but they rarely consider trying to take it further than that. The benefits of involving children with older people in their community are countless, and it is not only a one-way benefit. Children can learn such a lot about life in times gone by — history in the words of those that lived through it. Stereotypes can be broken down, with the children learning to appreciate older people as real live people and the older generations learning that the young are not all undisciplined and rowdy. With the breakdown of the extended family, many children do not necessarily have easy access to grandparents they can talk to and little children particularly can appreciate old people greatly.

Schools are often in need of practical projects, not only related to social care or suchlike but also projects involving, for example, history, drama, video, music, performance, poetry reading, public speaking, group work, psychology and interviewing. There may be opportunities for an oral history project, putting on a play based on memories, making pictures for the walls, making a film about old people, with old people, and so on. Remember, however, that children are not to be insulted by being put on display and you should not have them visit just to be looked at. Invite them in for a good reason and help them feel welcome and at ease. They will possibly be shy initially, but as it all becomes more familiar you will almost certainly see beautiful interaction between old person and child that may be very moving. Many barriers, and self-absorption, become fainter as young and old experience each other. Invite local schools to your summer event or garden party, to your display of memorabilia, to your residents' arts display and your annual talent show — and get yourselves invited to theirs. They will treat you as exalted guests, so do the same for them.

Mentally frail patients had a lively day presenting a puppet show for children from a local nursery school. The staff operated the puppets, made over a period of weeks out of socks and paper plates and papier mâché. The show was based on old songs chosen for the children by the patients. Well supplied with orange juice, the children watched the puppets and the patients watched the children.

An old people's home asked the schoolchildren to bring in favourite toys to compare with their display of old toys. Everyone played together: an 11-year-old trying to work a whip and top with expert guidance and, in return, explaining an electronic digital game to an 80-year-old gentleman. Many games, believe it or not, that were played in the earlier parts of the century are still played today, although sometimes the words and names have changed.

The innocent and straightforward approach of children can reach the parts of us that nothing else can touch.

Volunteers

There is a role for volunteers in the care of elderly people, not to help with physical care or dish out meals, but to provide a welcome breath of fresh air from the world outside. Many retired people are keen to use their skills productively and may have all kinds of expertise and knowledge that can contribute to your work. Be aware, though, that not all people will be comfortable in a hospital ward or residential home. For some, the reminder of fragile mortality can be a source of discomfort or even disturbance. For others, however, volunteering is an opportunity to be positively involved with the world and can offer them purpose and meaning in their own lives.

You should interview potential volunteers and make sure they are the right kind of person for your situation. Discuss their skills and interests with them, as they may have talents that would otherwise go unrecognized and they may be able to offer expertise in woodwork, gardening or some other practical skill. They may have arts or people skills to share. Others can be more effective playing a role in the background, helping with fund raising, with administration or in the kitchen. They may simply have lively and interesting personalities that generally improve the atmosphere.

Before agreeing to take on a volunteer, however suitable they appear, try them out in a few different situations to see how they get on with people. It is a good idea to agree a short probationary period just to make sure that they are going to be a help and not a hindrance. Judge their behaviour carefully and do not be afraid to confront them if need be. Help them to help you. If you can, devise a code of conduct that clarifies the rules of good practice that you expect in the treatment of clients. In the end it must be made clear to volunteers that the clients' interests come first. Always.

Agree formally with them what they are going to do and when they are going to do it. They are not doing you a favour. If they are clearly not suitable — perhaps patronizing, or unreliable, or even dishonest — you must ask them to go. They can be issued a contract and held to it. If they do not have rules and guidelines, they will not know where they stand.

Volunteers usually offer help when they are looking for something themselves, most often company, to be useful or to have an outside interest. Try to ensure that their needs are responded to. If someone is looking for social contact, do not stick them all alone in the office. Possible roles for volunteers include the following:

reading newspapers with people,
fund raising,
photography,
taking people out,
companionship,
storytelling,
listening to music,
driving (if qualified),
baking,
making a newsletter,
collecting reminiscences,
collecting and building a reminiscence resource.

Mr L, who had recently reluctantly retired from business, came to the recreation centre offering to help as a volunteer driver. Having once been the director of a small company, he could not help noticing, as the weeks progressed, a certain amount of chaos in the office and agreed to help out when he could. It turned out that he was also a good pianist, having been in a number of local bands. He had even been on the radio. How could he refuse to play a few tunes? It was not long before the 'Friends', knowing it was going to be cared for, donated a new piano. The hard-working manager of the recreation centre, so used to coping on her own, confided in Mr L and discussed issues and problems with him. He became a shoulder to lean on and a board to bounce off. Mr L had found a place, in his retirement, where he was loved and respected, and he was pleased to demonstrate love and respect in return. The recreation centre had to find another volunteer driver — Mr L was too busy.

It can be helpful to involve family members in your reminiscence groups, particularly if people are very frail. They can help you find out about individuals, and you can help them come to terms with what has happened. As with a volunteer, a participating relative will be more helpful if they have some understanding of the nature of reminiscence work and know what role is expected of them. Do not assume they know what to do. There is little as frustrating as a relative who help-fully answers the questions you put to a client, and it can be very diffi-cult to ask them to stop. Sometimes relatives' expectations will be a lot lower than yours and they may introduce all kinds of domestic issues into the situation. At the same time, they will have an intimate knowl-edge of a person that can really help expand your own understanding. It may also be very reassuring for some people that their family are involved. If the relative is involved in the work you are doing, they can reinforce and refer to it — and have something to talk about when they visit. You should discuss with clients what you have in mind, before ask-ing their relative in to help. They may not always be welcome.

Frank had a close relationship with his wife. She looked after him, dominated him, smothered him protectively and had always done so, even before he had his stroke. Wishing helpfully to be involved with the sessions, she came in and spoke for Frank, answered for him, made tea for him only. Frank, who needed help to regain some indepen-dence of action, was being carefully encouraged through therapy to make his own decisions and choices. His wife, meaning well, was encouraging exactly the opposite. This situation, seemingly destruc-tive, can be seen in a positive light. Frank was soon to return home to be cared for by his wife. Her involvement with the group meant that the clinical team were able to explain and demonstrate, tactfully, to Frank's wife an approach to his needs that was more likely to be ben-eficial to his rehabilitation.

Even if you decide it is inappropriate to involve relatives directly in sessions, and it is quite acceptable that you would rather run the reminiscence group without 'helpful' interference, it is definitely worth involving them in social events, parties, concerts and displays of work and so on as guests and helpers. I believe that family and friends can and should play a very important part in the caring and rehabilitation process.

Therapists and others

There is a point of view which argues that the notion of therapy has connotations of 'welfarization' and demeans individuals who have disabilities by reinforcing a dependent relationship with others. Despite better training in recent years, problems can arise when clinical practitioners only perceive individuals in terms of a medical condition, believing that, if there is not a measurable clinical benefit from the satisfaction of a personal need, it is not a therapeutic activity and is therefore of no consequence or value. Reaction to care practices that define a personality exclusively in terms of disability has led to a polarizing reaction that concludes that therapy is *inherently* a bad thing, used by the medical professions in order to stereotype disabled people as helpless recipients of care — that therapy in fact involves power. There is truth in this, usually in terms of effect rather than intention, but an approach that reinforces dependency would be considered bad practice by most therapists. It is not particularly helpful if stereotypical assumptions — in either direction — cause alienation rather than communication. All health professionals, though, do have a responsibility to have an awareness of disability issues and to be open to listening to the views of recipients of care provision.

Therapy is a clinical practice associated with disease and healing. The therapist's role is to work directly with a person who is injured or disabled through illness, old age or accident in order to help them regain previous skills (intrinsic therapy) and to help them learn new skills to replace ones that are lost (adaptive therapy). Hospitals will usually employ a variety of clinical therapists, who may or may not use reminiscence or creative arts as a tool in their work. Clinical therapists, such as occupational and language therapists, are members of well-established professional disciplines with strict ethical codes and professional training. No-one can do such work without a recognized qualification and each plays a distinct clinical role within an interdisciplinary team.

Art therapy and music therapy are also recognized professional disciplines requiring formal training and qualifications. They have a well-defined clinical function involving the diagnosis and treatment of medical conditions. Dance and drama therapy are still considered rather unconventional and do not generally have such a widely recognized and established body of professional expertise, although this certainly does not imply in any way that practitioners are less effective therapeutically or less professional than in other therapies. The true arts therapies generally are fairly rare and arts therapists will usually be found, it seems, working with people who have mental health problems. You will, however, find unqualified people using these titles and fulfilling this role. You may, as well, encounter people who are trained or employed in these disciplines but in fact fulfil a much broader role.

It is also quite common to hear people refer to reminiscence work as reminiscence therapy, a phrase presumably coined to give some kind of clinical credibility in a hospital or care setting. This annoys those reminiscence practitioners who insist they are not therapists, and annoys clinical therapists as well. Reminiscence work, except in certain specialized circumstances, is not a therapy and does not need to be. It can be therapeutic without being a therapy.

In order to try and address the broader needs of clients, hospitals and homes may employ people with titles such as social therapists, hobby therapists, craft instructors, activity organizers/directors or diversional therapists. These people may be trained therapists, or they may not. They are not considered part of a formal professional discipline as such, although they may well be grounded in nursing, occupational therapy or other professional practice. You may also encounter people with job titles such as arts development worker or hospital artist whose aim is to increase access to the arts in a number of different ways.

It is increasingly recognized that there is a desirable professional role to be played within clinical and residential spheres by people with expertise that does not find its source in the care establishment. Practitioners may well have little or no clinical or medical training (they are not therapists) but expertise coming perhaps from the voluntary or education sectors, architecture or the growing self-aware disciplines of hospital arts and reminiscence work. Artists are practitioners who work in a clinical or care context but consider their professional identity to be determined outside that context and whose position in relation to the clients, and to the staff, crosses traditional hierarchies. Usually their role will complement caring practices, but sometimes will be in contrast to, will even challenge, the attitudes and practices of professional care. The health services particularly have been enthusiastically embraced as a framework in which creative people with, sometimes loosely, a background and expertise in the arts apply their skills meaningfully for the general benefit of those who are sometimes perceived as a culturally dispossessed and neglected section of the population.

In many countries there are well-established arts organizations which have sophisticated expertise in setting up projects of all kinds in community, institutional, hospice and 'healthcare' settings, not only, of course, involving older people. There are experienced hospital artists and community artists who are used to working as facilitators, enablers or animateurs, that is, they do not work as artists in the traditional sense by creating their own individual work but use other skills in conjunction with an art form to encourage people to get in touch with their own creativity, to influence their environment and to express and enjoy themselves.

We were all quite apprehensive but slowly residents, and staff, who just came to see, or were passing by on their way to the dining room became interested, and Maggie's enthusiasm began to rub off onto the residents as they realized they could actually make something for themselves. Participants gained confidence week by week in a way that we could never have envisaged. Residents of all abilities and disabilities joined in, were encouraged by Maggie, and began to look forward to Thursdays, to the artist's visit. They were proud of their work, justly so and were glad to have been involved.

(Barbara White, Activities Organizer, Ringshill Nursing Home)

There are exciting opportunities for care and nursing staff to work alongside people with a background from outside the caring professions.

Maggie interacted extremely well with everyone she came into contact with. Indeed I felt that because of Maggie's qualities many more of my staff now see the benefit of encouraging clients to participate. I also feel it has been an education for us all. Indeed I have personally learnt a lot from Maggie. Because of my own enthusiasm I have tried to involve as many staff from Head Office as possible.
(Christopher Stannard, Director, Ringshill Nursing Home)

Reminiscence works as an art form

Much, though not all, reminiscence work is grounded in the arts because they represent an ideal vehicle for emotional and creative expression, for interactive projects and for recreation and enjoyment. Reminiscence work entwines, overlaps and blends with the arts and they act as good companions in a spectrum that ranges from individual expression to pure entertainment.

Reminiscence work requires the use of imagination, ingenuity, creativity, skill, sensitivity, perception, instinct and knowledge, with just a dash of eccentricity, risk taking, performance skills and aesthetic judgement. Without getting onto the subject of what art actually is, this sounds like an art form to me. Different art and crafts are rich with possibilities for animating and involving people — painting, drawing, screen printing, collage, music, songwriting, drama, performance, theatre, dance, dancing, poetry, creative writing, storytelling, ceramics, sculpture, mosaic, fabric work, sewing, appliqué, tie-dyeing, puppetry, photography, video, woodwork, stained glass work, cookery, reminiscence — which involve making, saying, writing, seeing, hearing, thinking, doing, playing, communicating, sharing, feeling, expressing, enjoying and reminiscing.

I feel that art as well as activities has a vital role to play in these settings. If it wasn't appropriate then nothing would have happened over the last six months. That all kinds of things happened and developed was due to the residents. They responded in a very positive way. They all had creative abilities and a lot to contribute.
(Carol Davies, Artist in Residence, the Rhyl Nursing Home)

Artists working in a healthcare context can play a wide variety of roles, sometimes in collaboration with a therapist, sometimes in a broader 'therapeutic' context and sometimes even in contrast to medical and care practices, as when an arts project may be specially set up to counter a 'clinical' atmosphere. To some extent a hospital or a residential home represents a microcosm of the broader community and the artist should be able to respond to staff, clients, volunteers and visitors, considering them all potentially able to play a part in promoting the health and vitality of that community. An artist working in a care setting may act as

- a therapist,
- a therapeutic resource,
- a teacher,
- a decorator,
- a designer,
- an entertainer,
- an activities organizer,
- a context for self-expression,
- a context for social interaction,
- a bridge to the wider community,

- an enabler,
- an antitherapist,
- a catalyst,
- an advocate,
- a mirror,
- a playmate,
- a stimulus for reminiscence,

and of course, an artist.

There can be advantages associated with involving people who are from 'outside'; do not have other duties to perform; can concentrate specifically on social/emotional issues; have plenty of time to pay attention to individuals; can introduce activities that staff cannot; have special expertise; can share skills with staff; and have access to a range of resources.

Although there is a tradition of multidisciplinary co-operation in care services for elderly people, different disciplines often refer to each other without actually working together. Reminiscence work, in its broadest sense, can create opportunities for different professions, who will have different perspectives on a situation, to blend their expertise, learning a lot themselves in the process. For example, a physiotherapist and a musician can work together to develop music and movement sessions, or an occupational therapist can work in conjunction with an arts organizer to improve the physical environment. How about the manager of a unit working with a reminiscence worker and a group of residents to devise new and appropriate activity programmes? The opportunities offered by interdisciplinary projects are largely unexplored and become very exciting if people are prepared to be honest, open and to respect each other's opinions and perspective.

The employment of an outside practitioner should be seen as a way of enhancing opportunities and not as a substitute for staff initiatives. A good project will ideally combine the experience and knowledge of staff in harmony with the skills and creativity of an outside practitioner.

Setting up a project
A co-ordinated arts and reminiscence project can

- attract resources,
- improve staff skills and confidence,
- stimulate creative activity,
- refresh,
- offer high-quality activities,
- offer insight into emotional needs of clients,
- create a context for social activity,
- support staff initiatives,
- improve the physical and social environment of care,
- offer a context for volunteers,
- take student placements,
- improve morale,
- offer a fresh approach,
- bring in special expertise,
- attract outside resources,
- make links with outside groups.

The artist (by which I mean anyone who uses arts skills and reminiscence techniques creatively while working with people), as well as possibly being entertainer or decorator should essentially be an 'enabler' using their skills to create a context where people can in some way experience their individuality, their culture and their commonality. For a project where you wish to involve clients, as direct participants, as audience or as advisers, the artist will have to be able to demonstrate a genuine interest in their views and their experiences. You are looking for someone with good interpersonal skills who knows how to involve people in an experience that will be pleasurable and satisfying. This will require that you have a careful selection procedure. You must make sure the artist understands the context they are to work in, the nature of their involvement and the boundaries of their responsibility.

If approaching or approached by an unknown group or individual without a recognized track record, do try to ensure that their practice is good. Find out where else they have worked, voluntarily or professionally, and check references, as you would if offering someone a job. There are a few, usually well-intentioned, people around who think reminiscence is a good idea but do not really understand the implications of what they are trying to do. A project that goes wrong, or is not completed, can put staff and residents off this work for ever. Find out whether they are known, supported or funded by reputable sources such as a local hospital, the local authority or a major charity. If they are not, it does not mean they are not any good or disreputable, but that they are unproven. Ask for references: this is just common sense.

If you are paying, agree with them exactly what you are getting for your money. Do not part with money in advance unless you are very sure. Even if you are offered a service for nothing, perhaps because a group has funding for work of this kind, as with booking anyone discuss your clients' needs and your expectations. Come to an agreement about what you are to get, when and for how long.

Considering different approaches

An artist or performer may regard a home or hospital ward as a gallery or a venue, ie. an alternative outlet for the presentation of the arts to the public, as with the theatre group that performs in old people's homes, or the mural artist who paints in community settings.

For others, the creative artistic act lies in working directly with people and making something together; examples include the writer who compiles a book of reminiscences and the visual artist who helps to make a mosaic.

Others again work by responding creatively to aspects of the physical or social environment, ideally incorporating the concerns or interests of you and your clients into a piece of work, as with the sculptor who makes a statue for the grounds or the designer who helps make the environment more attractive.

Finally, there are those who are essentially teachers, helping people develop technical skills, confidence and competence that can enable them to create and express themselves artistically, such as the music workshop leader or dance animateur.

The above approaches will quite possibly overlap and combine in any particular instance and there is no right or wrong type of arts worker. Whether an approach is suitable will depend on what you are trying to achieve. Before booking anyone, talk with them about what it is you are hoping to do and discuss their way of working to identify whether this is appropriate to your specific needs and situation. Many artists are capable of working in different ways, but need to be clear what is expected of them. Whichever approach is being used, whether visual artist, performer, dancer, actor, photographer, musician or writer — all of whom may use reminiscence as an aim, or a means, in their work — a healthcare or residential setting will bring them directly into touch with their audience, physically and emotionally, making this an exciting and demanding context for the artist.

When choosing an artist yourselves, rather than working with an established organization, you should evaluate, in tandem, their personal skills and their technical ability. Someone may be an excellent painter or musician, but if you want your residents, and the staff, to accept this 'outsider' you need someone who is also reasonably gregarious, demonstrates genuine empathy for people, is tactful and is a good listener. They should have an awareness and understanding of the concepts informing good practice in care, as well as a sensitivity and warmth that will help people feel at ease. They should like older people. They will also need to be able to tolerate the lack of continuity and disruption that is often an aspect of working in these kinds of situations.

Technically, the artist will need to be competent. They should know how to take someone's ideas and turn them into a product that people relate to and how to finish off work so that it appears complete and well presented.

Linkworkers

As I have said, it is important that any outside practitioner should be able to form a good working relationship with regular care staff. If staff work with an experienced professional artist or reminiscence worker, not only will they learn from them, but the artist in turn can benefit greatly from staff expertise and support.

It can help facilitate this if one or more staff are formally given responsibility to work on the project. I call them 'linkworkers': they link the newcomer to the venue. Linkworkers have the role of introducing the visitor to residents and other staff, smoothing out any scheduling problems, acting as a sounding board for ideas, acting as a support and companion and learning skills themselves so that the initiative can be developed in the future. Formalizing the linkworker role helps the staff by making it clear that this is indeed part of their job, and also helps the practitioner by providing a consistent friendly contact and source of reassurance. This makes it more likely that the venue will maximize the value of the input and carry on after the visitor has gone.

It is important to remember that *time* must be allocated for linkworkers to participate and that this is made clear and is acceptable to less involved staff. You could try and design a project to include *all* interested staff and ensure there are regular meetings between staff and artist(s) to iron out any problems and share perceptions of the progress of the project. These meetings should aim to be a relaxed and open forum for ideas and criticisms to be mutually explored and resolved.

Once a suitable practitioner or organization is identified, it is important that, together, you draw up a brief for the work. The artist and the venue must have a realistic discussion about what is expected from and by all sides. If a manager thinks an artist is there to do art, while the artist thinks they are there to do people, there is obviously a potential conflict of perception. Staff need to be clear about what degree of involvement is expected of them. They must understand what is disruptive and what is participative. Without this clarification it is very easy for misunderstandings and complications to arise. If everyone knows or is involved with what is being planned then problems are less likely. Linkworkers should bear in mind the following:

- Try not to take over or unduly influence the nature of the sessions. Let the artist control the situation, helping out tactfully when needed.
- Allow the artist to explore the nature of the group in their own way. If it is thought important that the artist have some information about a person, tell them discreetly.
- Allow residents to deal with the presence of a new person in their own way. Never ever force anyone to join in just because someone has 'come all this way' to do something 'for' them.
- Try and ensure people are ready and prepared for sessions.
- Use the presence of the artist as a spur for other things. Work with them to identify possibilities that allow you to have a party, invite the mayor round for tea, photograph people, have a special display, get on local radio, invite relatives in, go on outings. It is all too easy to drift into a series of recreational sessions when, with thought and planning, so much more could be achieved.

I felt it was better that care staff were not involved in the artwork unless they received some kind of training to develop their awareness levels. Sadly, they often came with preconceived and rigid views about residents. One of the most important things about art and activities is that the residents are met on equal terms as individuals and not prejudged. It is refreshing for them to interact with outsiders and often they find it easier to talk to these people about concerns and personal matters, as they are not seen as part of the institution.

(Carol Davies, Artist in Residence, the Rhyl Nursing Home)

It is a good idea to design a project to include some training and practical co-operative work for linkworkers. After a few professional sessions, they can be supported to lead sessions themselves. It may equally be of benefit to involve artists or reminiscence workers in a degree of basic training to enhance their understanding of both the client group and the issues with which staff have to deal. It can help with planning if the artist has had two or three sessions to get to know people, assess possibilities and discuss interests. This also allows residents to get used to the presence of a new face and decide whether to become involved.

In any project there should be achievable objectives, even if these are broad. Objectives should be open to change and modified as the project develops and might be something like the following:

- to enable residents to undertake creative activity on a regular basis;
- to introduce a variety of arts media and techniques;
- to enable residents to enjoy using the arts as a means of self-expression and communication;
- to work together with staff to develop arts skills;
- to encourage residents to join sessions (putting them under no pressure to take an active part);
- to encourage both individual and group work;
- to endeavour to create opportunities for people who already have creative skills;
- to include some reminiscence work in sessions. (Carol Davies, Artist in Residence, the Rhyl Nursing Home)

There must be clear working parameters that are acceptable to all parties concerned.

- Is the artist to work with the same people all the time, or with a variety of people, and with how many people at a time? Suitable numbers will be dependent on the space available, frailty of residents, the skill of the artist and the art media being used. Is one-to-one work considered acceptable?
- Is the project to run as a series of sessions over an extended period of time, for example once a week for six months, or as a block of time, such as every day for a week?
- Does the timetable for the project conflict in any way with the work of other people, such as therapists or hairdressers? Does the project take into account other demands on staff and residents' time? Does it clash with popular visiting times?
- Is the artist expected to gather people together for sessions, or is that up to the staff? Are staff to participate, observe or help in some other way?
- Is preparation and research time required? How much, if anything, is to be done by the artist in between visits and is this included in their paid working time?

- How much, if anything, is to be done by staff and/or residents in between visits and who is responsible for making sure this happens?
- Are there materials required? Is the artist to supply or pay for these? Is there a budget and in whose time are materials to be bought and/or scrounged?

Costs and fund raising

Different organizations and individual artists will set their fees in various ways. Single sessions will usually be charged by the session, but sometimes by the hour. A project over a period of time will probably be costed on a daily basis, plus costs of materials, travel and preparation. For a large, continuing project or residency, you will probably agree on an overall fee for an artist or organization, with a system of accountability, to do a specific job or for self-regulated input to a particular area of concern.

Some people will look at quoted fees and think, "Well, I don't earn that much an hour!" You may not, and neither, usually, do the artists. A freelance practitioner or organization has to cover *all* of the associated costs of employment, not just that of time spent on site. Not only are you paying for skill, experience, commitment and self-motivation (otherwise you may as well work with volunteers) but in most cases you are paying towards their overall ability to operate effectively: for holidays and sickness, for training, for meetings, for publicizing themselves, for preparation. They may be travelling several hours to get to you, using their own car, telephone, materials and so on. If you do wish to compare, compare a fee to the amount you *cost* rather than how much you *earn*. In the end, with proper checks and balances, you will get what you pay for.

The core costs of reminiscence and arts activities in old people's homes, hospitals and day centres need to be funded properly *as a key element of care provision*. This signifies to everyone that the social, emotional and spiritual needs of clients are being taken seriously, allows true expertise the opportunity to develop through a long-term strategy and takes the pressure of fund raising off people who could spend their time productively working with clients. Realistically, though, this work is not usually well supported financially, and there will be times when you need to raise funds in order to put on something special or make a purchase that could not otherwise be made.

First, and I have seen this done very effectively, raising money on a small scale can be organized as an integral part of an activities programme: for example, presenting a summer event, show or exhibition for which there is an admission fee or making booklets of recipes or poetry that you are able to sell. I was hailed once by a determined resident who insisted I come straight over and who would not allow me to go on my way before buying some raffle tickets. Participation in a fund raising process in this way can offer a strong sense of worthwhile involvement by allowing residents to make a useful contribution to the provision of resources.

Another way to raise funds is to apply to grant-making bodies. Before embarking on what can be an extremely frustrating endeavour, check first of all what funding sources there may be within your organization itself. You may find there are sources such as amenity funds, endowments or budgets allocated for special purposes. Just because there is no apparent money for one aspect of your work, do not assume that there is nothing for another. Budgets are often kept under different headings and it may be worth seeing if there is money unspent that was allocated for a different but comparable purpose. The people responsible for the allocation of finance may not be very forthcoming about what is potentially available. They, of course, must ensure that limited resources are used to the greatest effect and you will have to present a case that demonstrates that your project represents wise use of limited funding. A little persistent research may be required.

A variety of trusts and charities of all sizes can be approached for grants and donations, though some will not give money to statutory services or may specify that they will only consider providing a proportion of what is required. There are regularly updated books available listing companies and trusts that accept applications for grants and donations, along with other important details. Otherwise, there is usually some funding available via local and national government for arts and community projects. Sometimes there may be opportunities via hospitals and social services departments, or you may be able to apply for support from various lotteries.

Other potential sources of help are local companies and shops.

Ring up and try to obtain an appointment with the director or owner or, in larger concerns, with a public relations department, publicity officer or similar party. Sometimes if you are able to explain clearly what you are after to the person who answers the telephone, they will be able to give you the name of the person who is the best to talk to. Some of the largest companies allocate special funds for good causes and have an employee whose role it is to consider applications for financial donations. It is always best, unless company policy is clearly against this, to try and make personal contact so that your enthusiasm and commitment can shine through. Remember, you do not get any-thing if you do not ask, and they can only say 'no'. All you will have lost is the cost of a telephone call and some of your time. It is possible that a local or even a national company may be interested in forming a long-term relationship with a cause they perceive as being of worth that will reflect their image positively.

Fund raising is certainly worth trying if you need to purchase equipment or memorabilia, or perhaps to bring in an artist to work with you, but do note that some sources only grant money for capital projects. You might also consider setting up a group of interested sup-porters, possibly relatives or key local people, who can help to raise funds.

Applying for a grant
Whether you plan to apply for substantial core funding or for a small contribution towards something special, you must have carefully worked out a budget which clearly specifies what it is you want to pur-chase with the money and why. Have your requirements neatly listed and support these with relevant background information, such as pho-tographs, newspaper cuttings, details of other funding and so on that will help present, succinctly, an overall picture of who you are, exact-ly what you are trying to do and why. Try to get written support from others that can strengthen your case: from senior managers, key prac-titioners or influential people.

If you can obtain the information, look carefully at the nature of projects supported by the source you are applying to and any restric-tions on distribution. For example, a source may only support initia-tives in a particular geographical locality or may have a preference for, or indeed exclude, applications for arts-related projects or those involving older people. Emphasize an application in terms favoured by the source being approached and take into account the size of grants and donations usually given. It may matter at what time of year you apply: some sources only allocate funds for each financial year, others may meet quarterly; yet others will accept proposals at any time. Some will have application forms, others expect you to present a proposal in your own way. If so, keep it simple and realistic, and try to be quite clear about how much you need and why. Check facts to avoid wasting time on invalid or inappropriate applications.

Certain sources will only offer matching funding: that is, a proportion of what you need on condition you find the rest elsewhere. Do not forget, in making an application, to include *all* costs in your calculations. For example, if you want someone to work alongside you and you are employed as a carer, some of the costs are represented by the time you spend on this activity and some by the cost of the sessional worker. Then there are materials and travel costs to take into consideration.

Remember that, if you do get funding by applying for grants, you will have to keep proper accounts and may have to provide a report of some kind. It can be helpful to take a few photographs and note down feedback from participants (include related costs in your application). Keep funders informed of progress and invite them to see what you are doing. If you are able to form a working relationship with them, there may be all kinds of possibilities for future support.

Lastly, when applying for funding, be prepared for rejection and try not to take this as a criticism of your work. There is a lot of luck involved in successful fund raising of this kind and there may be many reasons why a particular source does not consider it appropriate to support the kind of work you are proposing. It is all right to approach a source again, taking a different tack, and do not be afraid to discuss your ideas with them. Do not get disheartened. If you believe in what you are trying to do, this will show and eventually reap reward. At least no-one can say you did not try. Good luck.

Contexts for Activity

Age appropriateness

At times I have encountered cynicism from care professionals who hold the view that some of the activities suggested by people like myself are somehow demeaning in themselves and not the kind of thing that people should be enjoying at 'their age' — not age appropriate. For example, during a singing session a doctor sneered loudly, in front of everyone (itself an insulting way of getting his point across) at what he called 'end of the pier music'. He meant that the music as he was perceiving it was somehow undignified, not refined enough. I *know* that the people having that singsong were engaged, contributing positively and enjoying themselves. Every bone in my body told me that the group was having a good time. The doctor, from his position of lack of involvement with the group, allowed his own prejudices to inform his judgement.

I believe that very little activity enjoyed by clients is inappropriate if it is broadly acceptable in the particular context, enjoyable or meaningful to the individual and not damaging or offensive to others. It is of more consequence to be sensitive to what is *not* appropriate than to what is. I will try to illustrate what I mean with what has become an oft-related classic example: the lively music has a strong beat and so the carer comes along and, taking hold of Harry's arms, forces him to clap along: "Come on, Harry, enjoy yourself."

To do this is *probably* wrong. It is clearly reasonable in this situation if Harry does or does not clap his hands. He does not need to do so either to enjoy himself or to participate effectively in the activity.

Clapping to music is usually a spontaneous gesture indicating enjoyment. If clapping enhanced Harry's enjoyment he would possibly do so *if it felt appropriate to him*. There should only be interference if through his behaviour he is spoiling things for others, for example if he is stopping them from listening to the music by making too much noise. It is much more likely that clapping at the wrong time would cause disruption rather than not clapping at all. It is inappropriate and threatens Harry's individuality if he is forced to behave in a way he has not chosen for no other reason than someone else's view of what he ought to be doing. The carer is taking away from Harry the decision he can and should make for himself as to whether he wants to clap his hands. It is not the music activity or the clapping that is inappropriate, but the control that the carer is taking.

Clapping because *he has been told to* is inappropriate; clapping itself is neutral, whether to end of the pier music or anything else. The judgement must be Harry's! Activities are not appropriate if they remove a fundamental right to make decisions and choices, dignity and self-esteem, or individuality. I am not suggesting that Harry should be simply left to his own devices. It is of course perfectly all right to suggest to him that he might like to clap along, or that it is all right to do so if he feels enthusiastic enough to want to. He can be asked whether he will and perhaps find to his surprise it is quite pleasurable. Perhaps the best technique is to indicate through your own behaviour that clapping along is a good and appropriate thing to do. Before you know it, the whole room could be joining in.

It is age appropriate to make your own decisions and not age appropriate to be directed and controlled.

Some years ago I was working on a long-stay psychiatric ward and encountered a patient doing a jigsaw of the English cartoon characters, Noddy and Big Ears. This offended me at the time. I felt she could have at least been doing a jigsaw with a picture of a favourite animal or a rose-covered cottage on it, although whether this was really a problem for the person doing the jigsaw I am now very unsure. I was making uninformed assumptions about what someone ought to be doing and, for all I know, she may have carefully selected that particular jigsaw herself for any number of reasons, perhaps because she liked the picture, liked the colours, had done all the others or was a big fan of Noddy's. Surely the key is not for me to decide what kind of jigsaw that person should be doing, but to ensure that there is a variety of jigsaws available so that a choice can be made from a reasonable selection.

I believe that the idea of age appropriateness has more to do with the way people are respected by those who care for them than with the intrinsic nature of activities in which people are involved. Appropriateness becomes a matter of concern when staff practice makes wrong assumptions about the capacity of people to understand what is going on and to make decisions for themselves. It is an approach to older people that treats them like objects that needs to be challenged: treating old people as very dependent, without respect, assuming they are not all there, unnecessarily controlling behaviour.

Patronizing attitudes may arise with a benign motivation that has its foundation in intimate physical care which, although often experienced as demeaning, is tolerated because it is essential. There can be a tendency amongst staff, as a result of having to help someone as one would help a baby or child, to continue this relationship in other contexts, such as socially, when it is not appropriate or benevolent. Staff need to be aware of this danger and cultivate skills that ensure that effective care is achieved while helping individuals to retain as much self-respect as possible. Furthermore, they must demonstrate a mindful, but not distant, approach to those in their care.

Contradictions arise because the concept of what is appropriate adult behaviour is very much in the eye of the beholder. Of course older people should be treated with respect for their age and maturity. Of course care staff should not 'talk down' to people, however 'childlike' they appear to have become. This aspect of good practice, that people should be treated with the respect due to mature adults, is sometimes inappropriately used as a reason to exclude older people from enjoyable and liberating activities.

The manager of a home where we were hoping to set up some arts-based reminiscence work condemned what we were trying to do outright. This intelligent, concerned professional stated intensely that his home was oriented towards normalization and that residents were expected to behave like other people. In his opinion it was not normal to look at old photographs and it was not normal to paint pictures.

Perhaps he thought it was normal for older people to sit watching television all day while waiting for a cup of tea.

There is no such a thing as behaviour that is specifically inappropriate for *older* people to engage in. Whether it is acceptable to behave in a certain way is largely dependent on the context in which it happens. What is acceptable in the social club is not acceptable in the church. What is acceptable in private may not be acceptable in public. It is the fact that older people in care spend most of their time in what we might call 'public' space that sometimes causes a discrepancy between admissible social conduct and the needs of the individual.

Organizing activities

It is important to devise a framework in which to structure what you are trying to do. Devise a plan, a timetable, but be prepared to make it flexible and open to change and development. Within this framework you should include opportunities for a variety of different activities that offer real options for making choices and decisions.

You should try, over the year (you do not have to do everything at the same time) to present a diverse broad based programme that includes a mix of activities which are social, creative, expressive, individualizing, physical, cognitive, emotional, spiritual, practical and entertaining. They should be devised to include the involvement of

individuals,
small natural groups,
small special groups,
the whole community of the home or ward,
residents doing things together,
staff and residents doing things together,
outsiders coming in,
insiders going out,
the local community,
professional practitioners and artists, and
contributions to others.

Try to devise a way of tackling activities that suits you and is realistically viable in your particular set of circumstances. Take into account the practical constraints upon you, the degree of involvement of other staff and the interest shown by clients. It can be helpful to distinguish between sessions, clubs and projects and to incorporate a variety of approaches to different aspects of a programme of activities.

Sessional work means offering the same activity regularly with minimal or only incidental development of the content of one session to the next. Examples might include hymn singing, bingo, reminiscence and exercise. This is a most common way of organizing activity programmes. A timetabled programme of regular sessions gives a shape to the week, offers something familiar to look forward to and a consistent structure to work with.

Although it may sometimes seem that regular sessions need the least preparation, in fact it can become quite difficult to maintain momentum over a long period of time. This is less of a problem, and may well be the only approach you can take, if you have a swiftly changing population of participants. This offers an additional benefit by allowing you to try the same subjects a number of times, thereby increasing your own knowledge and skill, your own repertoire. You will need to think of ways to maintain your own interest and, if a sessional activity starts to become stale and ritualistic, to discuss the possibility of changing it.

An extension of the idea of sessions is to think of activity groups as *clubs*. A club may ostensibly meet for a specific reason, but also potentially includes opportunity for all other kinds of aspects: eg. trips out, visiting speakers and social occasions. People can gain great pleasure and self-esteem from feeling they belong to something purposeful and distinctive. Possible clubs include the following:

- friendship club, social club;
- games club, such as darts club, dominoes club, bowling club;
- poetry reading society, creative writing club;
- drama club, playreading group;
- classical music club;
- memory lane club, oral history group;
- film club;
- debating society;

- gardening society;
- photography club.

You can take this further and elect officials, take minutes of meetings, collect subscriptions, raise funds and organize inter-club competitions and events. Devise your own name and logo and offer some real authority to the members about how things are organized.

A *project* involves working purposefully over a finite period of time towards an achievable aim. An example would be to compile a book or create artwork to decorate the clubroom. This may include a variety of different groups or individuals working in different ways towards the same purpose. If, for example, you plan to put on a show, you will need help making a backdrop and props, designing costumes, writing a script, devising a programme, rehearsing the pieces, sending out invitations, making refreshments, and so on.

Many older people are used to spending a great deal of time on their own. If your aim is not specifically to encourage interaction, you may devise a 'group' that is in fact made up of a variety of individuals working independently on work of their own to contribute to a greater whole. You may be collecting reminiscences for a booklet or display, or compiling individual life histories, or perhaps incorporating recollections into a drama event.

You might consider asking participants in regular sessions and club members to contribute to a larger whole. For example, a summer event can include displays of artwork, a presentation from the reminiscence club, a performance of music to movement, a poetry reading followed by a singalong led by the music club. Refreshments could be made by the baking group. Other people can be in charge of or helping with the raffle. Remember that some individuals can be responsible for making a direct contribution whilst others can play a more peripheral role. You should aim to devise projects that enable and encourage meaningful contributions that are appropriate to individual and group interests and abilities.

A project need not be complex, but you must aim to complete it; then you can have a welcome break and decide what to do next.

Building Support

It is difficult to work effectively when feeling isolated and it can enhance what you are trying to do if you can organize and negotiate support from as many sources as possible. It may help to try the following. Discuss your plans with colleagues so that their duties are in harmony with yours and they are not, intentionally or unintentionally, working against you. Develop or participate in a network involving other people doing similar work and share ideas and resources. Negotiate opportunities to attend occasional training sessions, even if you feel clear about what you are doing. It can be refreshing to step back from your work and look at it from a distance and talk with like-minded others. Secure the support of a senior manager. This can make it easier to get things done and to negotiate resources. A manager will also be able to act as support for the broad sweep of your ideas and represent your interests to other people in authority. Set up a support group consisting of colleagues and interested outsiders who can advise you, raise funds, help with publicity and generally back up your efforts. Make this group quite formal, with a chairman, treasurer and so on. You might consider involving clients, local business people, local dignitaries, councillors, artists, famous people and retired people — all of whom will have skills and expertise to offer.

If you have clear endorsement from clients, staff, relatives and local people, it will be harder for those who consider activities a rather expensive luxury to determine that you should be put to other tasks. The more effectively you are able to articulate and demonstrate support for your work, the more effectively you can negotiate for resources and justify your role.

Passive and active participation

It can be part of a programme to arrange 'entertainment' and, as long as everyone enjoys the show, it is considered that the activity has fulfilled its function. To be entertained in this way could be described as passive participation. Alternatively, we may concentrate on 'making things', requiring active participation. We will then consider that, if someone is not directly practically involved, they are not participating. Activities frequently and naturally tend to be organized from one perspective or the other, although the distinction is often blurred, but there can be opportunities for different kinds of involvement within a particular situation.

Listening to music is a passive experience. The musician, live or recorded, presents their 'product' to you, and you experience it without having to do anything except listen. If you talk about it, choose the programme, dance, clap or sing along to that music, it has become an active experience. Looking at pictures is a passive experience, whilst discussing their content or choosing pictures for an exhibition becomes an active experience. Activities should include opportunities for both kinds of involvement.

From chess to chocolate

Some people will be used to enjoying 'the Arts' in the cultural sense, with a capital 'A'. The theatre patron who has an intimate knowledge of a particular style of drama will experience a dramatic presentation differently from someone who has hardly ever been to a theatre in their lives. The lifelong enthusiast of jazz music will probably have a different perspective on music than someone for whom music holds little special interest.

Do not assume, and it is easily done, that "they don't like classical music" when what you really mean is "I don't like classical music". There is a place for a whole broad spectrum of cultural activity: from restfully passive to dynamically active; from popular to classically cultured; from those involving the whole community to individual acts of creativity; intellectually challenging and demanding activity as well as having a bit of fun. For some people, just to be gently involved in a group that is busy or interactive may be more than enough, but you must also try to create opportunities for a variety of options: from chess to chocolate, from Bach to bingo, from Dali to Doris Day.

Miss S sat by the window, gazing out on the view of the factory. She declined graciously to join in with groups most of the time. I sat and talked to Miss S one day. She was a kind, gentle soul, a retired schoolteacher. For her, the special needs reminiscence group and the playing games group — the only options available at the time — were not stimulating, seeming rather trivial. It was not that she found them beneath her, but simply of no intellectual interest. We had a deep conversation about industrial development in the twentieth century, and she gave me some useful gardening tips.

Present as diverse a programme as possible to your clients, try not to underrate an individual's capacity to understand and enjoy, and do not make assumptions based on your own artistic tastes. Try to create opportunities for those who need a little more than fun.

Getting Down to Work

> Nothing comes without its shadow; not every session went smoothly or without problems but there is a gift in everything — sun or shadow — and each session brought as its gift 'sharing' … the sharing of time one afternoon a week; of family stories: celebratory, tragic, humorous; of a spontaneous song.
> (Joan Poulson, Writer in Residence, Manchester Reminiscence Project)

Putting on a reminiscence exhibition

Putting an exhibition together need not be as difficult as it may seem. A great deal of enjoyment and satisfaction can be generated as the project develops and is finally put on show. You can create a general exhibition that broadly reflects the old days, using whatever material you are able to collect, or, alternatively, and this will be harder work but worthwhile, you can focus on a more specific topic. Choose a subject that is going to be of interest: this may be about the locality, such as our town or rural life or a less general theme such as cinema or shopping.

Introduce into discussion a subject or a variety of subjects on a number of occasions and elicit the main elements of interest, indicated by the frequency that they arise and the enthusiasm shown. There may be references to particular places, events or aspects of life — the Town Hall, the great flood of '47, listening to the wireless — that are particularly loved or remembered. Persuade the office to type up the information you collect (stories, anecdotes, facts and figures) preferably onto a word processor so you can alter things as you go along. To take this even further, contact your local library and discuss what you are doing and see what supportive information they can find, especially photographs but also maps, timetables and advertisements that relate to the topics and geographical area you are interested in. As the theme develops, other contacts may spring to mind, such as companies, shops, local newspapers and archives, that may be able to help.

You will probably wish to include artefacts and memorabilia in the display. Try the local museum but also, at the beginning of your project, make enquiries in your workplace and around the neighbourhood. You could be pleasantly surprised to find what people keep tucked away at home in case it comes in useful some day, and remember you only need to borrow things, not to keep them. See what photographs and memorabilia clients and their families have that they are willing to display. Some pieces will have a story to tell, whilst others can simply enhance the overall atmosphere and ambience of the exhibition. Personal memorabilia can be of great sentimental value, so do make sure you know exactly what belongs to whom and keep a comprehensive list. It can be a good idea, particularly if you have a lot of material, to stick a little label somewhere discreet and cross-refer this to the owners' names. Use a label that you are *absolutely certain* will not cause any damage. (You can get into terrible trouble and feel absolutely dreadful if you lose someone's special memento. I know ...)

As the exhibition unfolds, as things are brought in, show them to your group, discuss them, get their opinions; use the fact that you are building the exhibition to stimulate people's interest. The important thing, as in all suggested projects, is to try and keep people involved and informed and to work things out so they are included on the day. Your group are not the audience, they are the organizers (with you doing all the running around as usual).

You will need to work out exactly how you are going to programme the event itself. Will it be on for a day, all week, or for how long? Sometimes it does seem a shame to spend ages putting it all together, take a day or even longer to set everything out attractively and then take it straight down again. It always takes longer than you think to put up the exhibition and it comes down surprisingly quickly. Sort out what space you have, as you may have to arrange help to move furniture. Ensure that displays will be accessible to everybody and that the lighting is good. Have a few chairs available so that people who need to can sit comfortably to study and discuss what they see. Written information should be neatly mounted on card and in large print. You can enlarge text easily on many photocopiers.

You will probably find display screens useful (talk to your friendly librarian if you are stuck) and you will need tables for exhibits. Set everything out carefully, paying attention to the way it looks. Think about the presentation. Trestle tables can be covered with attractive table-cloths and pleasantly arranged objects, books and photographs, postcards, plants and so on, played off against each other so they look good together. A 'corner' furnished a little like an old room can create a special focal point. You would need a few bits of old furniture, a rag rug, some household appliances, perhaps a vacuum cleaner, carpet sweeper and suchlike. Possibly have a period tea set and a magazine from the 1930s artistically left open on a kitchen table, boots by the door and a coat and hat on a hook near the umbrella stand — the ideas start to flow when you think about it creatively. You could have a special corner dedicated to 'collecting' memories on the day.

Be aware that people will possibly want to touch and pick up things to have a closer look and this can increase enjoyment. Some things, though, will be too fragile or precious to be put at risk, so make sure vulnerable artefacts are kept safe, protected by plastic sleeves or on show in some kind of display case. You will have to consider whether you need a room that can be locked, or cupboards to put things away. You do not want to tempt sticky fingers. (I recall the woman who helped herself to a tiny little brooch that was on display in a hospital ward. She denied all knowledge on first enquiry, but I knew she had it in her handbag. Was I going to have to confront her and go through her bag? After several hours she returned and put the little brooch back. What a relief.)

Have key people stationed around the exhibition to welcome visitors and talk about things and, if people are very frail, have staff or volunteers available especially to facilitate involvement. Find some background music that suits the atmosphere or get the group, or perhaps someone who is unable to be involved in any other way, to choose some. A little bunting or a few flags can set it all off perfectly.

Are you going to charge an entrance fee? Even if it is not a fund raiser, a small charge often makes people take an event more seriously, and it will pay for the refreshments. Refreshments! Just biscuits, or are you going to make a meal of it? Perhaps you should have a word with the baking club?

Remember to prepare posters, flyers and advertisements and do not forget to contact the local press.

Let's hope everyone comes.

Writing a book

Compiling a book of reminiscences, stories, perhaps poetry, creative writing or recipes can provide a stimulating and realistic aim towards which to work. Nearly all of us like to see our name in print and it can help everyone feel important to give 'our very own book' to relatives and friends and even sell the item at the Summer Fete or Christmas party. Producing a book, or booklet, can be a very useful reason to talk with people: you are not just being nosy or therapeutic, but engaging people with a goal in mind.

For most people, the process of reminiscing together in a group while someone collects the stories will be the easiest and most enjoyable way to produce the information that is to go into print. After agreeing with participants that the group is to share reminiscence in print, run the group as normal, but, as you do, record stories and snippets about people that could be written up as a short piece. Make it very clear why you are writing things down and, perhaps on another day, read what you have written back to the person concerned to ensure this is what they intended to say. This reading back in itself represents an act of confirmation. Make sure you have permission from the speaker to publish or reproduce their material. Copyright lies with the source.

It can help you get started if you preface each recollection with something like "George remembers when ..." or "Lily recalls that ..." keeping to quite simple but clear statements. Here are some examples of some short reminiscences collected by professional writer Joan Poulson for the Manchester Reminiscence Project:

> We only had fresh milk on a Sunday. My mother made us rice pudding with it — our Sunday treat. It was lovely, with skin on made from nutmeg. She used to grate the nutmeg herself. The rest of the milk we used, our everyday milk, was tinned.
>
> We used to walk everywhere. You thought nothing of it. Some of them came to school on the tram but we walked.
>
> We all used to set off, the whole family of us — Mam, Dad, all us children, going off for the day out. We'd have a bag of sandwiches, some pop, or even just bottles of water. And we'd be laughing and looking forward to it. There'd be no snapping and quarrelling. My Mam was looking forward to it as much as the rest of us. It was a good day; nothing much to get ready, we didn't have much. Now when my grandson and his family are off out there's a commotion as if they're emigrating. Everybody's taking this and that. It's bedlam. They look worn out before they start!

Notice how the words are written as if they were being spoken and capture a sense of intimacy and personality.

If you are working with a group and intending to collect common group reminiscences that hold significance for everybody, it can be helpful to work to a theme and encourage 'what it was like' discussion. You might aim to discuss a subject generally with the members of the group and then try to write down different aspects of what the group is saying it was like. An example of this kind of writing could be the following:

> The streets were a lot quieter then, you might not see a car all day. Everybody played on the street and you could hear all the different games that were going on. You'd see the mothers bobbing in and out of the houses in their pinnies to see if the kids were all right on the street.

Even if these are the actual words of one person, they are summing up a common experience that applies to several or many people. You would want to check with the group that there is broad agreement with the statement being taken down on their behalf.

You may prefer to talk with each person one at a time in the group session, or interview people individually and get a comment from each person on a particular theme, as here on the subject of holidays:

We always got a holiday. Every year we went to Blackpool or Southport. We went on a train for the day.

I thought it was wonderful when we went to Morecambe for the day. We took our food with us, corned beef or ham sandwiches and biscuits. I used to love biscuits, I still do.

In the holidays my father used to say, "Where are we going tomorrow?" Then he'd say, "New Brighton!" We loved it. We went under the tunnel.

When working with people who have difficulty expressing themselves, you might find it easier to write about someone in the third person and personalize the story directly. I call these life and times stories:

Doris was born and has always lived in Fleetwood where her family roots go back for generations. Her father was very well known and respected in the town where he owned and ran one of the most thriving businesses. There was always a strong bond between family members and Doris recalls, with particular affection, the love and support she received from both her parents. Gardening became one of Doris's early interests and one she still retains today, but her greatest talent lies in her singing voice, which people have enjoyed hearing in concert halls not only in all parts the United Kingdom but in many different countries of the world.

You can compile the story over several sessions, checking each time that you have it right and gradually building a little word picture of the person. If people are unable to communicate at all, you might want to talk to relatives and find out some relevant information from them:

Frank has always lived in the area but both his parents came from Ireland. In his younger days, Frank enjoyed ballroom dancing, his favourite dance being the slow fox-trot at which he excelled. He recalls that it cost 1/6d for two people to go dancing at either the Winter Gardens or the Tower Ballroom in Blackpool. Frank's partner was his wife and they are soon to celebrate 40 years of marriage.

Notice that the story refers to the present as well as the past.

You will also find that reminiscences can have a variety of emphases, depending on the personality of the individual and the way you have co-ordinated the discussion:

Coalin, Tommy Coalin, the baker. The other side of the road there was another bakers, Jackie Adkins. The Queen's Head pub had also got a little butcher's shop down there. You come a bit further along and there was New Street next to Coalin's and a bit farther down on the corner of the street there was Gus Peppitt, hardware shop. Other side of the road, Plank the Baker. Farther down still on the right there was A Rogers the grocer's place. Across the way opposite, it was only like a little cottage, unless you knew the village well, she would sell sweets, toffees, bottled stuff, ice cream, anything you wanted. Lower down again on the right-hand side was Tommy Adlington, he was ... well, allsorts. The shop used to do sweets and everything you wanted and he would go out and sweep chimneys or do anything.
(Ted Cleaver, *Westminster Tales*)

What a memory for detail! The names and places. You could find your way round the village from that description. Compare this with the same subject, described by someone else; it is just as sharp, but less specific:

Village life has altered tremendously over the years. You made your own entertainment, your own amusements. Sunday School, that would have an outing in the summer and we'd have a Christmas concert which the children would act. We would have Maypole day when you would all dress up in your May clothes and your flowers and sing round the village with a big banner. The same with Sunday School day, you had the Sunday School banner and would sing. All those sorts of things have died out today. Cubbington gradually got more shops, gradually more houses and the village extended. Estates grew here and there and so it gradually altered.

(Dorothy Eales, *Westminster Tales*)

Both these reminiscences answer the question 'what was it like in the village?'

Some people may be quite capable and interested in writing down their reminiscences themselves. With gentle encouragement and a quiet place to go and work, they may well produce lots of information for you to draw on. You need to make sure that you demonstrate interest in what is being written and this interaction can become a very meaningful and profound experience for both you and the writer. Make sure contributors realize that you may be going to publish their words and that you have their permission. If you are not going to be able to use everything that someone contributes, which is quite likely, make sure this is made clear to them. People can experience a sense of rejection if you have to cut down the mountain of information they have given to you. One way to deal with this is to type up and present them with their own special publication of reminiscences that they can keep or give to their family.

Making the book
It is possible these days to create a very respectable-looking booklet using a home or office computer. The information should be typed into a good word-processing programme, edited to make sense but not to lose the 'flavour' of the language.

If you cannot produce it yourselves, borrow the office computer and, even better, the office typist as well, save the information onto disk and get someone experienced to do the desktop publishing. A desktop publishing programme can help ensure that the information is laid out artistically and decoratively, and can include drawings and even scanned photographs. A friendly computer buff and many voluntary organizations can do a professional-looking layout for you. It may even be a suitable project for a school, college or evening class.

High street 'printshops' offer all kinds of services at a very reasonable price and will design the document to your instruction, although you lose a certain amount of control by not laying it out yourself. They can often work directly from a computer disk. Once printed, your book can be bound with a coloured card cover. It is not worth considering professional printing for fewer than 500 copies.

As well as the method of production, there are a number of things you should consider. First, what size is the document? If it is over about 50 pages (sides) you may not be able to have it stapled, and will have to try another kind of binding — spiral or glue. Sticking to a standard size paper will save a little money and be less wasteful of paper. Recycled paper can be of very good quality. Next, what about the cover? Printing black onto coloured card or thick paper may look effective and printing two colours onto coloured card will not be too costly. Do you want the cover laminated? This can make a home-made product look very professional. Third, you need to think about print size. If your product is to be read by people whose eyesight is not very good, then the type needs to be larger than average without being so big it looks rather childish. Fourth, simple black and white drawings can be photocopied, or scanned into a computer system, very easily and effectively; are there any budding illustrators amongst your clients or the staff?

Finally, when your book is produced — 50 copies from the office photocopier or one thousand from the local printers — you need to have a party (making the most of things again) to let the world know your book is complete. If you have managed to get a sponsor or two, a grant from a trust or help from a local firm and so on, they will be pleased to be invited to the event, and perhaps more so if you have notified the local paper. If you are to invite people who are busy, give them a lot of notice — two months is not too much to make sure they can make it.

It is very very important that, if you have collected reminiscences for a purpose like this, you make sure you do something with them and do not just leave the project half completed. *People may have attached much more significance to what you are doing than you are aware. It is crucial not to build up expectations and then let people down.*

Individual Life History Books

It can be a profound and valuable experience for an individual to produce what is sometimes called a 'Life History Book'. This is an account, not necessarily in great detail, of aspects of someone's life, interests and personality. Information should be collected over a number of meetings and written down. A picture of the person will be gradually built up. As usual, make very clear what it is you are aiming to do and, once you start this process, be sure to complete it.

Agree when and how often you are going to meet. This need not be too frequent, but probably more often than once a week, depending on how much clients have to say. This process can become very intimate, creating an opportunity for staff members to come to understand the life experiences that act as a foundation for a person's present behaviour.

Once you have agreement from someone to try a life history, think through the questions you are going to ask and then let the process unfold naturally and enjoyably, bringing discussion back to the point of the exercise when required. Do not be too timid to ask questions that may seem a little intrusive, but be sensitive to the effects of what you are discussing and do not delve deeper than is comfortable for both of you. Be gentle, but do not be afraid of some intense emotion. As always, the situation should be in the older person's control.

A life history need not be very long and involved. You might start with factual details of where a person was born, where they went to school, what jobs they have had and if they married and had children. Even simple things such as the colours someone likes or their taste in music can help you tailor what you offer to that person and reinforce their individuality. It can of course go much further — and some people may wish to write things down for you, ready for your next visit. Eventually, go through the information you have been given, checking that facts and spellings of names and places are correct. Going through it all will also reinforce the progress made and minimize repetition of information.

It can be interesting to illustrate the document with photographs, newspaper cuttings, favourite poems and similar items and to do this well you will have to allow time for research. Agree with the person what form they would like the book to take. A big book written in free-hand may look very attractive to one, whilst another person might prefer something typewritten. Make sure it is bound nicely and has a good cover. This book can then stay with the subject, or if kept somewhere safe it should be easily accessible, to be looked at with them, read alongside them by new staff and the information gathered should be used as a basis for being responsive to that person. For example, you may find that someone has particular likes or dislikes that can help you decide what music to make available or what food to have on a menu. You may become aware of dates and anniversaries that could have an impact on someone's well-being.

Do not *assume* that an individual will want to explore their lives with you in any great depth. For many this will be inappropriate and possibly much too painful. But once people feel safe and comfortable, some will enjoy being the focus of attention and sharing aspects of their own special story. A profound, meaningful exercise, especially if you are working with people who are unable to remember or communicate information, is to talk to members of the family, again making very clear what it is you are planning to do with this information. Be prepared to provide support and guidance, as you are exploring *very* sensitive emotional territory. Emotions can run high as relatives may be experiencing grief and guilt as well as bitter/sweet recollections. Careful exploration of this kind has the potential to be deeply meaningful and will demand great tenderness on your part.

We invited Mr Jones to join us in a small group which included Mrs Jones, who was suffering from the advanced stages of Alzheimer's disease. Carefully, we asked Mr Jones about his wife, factual questions about where she was born and had gone to school. Mr Jones talked clearly and calmly about his wife who was sitting with us but was not *with* us. I could see the emotion in his eyes as he began to build us a vision of her: what she had been like, the good works she had done, the places they had visited together. Several times I felt I had to remind him that he did not have to do this and gave him the opportunity to stop, but he persevered. He talked about himself as well. We paid great attention. Towards the end of the session, as it was coming to a natural close, Mr Jones looked at me and said, "She's not there, is she, she's gone?" I replied, honestly, that I did not know. Her presence, since she was unable to participate, was based on an act of faith that she might have retained a flicker of awareness of her former self and might be reached in some way. The following week, Mr Jones arrived for a second session with some photographs of himself, his wife and the church in which they had been married 56 years before. Despite his pain, Mr Jones had clearly felt this was something he was able to deal with and voluntarily returned to talk to us again.

It is important that sessions like this, which have deep implications and are fundamentally risky, remain voluntary exercises and are handled with a high degree of sensitivity. In Mr Jones' case, where it would appear his wife was unable even to recognize him, the value of this process lies in what it can do for him. We created the opportunity for him to talk about his wife if he wished and eventually to meet others in a similar situation. He felt, I hope, just a little less isolated while coping with this sad and traumatic moment in his life.

Storytelling

Storytelling, although coming back into vogue, is still a very underrated art form. The oral tradition has a long and universal place in the history of human culture and, while nowadays we may tend to depend on the television to tell us stories, there is no reason that this should mean we no longer relate stories amongst ourselves. In many cultures and traditions, the oral storyteller is respected and honoured. Storytelling is, of course, the fundamental basis of reminiscence and older people may well have learnt monologues, have favourite tales to tell and have been handed down knowledge of myth, legend and tradition. Many of them are natural storytellers who can shape their material expertly.

You, or a member of the group, can tell or read stories to the others. I am aware that for some people reading aloud, and being read to, can cause a certain amount of embarrassment. This may be because we associate reading aloud with childishness. We read aloud to the young, while grown-ups are expected to read for themselves. This is a nonsense of course. If a person cannot read any more, should they therefore never again be able to enjoy a good tale? Silently reading a book to oneself is not the shared experience of hearing a story as one of a group. When reading to a group, you can 'transport' everyone, via imagination, to any time or place.

Key points when storytelling include the following:

1   Choose a piece that is not overlong. A reading should last no longer than 20 minutes, possibly much less, or the listeners' attention may begin to wander.
2   At suitable key places, summarize the story so far, especially at the beginning and probably at the end of each session. This will help ensure that people do not 'lose their place' and clarify the story for anyone who may have become slightly confused.
3   Discuss issues raised by the story as you go along, or have a discussion at the end. What would the listener do in a similar situation; has the story a lesson to teach us; and how do individuals feel about what has been said?
4   Choose something relevant and interesting, not childish but also not too complex. Remember that someone has to be able to read it out loud. Choose something you like yourself and pieces suggested by the clients.
5   Try books on local history, reminiscences, biographies and autobiographies, short stories and classic tales of myth and legend.

If you really do feel too insecure about reading out loud, there are taped books available in libraries and through organizations for the visually impaired. There are also stories read aloud on radio.

Projects arise naturally from storytelling: help individuals to record their 'story' onto tape and then to present this, followed by questions to the rest of the group; help both staff and residents to present a short talk on a subject of interest to them, followed by questions and answers; run a session particularly aimed at identifying folk tales and legends that have been passed down through the generations; compare folk tales from different cultures.

Poetry

Poetry speaks to the soul and can conjure up strong images and imaginative associations. The musical use of language allows for the expression of poignant and deeply felt emotions that are difficult to communicate in any other way, making it a meaningful and useful tool in reminiscence sessions. As an art form, poetry was much more familiar to people in the past than it is today and many older people will vividly recall poems learned in their schooldays. Even from a snippet of a line you may be able to trace the source and bring a hazy memory to life.

Perhaps you could set up a poetry group, not only to listen to poetry, but to read, recite and write it. Following a series of meetings by the poetry group, set up an event and invite visitors to come and enjoy recitations of old favourites and original compositions. This is a simple but very enjoyable way of passing an afternoon that focuses directly on people's individuality. You may benefit from some professional help with getting started on creative writing, so enquire at your local library about poetry workshop sessions. There are groups of poets who meet regularly to share their work and you could ask if they would like to come and give a recitation to your group. Go and listen to them first! Some poetry can be incredibly dull and obscure.

The following poem is an example composed in a creative writing session led by writer Joan Poulson. The poem is based on colours and suggests to the reader a whole spectrum of different experiences:

> Red of tomatoes
> Yellow daffodils
> Orange of the dawn
> Blue of the sea
> Green of the grass
> Indigo of love
> Violet of the valentine
>
> Turquoise is my Auntie Lillian
> Black is the dimmer nights
> White is the wedding dress
> Purple is the sweetness of the cooking

Beige is the lovely summer shoes
Brown is the chestnuts in the Autumn
Cream is the nice milky coffees
(M Howell, *Window on Winwick*)

And, in contrast, there is this little ditty donated by Henry Frumin:

A frog one day was crossing the road,
Along came a car and hit that toad,
Who managed to whisper, "This is no joke",
Drew its last breath and started to croak.
(*Ladywell Lives*)

Photography

Taking pictures with a modern camera is an accessible and relatively easy activity to try and photography's fundamental nature is the making of choices. Modern technology means that, if you wish, the camera can do everything required to produce an acceptable result, except for deciding what to photograph and actually pressing the button. An unsteady hand can be compensated for by setting the camera at a fast shutter speed or by using a tripod.

The exploits of a photography club can be an enjoyable reason to venture all over the place, indoors and out, talking to a variety of people with good and legitimate excuse. The act of photography draws our attention to what is around us, both on a macro and a micro scale. Simply to go outside and photograph small details, such as leaves, flowers, stones, walls, doors, colours and textures, reminds us that there is infinite sensation to enjoy in our immediate, even if apparently mundane, environment. Try a trip into the country or the park, equipped with cameras and sandwiches.

Of course, the results of your expeditions will need to be selected, cropped, enlarged, mounted and displayed. And you may have to persuade someone (a local company?) to buy you a camera and pay the costs of processing and enlarging. For some, but not really for the frail or very inexperienced, it could be possible to work in a darkroom, if necessary with a technician, to process black and white prints, as was popular in years gone by. Home developing was more common in the past than it is today and, once the techniques are mastered or regained, there are many creative ways of altering the nature of a photograph that are not that difficult to do: polarizing, tinting, masking out and all kinds of exotic practices. Unfortunately, most darkrooms are not designed for wheelchair access, although I have heard of special photography projects especially set up for people with disabilities. *You must ensure that all health and safety regulations are immaculately observed, especially where chemicals and toxic fumes are involved.*

The increasing availability of digital processing of photographic images should be explored. There is no shortage of projects where photography is concerned. Look at pictures and advertisements in magazines: you may pick up ideas. Go on a tour of the surroundings with a team of amateur photographers, photography assistants and general advisers. Indoors this could involve photographing aspects of life that make up the community: the staff preparing dinner, the manager in the office, people at work and play, the deliveries, the porters, the flowers in the window, the canary. Be as creative, and provocative, as the clients wish. The photographing of people, in formal pose or candidly as they go about their business, can be a fascinating way to make a statement about how you perceive others.

Photograph (taking care) the places where people used to live, work and enjoy themselves. Try 'life and times' photography: discuss with people their interests and past experiences, aiming to create an individualized snapshot. Collect together bits and pieces that reflect their interests and take, or help them to take, a still life photograph of a collection of meaningful memorabilia. Examples might include a sailor's hat, a key ring and old wallet, a pipe and a postcard from overseas, or perhaps a picture of a young couple alongside a china cup, a pair of gloves and some artistically scattered jewellery. This can be a very enjoyable and stimulating exercise if carried out in a spirit of fun, and not taken too seriously.

People can obtain great pleasure from giving a framed portrait of themselves, well turned out and looking good, to their children or grandchildren. If taking a portrait of someone and anticipating that the result will make people feel pleased, you need to capture that special moment when they are animated and focused. A tip is to get a spot of light in the eyes, as they do in fashion photography, but it is the 'right' moment that counts. You may have to take several pictures to capture this moment.

It is possible to encounter difficulty when showing some older people a picture of themselves. They may deny that this image of an old man with thinning hair or a greying old lady with wrinkles is themselves. Unless you are an experienced therapist, you are advised not to make too much of this. Do not challenge somebody's self-image in a confrontational manner, as this can be very destructive. How they see themselves is inherently their decision. Do not feel you must pursue the matter.

Special occasions can be an appropriate opportunity to get some good animated shots of an audience reacting spontaneously and these photographs can be displayed and used to back up a case for organizing programmes of activities or in support of fund raising efforts. They may offer affirmation to people by exposing them to positive images of older people achieving something special, working hard and enjoying themselves. When making a display, it is usually more effective to exhibit a few good and cropped shots than 36 photographs just back from the printers. Liaise with a good photographer if you need advice.

Sometimes being photographed can be disruptive of a session if it inhibits people, makes them feel self-conscious and distracts from the matter in hand. Usually, though, good photographers who are sensitive enough not to be intrusive, and possessing a genial personality, can enhance pleasure and satisfaction by their presence. The following points are important.

1   Don't use flash unless you have to, as it can disturb some people. If you do use a flash, warn people and stop if it causes distress.
2   Always get permission to take photographs of people in homes and hospitals, tell them what it is for and give them a copy. If pictures are to be published, some policies may require you to get written permission. If people are not able to give that permission themselves, you may have to get permission from relatives or from the manager.
3   Do not take pictures of individuals who say or demonstrate that they do not feel comfortable being photographed.
4   Unless you have clear agreement and very good reason, do not

use photographs that give a negative impression of old age. The art of photography is the art of interpretation.

Art

I don't think any of the residents had ever worked with clay before. The unfamiliarity was an added stimulus and also meant that people did not have preconceived ideas about their ability as they would with, for example, drawing. Some people did not find the idea of claywork appealing: "Not me." A number of residents who did not join in making ceramics did contribute their ideas to the design or took an interest in watching its progress.
(Maggie Warren, Artist in Residence, Ringshill Nursing Home)

Art activities can be stimulating and interesting, soothing and calming; be expressive, communicating ideas and feelings; can involve making choices; be sensual, involving colour, texture and shape; provide a sense of achievement; encourage dexterity and manipulative skills; create opportunities to control, explore and play.

The trouble with art is that many of us think we cannot 'do it', as if there is some mysterious quality only available to those who call themselves artists. Of course, as with any human activity, there are different degrees of skill obtained through training, experience and knowledge of the craft of a particular art form. Individuals also have varying talents and aptitudes and practice makes perfect. However, the real pleasure of art is that, to one degree or other, we *can* all 'do it'. We are bombarded by images created by professional artists, but should not let the fact that we are not trained illustrators or talented sculptors prohibit us from enjoying the satisfaction of producing and expressing ourselves through the creation of our own artwork.

If we perceive art as principally being the manipulation and exploration of various materials — be they paints, ceramics, leaves or bendy balloons for pleasure and/or for expression, we begin a process of making it accessible to everyone, regardless of their ability. This is the way art is enjoyed by young children and by artists when not constrained by expectations that their creation has to look like something.

Encourage group members to play with and explore, for the sake of it, the natures of different media and to enjoy them sensually.

See if it is possible to use people's past and existing interests to make a contribution towards the production of artwork based on skills acquired at home, at work, from hobbies and in education, such as woodworking, DIY, sewing, knitting, flower arranging, calligraphy or photography skills. Interestingly, some of the skills useful for claywork are similar to those used in cake and bread making; cutting out shapes, kneading, using a rolling pin and glazing. Take care as most people will probably not be able to use past skills to the standard they used to and confirmation of this can sometimes cause frustration. They may respond more positively to techniques with which they are unfamiliar, as they will not have preconceptions about their abilities. You can learn techniques, borrowed from professional artists, that do not necessarily require great skill to achieve an interesting and pleasing end result. This does not mean there is no potential for creative exploration. Examples include printing — monoprinting, roller printing, screenprinting; collage and montage; mosaics; ceramics, especially clay; fabric work, batik, appliqué; découpage; paper making, papier mâché, origami; and puppet making — hand puppets, shadow puppets.

A reminiscence emphasis may be directed to the content of the artwork rather than the process. Images from times gone by created or suggested by clients can act as the subject matter. If there is a figurative element to a piece, spend as much time as you like devising it with the group and relate it directly to the interests and experience of individuals. (I know of a man who only paints steam trains, and more steam trains ...) Brainstorm lots of ideas about what could be included. You can enable people to make a positive contribution even if they do not feel able or are unable to help practically.

Process and product

If a group is set up to make something, you need to be aware of the difference between *the process* — the quality of the group, the stages that you take the group through, what happens when your group meets — and *the product* — quality and presentation of the finished exhibition, book, display, artwork and so on. Although the product is always important and every effort should be made to achieve a good and positive outcome, it must not be achieved at the expense of the process. The process must aim to be as effective as you can make it. The product should be as good and successful as you can get without damaging the process.

I have sometimes encountered staff who are 'doing the work' for people to ensure there is a satisfactory result, and missing out the process altogether. It is not good practice to do this simply in order to create the impression that people have done it for themselves. You must never debase the process in order to achieve what you think is an acceptable product. Pretending something has been made by clients, especially if this was because you did not apply yourself to making this possible, is likely to undermine people considerably.

Having said all that, it is appropriate and good practice to involve people, openly, in an activity at a level that is in line with their capacity to be involved. This may well be as the source of inspiration for the art, not as the makers of it. 'Participation' does not have to mean 'hands on' involvement and memories and creative expression may be realized by working in conjunction with someone whose arts skills can illustrate people's ideas for them. One can participate by making choices of the way something should be or the colours that should be used, acting in an advisory capacity. You could get an artist to help you work from a group design. This can often be a most effective and rewarding way of working with people who are very frail and unwilling or unable to participate more directly. The emphasis must be on an empathetic response by an artist to participants.

It was decided that the group were to have a go at constructing a textile piece. When the artist actually began to work with the group it became apparent that they were too frail and had disabilities that limited their ability to participate directly with the physical construction of the piece. However, they were able to contribute their ideas to the content, to enjoy the company of the artist, to reminisce and to socialize. Once the group and group leaders had been reassured that this was all right, the session was adapted to encourage involvement of this kind. The artist openly made artwork, in a social context created by the older people, that celebrated their memories and stories. Music was played and reminiscence encouraged. The final product was a collection of fabric pictures, a tribute to the artist's skill, illustrating very directly things such as haymaking, village scenes, churches, family groups and portraits.

Think of artist and group as working together, each contributing what they are able:

I was struck by the amount of effort people put into working; they persevered in spite of disabilities. I noticed that people worked together or helped each other. For example, one lady held paper while another cut it. I had to modify my belief that I should never contribute to a person's artwork. It did prove necessary to prepare something for a person to use or to literally 'lend a hand'. In such cases I feel it is vital to be totally guided by that person, their choices and decisions, otherwise it becomes a meaningless exercise. This help is justified if it means that a person is enabled to express themselves or experience using the materials.

(Carol Davies, Artist in Residence, the Rhyl Nursing Home)

A group was struggling to get its first ever practical session started by making a collage based on a scene of a local town. Two participants had already asked to leave, two were asleep and two were very frail and not easily able to participate. Two were keen and interested. What might be happening here? Observation and discreet questioning revealed a number of issues:

1   The group were unsure why they were there. Previous meetings had been pure reminiscence sessions and, although it had been discussed the week before that they were to try some art, they had forgotten.
2   There had been no real attempt to introduce people gently to the scene that was to be made. It turned out that only one person could remember that particular scene: the theme was too specific.
3   The materials, a large piece of card and scraps of poster paper, looked intimidating and chaotic. The glue was sticky and there were no accessible facilities for cleaning hands.
4   The session leaders were sitting together much of the time, feeling unsure, and were tending to decide things for people in their anxiety to get a result.

At this early stage, more attention needed to be given to encouraging the involvement of participants. Although most were too frail to do much practical work, they might have been able to make a contribution if they had been helped to understand what was going on. Some appropriate music to listen to either while working or as part of the session could have helped relax people. The artists should have sat down and discussed the session before it started and put more emphasis on encouraging group interaction and less on trying to 'make the art'. I think that they were anxious to make an impression and were self-conscious when being observed.

When things 'go wrong' with a session it is not a failure, it is just the way that session worked out. It is perfectly acceptable to try things to see how they go and then adapt the next session in the light of the experience. It is not always possible to see how something might work until you have tried it.

Project ideas

1   Make a mural of, for example, painted wood, ceramic tiles or fabric pictures made up of single pieces worked by a variety of individuals. Put them all together to make one big piece. Work to a theme: a piece based on hobbies might include a picture of a cat, a flower, a hammer and a rucksack, representing the diversity of individuals in the group. You can create a large image made up of separate squares (montage) or a kind of formal collage made up of squares containing different pictures and scenes. If you are not an artist, or even if you are, do not be afraid to trace or copy images or parts of images. Artists usually do not make everything up in their heads; they use 'reference'.

2   To enlarge a picture; draw a grid of squares onto a sheet of tracing paper (the size and number of squares will vary according to the size and complexity of the image); lay it over the image you want to enlarge; trace the main lines of the image onto the grid. Make a larger version of your grid, keeping it proportionally the same and then copy the main lines that are in each square and you will create a large version of the image. The squares containing parts of the outline can be completed by a variety of people and then all fitted together like a giant jigsaw, producing an exciting and original result.

3 Draw or paint memories, such as the homes where the people used to live, a typical street scene, a garden or a key event. (Do not forget to reminisce as part of the process.) Scenes from memory can also be recreated by using sewing and fabric skills. There is no reason why a piece should not be made using a variety of different techniques blended together.

4 Members of staff or an artist can create artwork based on the memories and stories that are told and make a piece as described by the group. For example, in a kitchen scene you can find out what things would have looked like: what colour and style of furniture and doors, wallpaper, lampshades, fittings and so on; what equipment would be used and what products would be on shelves and tables; what hairstyles, clothes and shoes the occupants might have worn and what they would be doing.

5 Sketch the storytellers, as portraits or 'in action'. Mount these as a display or frame them as gifts. They make an interesting alternative to photographs.

6 Painted or mock stained glass can filter the sunshine to make forever variable tones of light on the walls and across the floor. The leading, the outline of the images and sections, stands proud so that people whose hands are not too steady can accurately fill in a pattern or picture. The fumes can be rather unpleasant, so make sure there is plenty of ventilation. You can sometimes buy the appropriate materials in a craft shop, though you should seek professional advice before embarking on this.

7 Use cake decorating equipment and a medium such as Polyfilla to make a work of art. Pipe filler onto a piece of wood or stiff card. Paint it when dry or cover your creation with aluminium foil and press the foil down with thumbs or a spatula. Some very attractive results can be obtained through this process and for many people the experience of piping the filler will be very familiar.

8 Try painting to music, letting the music influence the colour and style of the work.

9 Using a large sheet of paper, one person draws a shape or pattern, the next 'answers' the shape and so on until you have a mass of shapes and patterns. This is fun and involves group interaction.

10 Make a garden picture containing individually made butterflies

and flowers. Print patterned tablecloths, cushion covers and anti-macassars. Use mosaics to make table mats, teapot stands or coffee table tops. Compose a collage of photographs of local and significant scenes and images.

11 When you have completed a product, celebrate the achievement. Use the occasion to create another occasion. You can unveil the 'painting' to invited interested guests, have some music and bake a cake. You might even get into the local paper.

I found that people enjoyed looking at their finished work and it clearly had a lot of meaning for them as well as providing a sense of achievement. It was also a clear indication and reminder of what had been done in previous weeks.
(Carol Davies, Artist in Residence, the Rhyl Nursing Home)

Before initiating practical arts activities, it is worth asking yourself one important question. Is it only you who feels that people 'should' be doing something practical? In a survey of clients in a hospital day centre, less than half expressed any interest whatsoever in practical activities, whilst over 90 per cent said they wanted to be involved in social activities — though of course, they are not mutually exclusive. A practical session can be an enjoyable social occasion as well. I have at times encountered staff desperately trying to stimulate painting (usually) amongst a group in which, I guessed, only half were actually interested.

Art sessions are often not made as much of as they could be and can be easy to set up if you bear the following in mind:

1 Start off gradually with socially based groups having fun with materials and gently explore other possibilities as people gain confidence and you begin to get an idea of what their true capabilities are. Do not expect instant success and do not give up after trying once.

2 Unjustifiably, certain materials, usually the cheap easy-to-buy items you will have access to, have associations with childishness: materials such as poster paints, crayons, sugar paper and so on. This is unfair, as every medium has the potential to be used imag-

inatively and expressively. It is possible, though, unless you really know what you are doing, that play school materials will tend to produce a result that looks a bit childish. Try others.

3   Do not use materials that are not suitable for the job. I know it can be expensive, but try and use a variety of good-quality materials. Consider incorporating natural and 'found' materials, which can be pleasant to use, free and interesting to collect.

4   Presentation can make an enormous difference to the way something looks. A frame does wonders for a drawing or painting and a simple collage can look a lot less school-like when mounted firmly and varnished.

5   Have some examples of finished work to show the group, especially if you are using an unfamiliar process that will end up looking very professional.

6   Some people are anxious not to get their hands and clothes dirty and this, more often than you might think, can be a reason for declining to participate. Have everything prepared and sorted so that choices of material, brushes and so on can be easily made. If materials are potentially 'messy', have facilities for keeping clean readily and obviously available. Plastic aprons can be used if you have to, but why not get the sewing group to make some pretty or individualized aprons? Allow cleaning up time at the end of each session.

7   If you have a visitor, such as someone to take a few photographs, or a relative, exploit the presence of that person. Introduce everyone and encourage discussion about the work they are doing. Remind people of their achievements and let them 'show off' what they have made.

8   Do not expect anything you try to organize to appeal to everyone all the time and remember that the art is a means to an end. You are looking for as many opportunities as you can find for the generation of pleasure, interest, self-expression and engagement.

Drama and theatre

Drama and theatre is the stuff of life: 'All the world's a stage' and all that. It can allow us to express the dreams, and nightmares, of our inner selves; to free our minds from the restraints of daily reality and temporarily construct an alternative; to suspend disbelief and to enter a world where imagination can take us wherever we wish.

Whether through the presentation of live theatrical performances or by devising and performing productions, reminiscence-based or not, drama is rarely exploited for the enjoyment of older people. There is no real reason why there could not be many more live theatre events and projects organized for, with and especially by, older people. There are theatre groups and performers, traditional, community-based and amateur, who would be more than pleased to take bookings from institutional venues. You may find that local theatres have first night offers available and I have known occasions when the cast of a play have taken aspects of their latest production into community venues. Some of the larger theatre companies sometimes organize workshops and presentations especially devised for institutional venues.

Costume, scenery, lighting, music and storytelling can be combined to create a memorable and stimulating experience for all involved. If you have the confidence, plenty of time and are moderately extrovert, there is no reason at all why you should not try to dramatize the experiences of clients. However, I suspect that most of us would feel more secure working with professional practitioners who have had experience and training in techniques for involving people in drama-based activities. A good drama practitioner should be able to devise a context that encourages participants to provide the material that is then adapted as the basis of a performance. The best will expect to work closely with you and design a project that suits the group's abilities and draws on the experience of the participants. If appropriate, the project can be designed to involve them directly in the final presentation. This may well then be suitable to go on tour — I know of a group of players who are well into their third age.

You could also work in conjunction with other groups — perhaps schoolchildren or other older people — who can directly re-enact stories and memories on behalf of the storytellers.

Community plays involving a variety of local people from all kinds of circumstances working together to produce a big event are becoming increasingly popular. Keep an eye on the local paper or on information circulated by arts organizations, as the organizers of such an event are going to welcome contributions and may have expertise available to help you get involved.

TIE, Theatre-in-Education, is a recognized practice that places drama practitioners in schools and youth projects. It would seem only to require a slight adaptation to be a resource for older people.

Reminiscence theatre involving the dramatic interpretation of memories can make reminiscence a vital living experience, as well as being immensely stimulating and enjoyable. I suggest that if you are interested in this (and I hope you are) you talk to local arts organizations to explore the possibilities. Talk to the local amateur dramatic society, arts centre, theatre, college or school.

The Certain Curtain Theatre Company were booked for a six-month residency in a large psychiatric hospital. Each week they presented a little 'playlet' lasting about 20 minutes, followed by a discussion with a group of patients. Stimulated by the dramatic action, patients and staff discussed and explored their response to what they had seen and heard. Material gathered in the discussion was then used as the basis of the following week's presentation. After a number of sessions, enough material had been collected via enjoyable participative sessions to devise a complete production, which then toured the hospital wards.

When planning a drama project, do not always go for the obvious 'show for old people' or 'old time musical hall'. Although theatre involving music and theatre based on reminiscence are bound to be favourites, try to present as broad a programme as possible. How about a 'whodunit', a comedy or even some Shakespeare? I suspect that there will be some very exciting possibilities waiting in the wings if you have the enthusiasm to initiate working relationships with the right people.

Making a radio play
Composing and presenting a play for radio (or perhaps it should be for the wireless) has the advantage of containing all the constituents of a stage presentation while being much easier to put together and present. It minimizes problems of stage fright and requires no movement. Elaborate setting and dramatic events can be suggested through words and sound.

With a group, set a scene that has general appeal. You might consider a love story, an adventure or just an everyday event from days gone by. You may base your drama on something that happened to someone in your group. The group will then need to decide creatively when and where the scene is to be set and the identities of the main characters. Start to fill out the background: what kind of people they are, what is happening to them now and has happened to them in their lives. (Again, remind yourself that the process is important: the play itself is an aim to work towards.)

Over a number of sessions, begin to elaborate on the story, taking into account the environment and experiences that people would have had at that time. These may well be based on real experiences of members of your group and characters may be based on them or on people they knew. Fill out the scene around the main story by seeking information from people. If your story is, say, about someone who is just starting work, aim to develop a picture of what doing that work at that time would be like: what time would they get up, how much would they be paid, how would they get to work and what would they have for dinner? To take it further, imaginatively decide, drawing on people's experiences, what kind of house the characters live in, how their parents behave, what is on the radio and in the newspapers, what is on their minds, and so on. This can be an extremely interesting process.

Compose a simple script making a note of all the sound effects you are going to add. These need not be literal. You could record the sound of the kettle boiling or you could represent this with musical instruments or voices. If there is a window cleaner in the story, you can illustrate this with appropriate songs like *When I'm Cleaning Windows* or, if the story is set by the sea, with *Oh I Do Like to be Beside the Seaside* and so on.

If you plan to re-enact the script live, or put it onto tape, you will probably need to practise with microphones, and people should have their parts clearly written out on cards. You may need to have someone to act as a prompter. Costumes are not required, although for a live event you may want to clarify roles with hats, scarves and simple props to give a visual context. It can be performed by the writers themselves, or you could involve staff, students or schoolchildren.

If you are impressed with the result, there is nothing to be lost and everything to be gained by sending a copy to a local or national radio station. You never know!

Dance

Dance allows us to express ourselves through the movement of our bodies. Moving in sympathy with music, we are able to embrace the life-enhancing and energizing forces of harmony and rhythm within the very fabric of our being. "Sit down and dance with me," sang my friend Terry McGinty — we do not have to be on our feet to want to go to the ball. It must not be considered inevitable, because older people may not be able to get up and tango, that dance — literally music and movement, as a passive and as an active occupation – is therefore not a suitable option.

Dancing, in the reminiscence sense, is an activity that has had a fundamental place in the lives of the current older generation. The ability to dance properly was seen as a social skill and essential requirement if you were hoping to associate respectably and, as the craze for jazz dancing grew, not so respectably, with a member of the opposite sex. In their lunch break, young people would dash to the dance halls, changing into their dancing shoes for a few brief moments of glamour and fantasy during a dull working day. Saturday night saw crowds flocking to the Plaza or the Palais, names that themselves conjure images of high society. For others, the local hall and a 78 record or two would have to suffice. The leading musicians of the day were dance bands and Fred Astaire and Ginger Rogers were idolized by millions. Dance troupes of girls were a popular social phenomenon in town and country, and are still to be seen today, bringing a little military precision to display dancing. Long lines of high-kicking ladies sparkled provocatively on stage and screen.

Dance as a creative art form and particularly as a participative activity is not something usually associated with older people, especially in institutional settings. Many people will be unsure and lacking in confidence, but this is no reason for older disabled people not to enjoy the pleasure and expression of moving to music. This is an area where I would strongly recommend you draw on the skills of an experienced practitioner who will work with you to help develop techniques for gently 'enabling' participation. There are a number of skilled 'dance animateurs' employed by local authorities and arts organizations.

Of course, the display of dance is something that can easily be incorporated into entertainment programmes. Local ballet and tap dancing schools, country dancing clubs, ballroom dancers and other professional and amateur dance organizations could be approached.

Projects could include a tea dance, a ceilidh or a barn dance. You could book live displays of traditional dance from many countries. You could start music and movement sessions. Try wheelchair dancing. Devise a display about local dance halls or the costume of dance. Teach young people how to dance 'properly'. Contact a local school of dance. Enquire about the services of a dance 'animateur'.

With encouragement, so that we do not feel silly, most of us are able to move to music and rhythm, enjoying pleasurable exercise and physical expression. We can dance inside.

Music

Music seems to reach places that other attempts at making contact do not. People who appear to show very little awareness of the world around them at other times will, often almost imperceptibly, indicate acknowledgement of musical communication. From a simple rhythm that encourages a foot to tap, to a trigger that transports us to other places and other times, music has a fundamental place in almost all reminiscence work in all contexts. There are four main ways of perceiving music in relation to work with people in institutional settings: appreciating music — listening to and talking about it; making music — playing, composing and singing; music and movement — dancing and exercise; and music to create atmosphere.

Using music in sessions

Music plays a profound part in the lives of nearly all of us. The tastes in music that we have very directly reflect our culture, our ethnicity, our individuality, our generation, our education, our experience and our emotional state. We gain a great deal of pleasure, satisfaction and a sense of achievement from music. It is very helpful in reminiscence sessions. You can listen to it, talk about it, make it.

If you can play a musical instrument, do not be shy; bring it in. Some of the old tunes are marvellous to play and imagine, and you can practise at work. Amongst your clients there may well be people who have learned to play instruments; the piano, harmonica and accordion are particularly popular. Whether a person is able or confident enough to play nowadays is a matter for you to discuss with them. The frustration of being reminded that you are unable to play as well as you used to could lower self-esteem.

Music, live or on tape, can mark the beginning or the completion of an activity. At the beginning, it can help to put people at ease and can set the tone for the event. At the end, expressing a sense of achievement, a good singsong allows us to express our exuberance, and listening quietly can enable us to relax and unwind.

You do not have to be a musician — there is about 80 years' worth of recorded music available, waiting to be listened to. Do not just go for the *Sing Something Simple* school of music; look for authentic and original versions. The better portable cassette machines reproduce very well and can be locked away when not in use. There is no reason why every residential and nursing home, hospital ward, day centre, club, group, and activities organizer should not build up an extensive collection of recorded music to suit all tastes and occasions.

Most people relate easily, but not exclusively, to the music they grew up with in their youth but one should not make assumptions about what this music might be. It may be the popular music of the time but it is also quite likely to be music learned from and associated with parents and family, dancing, school and church. There may be the influence of a strong culture of traditional music.

As regards possible projects, if you have access to people with musical skills, the staff and/or a musician can learn pieces that people particularly like and put on a performance especially for that group. Make sure that suggestions performed are acknowledged as a contribution from the people who have chosen them. In cases where someone is unable to request a piece but is clearly interested in being part of what is going on, there may be songs that they relate to in some way, songs that refer to, for example, their name, place of birth, a particular interest or element of their background: songs and tunes such as *My Little Margie, 'Enery the Eighth, Alice Blue Gown, Stella by Starlight, Bluebells of Scotland, My Wild*

Irish Rose, Chicago, Food Glorious Food, Cruising Down the River, Chattanooga Choo Choo — you get the idea. But do make sure that the person likes your choice and avoid silly or patronizing associations.

Invite a local school orchestra to present an evening of classical or jazz music based on pieces chosen by the residents. Alternatively, some thorough research through tape and record collections, including a visit to the library, may enable you to put on your own short disco, featuring favourite tunes and songs especially chosen for the occasion by the group. Expand on this by turning a session into your group's own *Desert Island Discs*, with choices of music accompanied by stories and recollections associated with the music.

'It's a Long Way to Daisy Daisy'

> The performance isn't really about music. You are having a conversation with a musical instrument in your hands.
> (Terry McGinty, musician)

What is the problem some people have with singalongs? They are so often criticized as an activity that stigmatizes elderly people, as if they were some kind of last resort when all else is lost. Enjoyable, well-run and interactive community singalongs have a great deal going for them.

- They are good for morale: singing as a group in time of difficulty has always boosted people's sense of 'pulling together'. A singalong takes the mind off trouble and strife.
- The physical act of singing is good for you: it clears the head, fills the body with oxygen and uplifts the spirit.
- Doing a turn offers a chance to show off and bask in the limelight for a moment.
- Singing together, perhaps round the piano, was commonly a form of entertainment before the overwhelming presence of television.
- You do not have to be good at singing to sing together.
- Singing stimulates part of the brain and is accessible to some people who otherwise find difficulty communicating.
- Songs can remind you of times gone by.

- A singalong is interactive and communal. You can still participate even if you are of great age and frailty.
- Singing together creates opportunities to make decisions and choices.
- Singing can be an opportunity to give and accept a gift (of a song).
- One sings when one is happy; equally, singing can help you feel happy.
- Singing is expressive and allows the sharing of emotions with others, safely and acceptably.
- Singing encourages, by the music chosen, a sense of shared identity through generation, culture and social background.
- Singing is enjoyable and continually astonishes care staff by enlivening old people.

A singalong is one of the most popular, favoured and stimulating activities that is enjoyed by older people in institutional care, except:

- by those who do not want to do it;
- when crass assumptions are made about who likes what;
- when dominated by staff;
- when it is not interactive;
- when the musician, if there is one, is really, really bad; and
- when it is the only activity deemed suitable.

It is frequently assumed that certain songs are the anthems of a generation. The ubiquitous *Daisy Daisy* came out in the nineteenth century and certainly these days, while enjoyable in many circumstances, tends to have connotations of institutionalization. Another favourite, *It's a Long Way to Tipperary*, although a song of perseverance, was, by some accounts, deliberately written as a propaganda song for troops (some say in the First World War, other have told me the Boer War) and evokes strong connotations with war and loss for many people. I have known this song to stimulate intense feelings of grief. Both songs are popular and well known by all age groups. They are loved by some, and equally loathed by others. They can be appropriate at certain moments, in certain situations, for certain people, but they 'belong' to an earlier generation. If someone asks for songs of this kind, this is perfectly all right, but do avoid making stereotypical choices on behalf of people. Recently, I discussed with a woman who had requested the song *Daisy Daisy* why in fact she had asked for it. Did she like it a lot or was it perhaps a song her family had sung? "Oh no," she said, "I hate it, can't stand it. I thought the others might like it."

People often find it difficult to articulate what is it they 'like'. Ask someone what their favourite song is and you will often receive a blank look. If you asked me what my favourite song was I would give you a blank look as well. It is rather a hard question to answer just like that and, if I give you one, am I stuck with it? For ever? The music someone likes will quite possibly depend on mood and context. Someone may have greatly loved Mozart, but preferred *You are my Sunshine* on the dance floor. They may like to sing novelty songs but listen to big bands. Most old people are no more one-dimensional in their tastes in music than they are in other aspects of their lives. There may not be one single favourite song, although a particular piece may be well liked or associated with a person or a moment in the past. Some people may have been, or still are, avid fans of a particular genre, artiste or era. Even if someone particularly likes one kind of music, this does not mean they do not like another: give people the benefit of the doubt.

Also take into account that people will request music that is determined by the choices being made available. During an old-time singalong, people may make different requests than they would while listening to classical music. Because someone likes a rip-roaring version of *She'll be Coming Round the Mountain* in the afternoon, this does not mean that later in the evening they will not prefer to relax to some cool jazz. Set up situations where people are exposed to a variety of different musical genres and they are more likely to demonstrate by their reaction what they are enjoying at that particular time. It is so easy with recorded music to turn one recording off and put another on that there is no reason not to explore every possibility. Find out who and what was liked and gradually build up a collection of styles and genres from which to choose.

Try exploring traditional jazz, folk music, traditional music, classical music, hymns, choral music, gospel music, sentimental songs, crooners, ragtime, blues, rock 'n' roll, pop music, opera, songs from musicals, country, country and western, Cajun, Latin American, music from different countries and cultures, ballroom, big band, salsa, 1920s, 30s, 40s, 50s, 60s, 70s … I am not too sure about punk and heavy metal yet, but relatively recent pop music is often more popular than you might think — and familiar — being perhaps the music their children listened to.

Even specialized music such as modern jazz, some of the less 'popular' classics and 'modern' music may appeal to some individuals. (Just imagine for a moment how you would react if you had spent your life as an aficionado of Stockhausen and were expected to get enthusiastic listening to Perry Como!)

Making music

Let us consider for a moment the possibilities of *making* music, by which I mean performing and composing. This activity, like many others suggested, is not strictly an act of 'reminiscence' in the direct sense but, like reminiscence, it draws on the strengths and emotions of the individual or group, encouraging expression, communication and socialization. Music is essentially an emotional language that enables and stimulates expression of feelings and communication between people. It is a rhythmic language, using sounds, tones and textures to say something that may not be describable in words. We may communicate, generate or vent an emotion, interact with another so that an action asks for a response, or work in harmony with others.

If you are planning to lead making music sessions (as opposed to singing) you will probably have to reassess the conventional view of what music fundamentally is. So, perhaps, will members of the group. You will need to discard the common perception that music involves composed works played on well-known musical instruments by people who have spent years developing technique and competency in performing recognized styles and fashions. Forget about rock 'n' roll, jazz, classical music and genres which, after all, only represent stylistic conventions and traditions.

Making music involves the manipulation of sound, harmony, rhythm and syncopation. It also involves singing, banging, shaking, rattling, exploring, playing, communicating, expressing, making, working together and having fun.

To lead a music workshop session of this kind you must take musical command of the situation or you may end up with a lot of people thundering away at random — not in itself unenjoyable — but not really leading anywhere and ultimately frustrating.

The collections of musical instruments available to most of us, pre-computer, are frequently the same instruments that are used in primary school. They will normally consist of untuned and tuned percussion — drums, woodblocks, chime bars and so on — though you may have access to instruments such as recorders, guitars or keyboards. The tambourine in particular is unfairly closely associated with a negative perception of 'old people in groups'. In reality, by using easily understood instruments, there is more likelihood of people being truly able to make expressive music than when using conventional orchestral or harmony instruments which take time and talent to master, although this possibility should not be ruled out altogether! There are techniques that 'workshop' musicians use, such as only using the notes on the pentatonic scale which do not go out of tune, to help people succeed with melody instruments.

I strongly recommend that, if you intend to introduce this kind of music making, and it can be tremendously satisfying, you:

- go on some music workshops with an experienced practitioner and learn some practical techniques;
- work alongside a music practitioner with the aim of learning from them by experience;
- work closely with a musician and work out ways of making music together; and
- seek out a music therapist/practitioner and have a long, frank discussion with them.

Sound pictures
One way to break out of the limiting cultural concept we have of music is to use instruments to create a sound picture. This means that sounds are used to communicate a chosen image. For example, a common one often chosen is 'the storm', where instruments are used to suggest weather — a rising wind, gathering clouds and heavy rain, lightning and thunder — increasing intensity in a

crescendo and then gradually returning to a peaceful calm. It is very satisfying.

Choose with your group which instruments represent the elements of the storm (perhaps tinkling sounds for the rain and big crashes for the thunder). However, be rather more sophisticated than that and remember that instruments can suggest, rather than sound like, trees in the wind, people running for shelter, leaves fluttering to the ground, and so on. You are not making sound effects (though you can do that, of course) but representing textures, feelings and atmospheres with sound — much like the greatest composers.

Be prepared to fend off criticism from ill-informed people who describe workshop music making as just a noise. It may be some comfort to discover that it is often trained or experienced musicians who have the greatest difficulty in putting aside their cultural concept of what music should be and escaping the traditions and structures that, in this context, can actually leave making music inaccessible to everyone except 'musicians'.

You are using pure folk instruments that are hallowed by time. Any suggestion that these are not proper instruments is widely off the mark. You are using instruments that may be simple but are accessible and fundamental to all music making.

The making of music can have profound emotional and spiritual meaning and should not be restricted by assumptions of what is proper music. It should be available to all of us, regardless of age and expertise.

Arranging performances

Most performances are likely to be of music, but the principles discussed here apply equally to any guest who is to perform a 'one off' entertainment session, whether it be drama, dance, poetry, a talk on local history or any other kind of presentation. There are many performers available in the community, professional and amateur, possessing a variety of styles and qualities, some of whom are more likely than others to be attuned to an audience of older people. You are looking for those who grasp the situation effectively and agreeably.

Try to avoid always booking the same type of act (variety is the spice of life) although, if there is someone that you can see is particularly popular, there are advantages to allowing them to get to know the audience well over a period of time through a series of regular visits. It is important, as with all this work, that a performance is taken seriously and organized so that things go reasonably smoothly and as many people as is sensible can get the most from the booking.

When booking a performer, ensure that you have agreed the fee, if there is one. Agree whether this is inclusive of travel and how and when payment is to be made. Send a written confirmation with details of the venue, times and, if need be, clear directions. It is well worth contacting the performer a couple of days before the event as a reminder.

It is a good idea to make sure someone, a linkworker, is identified to 'host' the performance, welcoming, looking after and acting as a link between audience and visitor. Do not assume that a performer understands the way your unit operates. In many clinical and residential settings, the daily routines have to, or sometimes expect to, carry on regardless of what else is happening. Ensure that the performer is warned of any anticipated disruptions, for example if people are to be taken away for treatment or have appointments with the hairdressers, and that everyone, including the individuals concerned, is aware of this. Of course, some disruptions are inevitable, but see what you can do to minimize those that are not.

A performance in an old persons' home or a hospital ward is usually much less formal than in a concert hall and in a relatively small, intimate setting it can help visitors form a bond if they are introduced to people. Some will feel able do this for themselves others may wish to be taken round, especially on their first visit. This makes the whole experience a friendlier and less intimidating one for both parties. This can be crucial in situations where people are considered 'confused'. To not inform people who it is that has come to visit them could be construed as rather impolite and represent yet another lack of acknowledgement of the status of the clients. *You* would certainly want to know who it was who had turned up in your living room.

Does the performer need time and space to change clothes, warm up, arrange equipment and so on? Some performers like to arrive and get started straight away, others like time to acclimatize themselves. Although I would normally encourage chatting time before the show some performers are unable to interact spontaneously until they have done their act. They may appear to be almost in a kind of trance. After the show they may be relaxed, but before it starts they feel vulnerable, nervous and preoccupied.

From the outset, staff and performer(s) should make sure they are clear about the structure of the session and this should accommodate both the needs of the venue and the needs of the performance. Agree a starting time and clarify whether this is the time the act commences or the time the audience will begin to arrive. Discuss with the performer when and if they want a break and do not assume that, because you normally have tea at three o'clock this will fit in with the programme they have prepared. Some shows have a natural interval, while others need to be continuous over a specific span of time. Whatever your arrangements are, discuss them, so that at least your guest is not taken by surprise and brought to an abrupt halt. What time is the show to end? It can be offputting if people are getting restless because it is 'time to go' and a performance should ideally aim to finish so that there is time for some conversation and to say goodbye. If you encourage the performer to stay and chat afterwards, and this can be part of the agreement, a passive event (the performance) then also becomes an active event (the social interaction).

Make sure a performer has access to some water. It can be very hot in care settings and singing or talking in public can make the throat very dry. Think about the suitability of seating arrangements — would it be best to have a formal layout, a circle or semi-circle, or seats casually scattered, café style? Arrange the layout so that necessary interruptions can be kept to a minimum. Ensure everyone will be able to see and hear and take account of high-backed chairs.

The performer should have some space for themselves and not have to work with their back to a member of the audience. They will probably be able to be seen and heard by more people if they are facing a semi-circle or the longer side of an oblong. Have a wide, shallow audience rather than a long, thin one as it is easier to make contact from side to side than from front to back.

Let the potential audience know in advance that there is to be a special event — even people you think are likely to forget. Remind them. This helps build a sense of anticipation and provides some time for them to decide whether they want to go to the show. Use the fact that an event is planned to animate people and put up posters or make invitations.

The following questions should also be considered:

1   Perhaps people would like to wear their best clothes.
2   Are you going you invite relatives or people from another department, floor or ward?
3   Are you going to serve alcohol? If so, this can be a special event in itself, so make it part of the entertainment. If this is likely, in your experience, to send everyone to sleep or to the toilet then the timing may be crucial: beginning, middle or end?
4   Have you thought about the lighting and can you do anything to enhance atmosphere? Should light be bright or soft? Should the performer be picked out? Sometimes it is best if the audience is in rather subdued light as it can encourage relaxation and audiences are rarely at their best when brightly lit.

Never ever force anybody to attend or stay in a performance. If someone has to leave, wait for an appropriate moment and give them an opportunity, if they wish, to bid farewell to the guest. Ensure that someone taken out for an appointment understands where they are going and why. Do not just walk in and remove them without explanation. This behaviour by staff is very common: I have on too many occasions watched a distraught person being mysteriously punished by being removed (without an explanation) from a singalong in mid-song, in front of an astounded performer (me!).

To get the best from a special event, staff should be encouraged not to use the presence of a visiting entertainer as a chance to take a break or do some other work, but to use it rather as an opportunity to participate in a shared experience with those in their care. Ideally, staff should try and find time to sit amongst the group and gently encourage participation (if appropriate) by directing attention to what is going on and to reassure anyone who gets confused or disoriented. They should not hover at the back.

Although staff may help to keep extraneous disruption to a minimum, they should allow the performer to control the situation within the group unless they are clearly looking to them for assistance. They should not subdue anyone's enthusiasm unless it really has become a problem for the performer or is spoiling everyone else's enjoyment. Staff should bear in mind that the prime contact is between performer and client and should make sure they do not, by trying to be helpful and encouraging, actually disrupt the act or undermine the authority of the session leader.

I was playing my guitar on a long-stay ward with some very frail participants. One woman had just, very nervously and with a lot of gentle encouragement, in a beautiful voice, given us the song that her husband used to sing to her when they first met. The atmosphere was rich with emotion and the whole group was almost in tears. In walks Doris: "Come on everyone [clap, clap]. Pack up your troubles in your old kit bag ..." The gentle atmosphere is gone in an upheaval caused by a well-meaning but insensitive contribution. The behaviour of staff, well-intentioned or otherwise, can drastically affect the nature of the performance. Staff should not (and these have all happened): walk through the event jangling keys; sit at the end of the room chatting and laughing; clean the floor round a musician (while I am playing); physically move a performer (a wheelchair user) halfway through his act; stand in the middle of the room having a conversation with an ambulance driver; delay sending a group of patients to a concert, thereby causing late arrival, because staff are watching a favourite soap opera!

As a performer myself, I have noticed an interesting distinction between the way people brought up before the Second World War respond to a performance session compared with those brought up after the war. The former seem to have a more developed instinctive understanding that an audience plays a role in bringing the best out of a performance and are intuitively inclined to 'work with' a performer. They are also much more willing, when asked, to interact, join in, ask questions, make suggestions and comment. These older groups will tend to help an entertainer act as a stimulus for an interactive experience. Younger groups are more likely to challenge the act to entertain them and react in a passive manner. Before the war, people generally made their own musical entertainment, singing round the piano or the accordion. Public entertainment would often be live and an audience response would be direct and noisy. Even at the cinema people would cheer the hero and boo the villains. Entertainment was generally experienced as a communal and live experience. It was also relatively rare.

Younger people tend to have become 'consumers' of entertainment. We sit passively in front of the television and there is no point in responding to it. I do admit to talking to the television now and then, but it has never answered back. We have no effect at all on what is presented and can only make selections, choosing to watch or not to watch. The music we hear is predominantly recorded. Even live theatre and concerts are often of such a scale that our individual input is not very significant, although we may clap along or shout a response. Younger people no longer know how to work alongside a live performer to create a mutually satisfying experience. We are stimulated and satiated by a previously unimaginable quantity of professional media products and presentations which only allow us to choose, not to share or form a creative relationship. As a consequence, we have become less able to accept and enjoy the amateur, scared of singing publicly and less able to make any kind of contribution.

Getting bigger

At times you will want to organize a celebration involving the whole caring community, a chance for everyone to get excited, dress up and 'go out' for a grand occasion. When everything is right — good music or entertainment (loud enough to talk over but not so loud as to be oppressive), plenty of food, drink and sociable company, with space to breathe — a 'big' show or party can be the tonic one needs, allowing the whole gang to get together. You really can try to make the most of a large event, inviting relatives and friends and helping to form a relationship between a residential unit and the surrounding community. It can be a chance to bring the outside in with the ultimate benefit of reducing the isolation too frequently experienced in institutional settings.

When you have a 'special', for example that favourite band you cannot often afford, that prized offer from the arts people or a celebration to mark an important occasion, make sure you really lay everything on to make it *feel* special. Do not be embarrassed to seek out the support you need; and it is quite reasonable to get the assistance of other staff agreed officially. It may be appropriate to work with a volunteer agency or the local school. Ask them to help out on the day as escorts and enablers but, as with any volunteer help, make sure they are clear what is expected of them.

Involve clients in the event, welcoming visitors, running a stall, handing out the programmes, selling tickets. This will help them feel they are a part of what is going on. Let everyone know what is planned so they can look forward to it. Make posters and display them and ensure schedules are adapted to allow plenty of time for everyone to get ready.

If organizing a formal performance, such as a play or a recital, ensure that everyone is comfortable and is able to see and hear properly. As much as possible, organize the room so those that may wish to leave can do so without fuss. If the event is essentially social, as with a tea dance, you will need to create an informal atmosphere. Consider grouping people taking into account friends and natural associates. It is most important that everyone can interact with someone. Not everyone can easily move to a different position and some may appreciate someone sitting with them to help them enjoy the show with an occasional explanation, drawing attention to what is going on or simply keeping them company.

Take care to book an appropriate act for your requirements. There is no point in having an act that requires a silent audience in order to be heard when what you were expecting was a good dance band. Some artistes need people to pay close attention while others thrive on an informal, noisy atmosphere. Is the act going to be loud enough, or too loud? Many people together can absorb a lot of sound. Modern buildings are often designed to subdue sound rather than carry it, while older buildings may create echo and make it difficult to hear properly. It is in everyone's interest to liaise with the players and sort out all these kinds of details in advance.

The social aspect of a formal show, if there is to be one, normally occurs afterwards, when we talk about it and discuss our opinions. After your own 'show', make sure there is time available for refreshments so that people have an opportunity to be with each other. Try and ensure that follow-up involves a little more than: "Did you enjoy that, Doris?", which is often the limit of any critical evaluation of a show, performance or event. Discuss feelings and opinions for the pleasure of it and take these into account next time.

Try not to limit what is possible by always going for the obvious and you will find there may be many opportunities for special events. Consider the following suggestions:

a theatre group presenting a play,
a display of dance,
a festival of reminiscence,
a classical music recital,
a feature film,
a local choir,
a garden party,
a juggling workshop (do not be sceptical, we have done it); acrobats we have not tried this), a display of circus skills (but I have seen this).

Just being there is not enough
It is possible to be very alone in the midst of a large number of people. We must take particular care that the scale of an event — the size of the audience — does not cause isolation. People are not always offered a chance to be individuals in large groups and can get quite distressed if packed too closely together like sardines. You may think you are getting value for money by crowding in as many people as possible, but you need to be very honest with yourself: are you just trying to make sure everybody gets something when there is not enough to go round? Some people thrive on crowds, others hate them. Be aware. Consider seriously whether it could be more appropriate to present an event for a smaller group so that the participants can get more from the session.

At one event I attended the manager was so keen to make an impact that he invited the mayor, the vicar, the boss and a handful of other important people. A good idea, except that they were seated in an imposing row in front of the residents, blocking everyone else's view. This was rather daunting for the performers and the visitors appeared to be as embarrassed as I was.

Putting on your own show
Over a series of sessions, discuss with the group the music that they have loved and enjoyed over the years. Unless you have a musician

available, take in some 'various artistes' tapes to listen to which will remind people of some of the enormous variety of styles, performers, songs and music that is available. If someone sings you an apparently obscure snippet of a song they remember but you cannot identify, see if other members of the group can identify it for you. Pinpoint some favourite and meaningful songs, music, stories, monologues, jokes and poems — 'party pieces' — and devise a programme for a variety show made up of a selection of 'turns'.

Nelly sang a few lines about seagulls and we always thought she had made them up herself. Several years later I found out it was a snippet of a very old song called, wait for it, *Seagulls*. If we had known, we could have sung along with Nelly in the way she wanted and helped her finish her song.

Some people, like Nelly, will feel secure singing and performing in public, and a favourite which has been remembered for 50 years will not need much rehearsal. With those who are less sure, help them to 'polish up' their piece by rehearsing it with them a few times, but not so often that it loses a sense of spontaneity. Some may need reminders of half-remembered words and tunes. For those who do not feel up to performing themselves, you can arrange for someone else to sing the song or tell a story on their behalf. Some chosen songs can be sung by a group, the 'chorus' of the show, perhaps in a special finale or at key points in the programme. Each piece should be acknowledged as a contribution made by the person who chose it.

It can help to give a little added security if you type up words in large print and stick them on a piece of card for use in rehearsal and on the 'big' day. Passing songsheets round the audience encourages audience participation, especially if the audience includes younger people who may not know the words.

Is there any musical or theatrical talent in the house? If so, are they able to remind others of long-forgotten songs or monologues? Are they really unable to perform any more or are they just a bit rusty and suffering from a little false modesty or low self-esteem? These people may be very interested to meet or work with fellow musicians and per-formers.

It is best if you can find a good musician to help throughout the project, but if this is not possible it is worth trying to find someone who can play on the day and for at least one or two rehearsals. A versatile musician will be able to accompany people as they perform their choices but will appreciate being made aware of the chosen programme in advance so as to be able to prepare. A good idea is to have a microphone available to ensure everyone can be heard and do a sound check in advance; otherwise you may suffer from feedback. Adjust the position of loudspeakers (best in front of the microphone) and volume levels to minimize the danger of this. Make sure the microphone has a long lead so it can reach the performers.

Depending on how elaborate the whole project has become, make sure you rehearse the show as a whole a couple of times at least and time it. The rehearsals themselves can be great fun and build a sense of anticipation as the day approaches. Spend time preparing for the event. It need not be large, but it should be special, and it may be worth decorating the room, baking a cake and inviting friends. If you are really 'going to town', you may want to make some attractive costumes for the cast. A simple cape with a clasp can make a colourful outfit without complication. Have a grand finale involving the whole cast and audience in a singalong including those songs that can be enjoyed by everyone.

It can help a caring community to strengthen its common purpose if you are able to encourage staff to get in on the act. Does the porter do a tolerable Elvis impression or a Beatles song? Is there a Sinatra or Gracie Fields in the kitchen? Will the priest perform *Albert and the Lion* or give a recitation of poetry? This kind of involvement is *not* wasting staff time, it is using it more imaginatively than is sometimes considered appropriate! If staff are to perform, keep them under control. It is my experience that staff can sometimes let their hair down somewhat and go a bit over the top, becoming too raucous, too silly or just too loud and fast. The clients must take centre stage and you should be very careful not to transfer ownership of the event from them to others who get involved.

I knew a very successful scratch band once put together in a hospital, with a mixture of kazoos and percussion instruments. It was successful in the sense that everyone thought they were good and the participants enjoyed themselves. Only those who were really keen to play were in the band; other people were doing different activities related to the whole: reading monologues, making costumes and so on. The venue had a tradition of live performance and the staff were used to getting up and singing or acting, and nearly everyone was involved in the event in one way or another. There was a good piano player working with the band and the drummer, Margaret, played a small but real drum kit. Plenty of hard work was done by the staff to pull them into shape musically and the Withington Wanderers played to capacity audiences in Burton House for several years.

Gardening

This is an activity that should not be overlooked. Many of the large old hospital gardens and farms were tended by patients, and gardening and even farming, rightly so in my opinion, was once considered a life-enhancing element of institutional life. Gardening is an activity favoured by many older people, but this is often forgotten in homes and hospitals where professional gardeners work the grounds. Many people come to enjoy gardening greatly as they get older, whether they have an allotment, a vegetable patch, a display of bedding plants or spring bulbs. It can act as a very suitable setting for all the benefits and potential for achievement sought by the activity organizer.

Gardening gets people out into the fresh air and it can be creative, interesting and immensely satisfying to choose plants and tend them to maturity. The rich perfumes and fresh tastes of home-grown produce are one of the great pleasures of life. You may have to consider building raised beds that can be reached easily from a wheelchair and the heavier work will have to be done by one of the youngsters. People could have their own little patch and, remember, many vegetables and flowers are suitable for growing in containers. Herbs are easy to grow and have the added bonus of taste and aroma. They will grow indoors, as will bulbs and lots of other plants. If access to outside is lacking, you can make a garden inside.

In the generally warm environment of homes and hospital wards, with care, you should be able to produce some exotic specimens. It would be so restful and soothing to be able to go into the conservatory and sit in the cool and humid shade of living and aromatic plants. What a respite this could be for those who are frightened, tired or depressed. Think about the possibilities.

Day trips

For people who do not get around much, the chance to get out can be a welcome relief from everyday routine. It can also become an almost intolerable ordeal. We have all done it — crowded into a noisy minibus and travelled for hours wanting the toilet and feeling a bit travel sick. I have accompanied some very unhappy people out for their annual jaunt. To avoid this kind of scenario all you have to do is be prepared:

1   Do you really have to travel so far? Many places have local areas of beauty and interest that we tend to forget or take for granted.

2   Make sure there are adequate staff or helpers and do not go in a big group. (The frightened and pitying looks that massed ranks of wheelchairs can attract can be quite unpleasant.) Travel if possible in small groups, so that there is the time and opportunity to talk to each other, and ensure that the people involved know where they are going and why.

3   Allow plenty of time for tea and rest rooms and, if you are hiring a coach, make sure it is going to be suitable for your needs: accessible, spacious and with air conditioning.

4   While out and about, draw attention to subjects of interest, such as outstanding and historical buildings and beautiful scenery.

5   Take into account different likes and dislikes. If, for example, you are by the sea, some people will love to sit quietly and take in the air. Others will much prefer a hot dog or a candy floss, followed by a flutter on the slot machines.

6   Check the accessibility and policy on group visits of the places you intend to go to. It is more than frustrating to turn up and be unable to get in without making prior arrangements or, worse, getting turned away because they are unable to accommodate disabled people. Some places will welcome groups only with advance notice and may even, if forewarned, provide refreshments and escorts.

   (As I write, saying so confidently that there is no need to travel very far from home, on my wireless comes a story about residents of an old people's home who have just returned from an exchange visit with a residential home in France. As the man said, it was very cost-effective because all the appropriate facilities were already there. Come to think of it, a few years ago I went to Lourdes with a group and we had the time of our lives. I went as a volunteer and raised the fare by asking everyone I knew for a contribution. All things are possible.)

Debating society

Old people are young people who have grown older and in any residential or hospital community you will find people with all kinds of interests and approaches to keeping themselves stimulated. For the more intellectually inclined, you might consider starting a debating group that will meet regularly to thrash out different issues of concern to society at large. Your aim is to create an opportunity for people to express their knowledge and intellect through constructive discussion. This could be a positive way of engaging those who find it 'difficult' to tolerate some of the less communicative clients or find the general level of intellectual activity undemanding.

It can be particularly interesting to associate relevant events from past times with issues that are topical at the current time. Politics, religion, sport, scandal and changing values are always good subjects for debate. You could discuss issues associated with ageism and consider the political and social influences affecting hospitals or residential care and the way these have changed over the years.

Scan the papers, local and national, for ideas. Do not only associate topics with people's chronological age but also raise issues that are controversial and topical in the present. Encourage opinion that is reinforced by knowledge and experience. It may be helpful to have an authoritative 'chair' to mediate and ensure everyone gets a fair chance to make their point.

Good practice: a summary

The main points of good practice for organizers of activity programmes are as follows:

1   Participate yourself.

2   Spend time learning how to do it; involve people who do know how to do it, and work alongside them.

3   Make events part of a continuing process of involvement and interaction. Remind yourself that the aim is not simply to make music or a piece of art, to go on a trip or take in a show. The activity is part of a process that creates opportunities that enable people to make decisions and make choices; to be recognized, acknowledged and stimulated; to be individualistic and/or part of a social group; to express something of their own tastes and interests; to be reinforced; and to have a satisfying and enjoyable time, with particular emphasis on the last one.

High Dependency Settings

MANY ACUTE DISORDERS CAN be diagnosed and treated effectively and the sufferer helped to return to normal or at least helped to manage distressing and disabling symptoms. Other illnesses and injuries can have tragic consequences, leaving the individual in need of long-term and continuing care. Especially upon reaching a great age, a person may acquire multiple disabilities and associated symptoms. The more serious psychiatric disorders will require professional therapeutic intervention.

In this book it is not possible, and not necessary, to examine in any great depth the different symptoms and illnesses usually associated with old age. Generally, I would suggest it is often better if the reminiscence worker does not know too much about the details of someone's clinical condition, so that they do not try to adapt their responses to the illness rather than to the 'wellness' of the individual. Also, as I have said elsewhere, elderly people are often stigmatized and labelled in terms of what is wrong with them and reminiscence and arts activities are situations where they should be relatively free of clinical attention. There are times, though, when a general understanding of some of the implications of disabling conditions will help a practitioner to respond more effectively to clients and patients.

Stroke

Stroke is one of the most serious and baffling illnesses that can afflict anyone. The brain damage caused by a stroke can have quite bizarre effects. A person may find their own behaviour inexplicable: for exam-

ple, emotional sensitivity may be heightened, or there may be awareness on one side of the body only. Speech can become absent, slurred
or incomprehensible. There can be personality changes or exaggeration of existing traits. A person may experience being trapped inside
themselves and, although their inner self is aware and conscious of
what is going on around them, they become unable to react, articulate
or express themselves — or their expression becomes inappropriate
and incomprehensible. A man who had recovered from a severe stroke
told me of his intense frustration as he sat there, frozen, while people
talked to him as if he were stupid, talked about him as if he were not
there, and assumed he did not care. And he could do nothing to challenge these assumptions.

A stroke is sudden, possibly disabling a fit, healthy and independent individual in an instant. This can be very traumatic for the sufferer and for the family. There is no gradual process of deterioration
which can allow at least some opportunity to come to terms with what
is happening to you or one that you love.

It is understood that for people who are recovering from a stroke
one of the greatest hurdles to overcome is an extreme apathy caused
by a fundamental loss of confidence in oneself. This can often be a hindrance to learning to cope and to getting better. Involvement in reminiscence sessions can help a person regain confidence, practise speech
and communication, practise social interaction, practise paying attention and practise listening, so rebuilding confidence and social and
motor skills. Remember: *the reminiscence worker's role is not to teach
someone to speak* (leave that to the therapist) *but to create an opportunity for them to communicate*. You are not rebuilding their confidence;
you are creating a context in which *they* can rebuild their confidence.
You may have to practise communicating yourself, perhaps also using
a writing pad, and may have to learn to interpret what is said, helping
to articulate and express as effectively as you find possible. It can feel
somewhat embarrassing not to be able to understand the words someone who has had a stroke is trying so hard to say, and the temptation
to agree in an indeterminate manner can be very strong. For example,
if you are being asked for a glass of water and are trying to be polite
you reply, "Yes, isn't it?" The situation is perplexing enough without
adding further confusion. We should all try to avoid this, although I

suspect we have all done it. No-one is going to criticize you for trying to understand, although people may become frustrated and angry when they cannot be understood. Try to make sense of what you hear: you may be able to ask questions and, with inspired guesswork from 'yes' and 'no' indications, work out what someone is trying to communicate. If in the end you are, regrettably, but understandably, unable to make sense of what is being said, be honest: "I am very sorry, but I cannot understand what you are saying to me." Try again, without embarrassment, as experience of the individual's way of using language may make communication easier in time. Try other ways of communicating, for example by using pictures. I watched once with fascination as a music therapist taught, with some success, how to sing as a substitute for speech. It sounded strange but worked!

Stroke is unpredictable and mysterious. I recall an old man who had recovered from a severe stroke which had left him frozen. He recovered so well that he gave lectures to care staff about the experience. This rational man told us emphatically that he knew beyond any doubt whatsoever that his father visited him, sat on his bed and reassured him. Who are we to dismiss this reality? His father certainly helped him through this crisis more effectively than anyone else could.

Depression and anxiety

Depression and anxiety are generalized symptoms commonly experienced by older people in care. There are a variety of causes of these conditions, with great variance of degree. Conditions may be considered acute or chronic depending on the cause, duration and nature of the problem.

Depression and anxiety are common amongst elderly people and 15–20 per cent of us are likely to suffer some degree of depressive illness during our declining years. Pessimism, low mood, low activity, loss of appetite, insomnia, loss of interest, loss of weight, constipation, increased somatic concern (concern with bodily functions), hypochondria and increased dependence on others can all be symptoms of depression and indicate a need for medical attention and treatment. Anxiety, which can be a symptom or a cause of depression, may, when extreme, express itself through phobias, fearfulness or panic attacks.

Both depression and anxiety, which are frequently interrelated, can often be reduced by dealing with the cause, if necessary with drugs or appropriate therapeutic intervention and by making positive changes to care procedures.

It is important to recognize that depression and anxiety can be a reaction to the difficult transition from independent and self-regulated living to residential or hospital care. They can be reactions to grief, separation from family and friends, loss of independence, purpose and social standing and physical and mental deterioration. Although to some extent it may be considered normal to react to negative experiences in this way, it is crucial to recognize that most elderly people do not suffer from extreme psychiatric disorders. Such difficulties must be considered, not as an inevitable consequence of ageing, but as problems that have a cause and therefore, potentially, a solution. We must try to ensure that help is available that enables people to deal with issues associated with old age so that depression or anxiety states do not become chronic psychiatric disorders. It is equally important that every possible attempt is made to ensure that the care being given and the environment in which a person spends their time is not exacerbating avoidable unhappiness and dislocation.

Sometimes people who have lost control of their affairs will worry persistently about a matter that is simple to resolve and a little information may help them understand that the problem is being dealt with. Remember, too, that concern may be about things that happened many years before. Try very hard not to be judgemental and do not treat their difficulties as trivial. Even if you cannot do anything about a problem directly, just being able to share the burden may provide some relief. Continual reassurance may be necessary, but people who are clinically depressed do not usually need 'cheering up'.

Taking into account the cause and degree of depression, you will have to work out, with the client, what activities would suit them best. For some people, although they may have initial reservations, something lively and social may be just the tonic they need. For others, especially where the depression is accompanied by anxiety, a lively social occasion will be exactly what they would hate most of all. It is probably best, at least to begin with, to work for a short time on a one-to-one basis, so that you can really concentrate on what the problem is for this person. Very gently, you may explore their feelings and concerns. A life history exploration could be a good idea, enabling you to help someone recall times when they were not depressed. Thinking of those you have loved and who have loved you, of the things you have achieved, the obstacles you have overcome, even if accompanied by sadness and regrets, can help to revive emotional activity. This can sometimes begin to alleviate the sense of being emotionally 'stuck' which often characterizes chronic despair.

Listening to some profound and moving music, being brought to tears by the sight of young children or animals, artistic expression, reminiscence and experience of the effects of nature and beauty can help the inner person tentatively to let a chink of light into a darkened room. A change of environment, or even a thoughtful response from someone who makes it clear that they matter, will sometimes reach through the veil of despondency. Then, perhaps after a release of tears and emotion, the individual may want to relax and make some contact with others, *gently*, because they may still be rather fragile.

When depression is chronic and does not respond to tender loving care, it may be that drug treatment, professional counselling or even psychotherapy is indicated.

I don't really remember much about being in hospital until one day, it was Autumn, I was sitting outside in the gardens. It was just before I was discharged and I sat there on a form with my coat and scarf on. Suddenly I saw the leaves tumbling off the trees, the colours of them. And I thought, what a wonderful world I was living in. I saw all the trees and the grass, the sky, everything, and it was as if I was seeing it all for the first time. It was just wonderful, it changed me, that experience, all of it. I don't think anyone can really understand mental health problems unless they've experienced for themselves what it is like to be there. (Anon, *Window on Winwick*)

Confusion and dementia

Confusion is a word used to describe a group of symptoms of different illnesses. In cases where onset has been sudden, or 'acute', and mental function was previously considered normal, it is essential that the underlying cause (which may well lie outside the brain) is identified and treated quickly. If mental deterioration is 'chronic' or progressive, occurring over a period of time, and there is no other apparent cause, the problem is usually associated with organic brain disease. Severe chronic confusional states tend to be linked to dementia. Some dementias are reversible, others not, and Alzheimer's disease, which is not yet curable, should only be assumed when all other possible causes, including depression, have been investigated. Be aware that drug treatments themselves can cause confusion.

Confusional states are symptoms that are often associated with disruptive or apparently inexplicable behaviour, reduced attention span, memory loss and intellectual deterioration. Degrees of alertness may range from apathy and drowsiness to hyperactivity and this may fluctuate greatly, including, importantly, periods of lucidity. Although the majority of elderly people do not suffer from chronic symptoms such as dementia of the kind associated with Alzheimer's disease, it has been estimated that one-third of residents in non-specialist residential care could be described as being moderately or severely confused.

The 'mentally frail'

As changes in legislation and expectation lead to the contraction of long-term institutional care, those who have psychiatric or cognitive impairment, suffering from dementia or severe confusion, those people we may call 'mentally frail', will almost certainly continue to be cared for in long-stay hospital or nursing home settings. The proportion of confused and dementing patients in care will become very high, with increased demands put on the nursing and care professions to devise ways of responding to the emotional needs of these people. In an area of work where a high level of physical care is required, demands on staff are already, and will increasingly be, very intense.

It is not accepted that reminiscing, as an activity in itself, directly influences the progression of the disabling effects of dementing types of illness or that it can directly improve memory. What it can do is help focus effort on areas where achievement is possible, such as the use of long-term memory, recognition, emotional contact and creative expression. Often residents can be excessively dependent and withdrawn and not show any interest in participating in activities that are available. This may be because of genuine lack of interest, lack of confidence, no understanding of what is actually being asked of them and, sometimes, because of the way that activities are presented and organized.

I have done similar work with elderly people before. I was initially disappointed that the residents seemed reluctant to make decisions about the work, make uninvited contributions, or progress independently. However, I think these things did begin to happen as the residency progressed. I adjusted to people's individual capabilities and they gained confidence.
(Maggie Warren, Artist in Residence, Ringshill Nursing Home)

The perception of what is 'appropriate' is sometimes determined by staff in a very narrow sense and activities may be considered a waste of time and approached without any real thought and design: "Oh, our people can't do anything" is frequently a response to suggestions for projects. Sometimes staff will resist activities that might make people, seemingly, more difficult to manage because they have been stimulated or encouraged to make their feelings and opinions known. Sessions based on reminiscence may be seen as of no value to people whose memories are severely impaired. There is, however, a general acceptance that altering the nature of the environment, and here I mean the overall context of care, can have a positive effect on well-being. Atmosphere can influence mood and reminiscence work can increase the level of communication between carer and cared for.

We must acknowledge that living in care, however well managed, can have an adverse effect on an individual. Someone who is inherently passive will probably appear settled and adjusted relatively quickly and will be seen by staff as helpful and co-operative. They may, in fact, be pliant and submissive. A person who has always been fiercely independent and highly motivated may experience intense frustration and resentment and will probably be seen as 'difficult' as they strive to retain a degree of control, however confused, over their daily lives. There may be personality changes, exaggeration of existing personality traits or a resistance to increasing dependency that at times brings the older person into conflict with care staff and other residents. In order that a spiral of struggle does not arise, it is important for staff, through professional training, to understand what lies behind perceived behaviour problems and to respond carefully, humanely and creatively. Usually, experienced and sensitive care staff can learn how to negotiate the delicate balance of control and forbearance required to deal responsibly with such conflict.

I take it as self-evident that a degree, at least, of the loneliness, frustration and emotional unhappiness too often associated with mental frailty can be mitigated by thoughtful attention to the environment and warm, responsive behaviour from others. Some of the behaviour we view as difficult is caused by the nature of the places in which we keep people and the way we look after them. It is the interpersonal environment — that is, the way people are treated — that is most amenable to exploration by care staff. Quality of care lies predominately in the *process* of care, the way that people do things to another. The quality of interpersonal contact between nursing staff and patients with cognitive problems is often less than ideal and not usually considered of great significance. Anyone who has spent time on a 'psychogeriatric' ward will recognize this.

It need not be like this. It is a perfectly legitimate component of nursing practice to influence the interpersonal experience and the environment of patients in order to maximize individualized care and attention. It is all right to spend time with people. The cultivation of a positive approach that confirms and comforts rather than alienates can have a beneficial effect for everyone. The way someone is treated will have an effect on their behaviour.

In a high dependency context where there is a great deal of confusion or frailty, the process of making contact is all-important and the actual nature of this contact is not particularly significant. It is not the reminiscence, the music, the art activities that make the difference, although a variety of stimulation is desirable, but the emotional connections that are made. If the staff are motivated, some patients will be influenced by the improved atmosphere and become more responsive in turn. Staff may begin to alter their assumptions about what is appropriate and begin to appraise the nature of the caring process. A good atmosphere will improve everyone's well-being.

Care staff must be encouraged and trained to interact with patients with a positive attitude and with regard for dignity and individuality, despite the limitations of the patients' ability to be responsive. They should aim to create an atmosphere of mutual trust and respect, with clear expressions of human warmth and consideration. Opportunities to share emotional experiences will help to lessen the frustrations of communal living, for staff and patient alike. Comparisons of situations where there is a high degree of interaction and stimulation with those where very little happens have shown much greater work satisfaction amongst nurses on the high stimulation wards. On low stimulation wards, care was seen as having low status and being stressful; where there was a high level of interactive activity, care was more likely to be seen as an interesting challenge requiring a duty of good practice. Raised morale amongst nursing staff can only have a positive effect on work practices and patient care, and it is likely that the kind of management approach required to bring about a high stimulation or 'therapeutic' environment will help develop positive attitudes amongst staff.

Little research and experimental work has been carried out to explore, in depth, the effects of change in the physical or interpersonal environment. The discovery of creative and innovative solutions to the emotional concerns of the mentally frail is restricted only by the limits of our imagination. Consider the importance of the following:

- Colour schemes and artwork that could help ease disorientation: for example, clear, but attractive, identification of dining areas, toilets, bedrooms, communal and personal spaces.
- Space and light that help calm and relax (a sense of inhibited, cluttered personal space can cause aggression and frustration).
- Minimizing unpleasant noise and echo that is disturbing and irritating.
- Quiet areas where people can go to be private and alone to calm themselves and to not affect others when feeling frustrated or angry; places amenable to reflection, meditation and peace.
- Familiar, pleasant and interesting surroundings that may help lessen confusion and increase stability.
- Landscaping and innovative design that can make the experience

of encountering a 'safety barrier' feel less like entrapment: the inevitable boundaries of a space can be designed to feel like a satisfying place to arrive rather than an unpleasant restriction.

● Ensuring that inappropriate medication is not the cause of so-called bad behaviour.

Lucid Moments

She stands
with her hand
on the handle
of the door
waiting.

Is she hoping?

Ah, there's a question.
But she's clearly waiting

for someone to unlock the door,
let her go home;

would stand there
for hours
if they left her
alone.

Tree gnarled
shrunk
in the fifty years

but can even now
in her lucid moments
relate —
That's the term,
relating,
talks of the cottage

outside the village
where she and her brother
fed the hens every day

went to school
together

grew up

(Joan Poulson, *Window on Winwick*)

Organizing activities

I do not wish to make too much of differences between practice in residential care and what I refer to here as 'high dependency' settings involving a high degree of nursing or psychiatric care. There are differences, but they are not distinct and there is not a cut-off point between being 'sturdy' and being 'frail'.

Throughout this book I have been trying to demonstrate that we must adapt activity programmes, through knowledge and understanding, to the needs and capabilities of individuals. Suggested avenues for exploration will suit some people, seem trivial to others and will be too demanding for yet others. You must adapt possibilities to your own particular situation. There is not a special category of activities suitable for the mentally or physically frail; it is rather a matter of degree and intensity.

The most important foundation for those who organize activities with very frail or confused people must be the cultivation of a positive attitude to the challenge of this role. An innate faith that contact, however brief, made at a very fundamental level between human beings has intrinsic value can make all the effort meaningful and worthwhile.

The expectations you have of what you are able to achieve have to be modified. If, for example you are able to stimulate very little apparent direct response from a person, you will have to look for more subtle signs of encouragement such as eye contact, the tap of a foot or small changes in behaviour. These responses may, in fact, represent a major achievement for those concerned. Also any effect you have may well be temporary; as soon as the activity stops, people may return immediately to the way they were behaving before. Be careful about making negative assumptions when this happens, because you cannot be sure that, because someone appears to forget what has happened, there has not been any emotional effect. If you forget you have just eaten, you will still be full of food and take nutrition from it. It is also evident that sometimes, perhaps, more often than we tend to assume, mentally frail people are more aware of what is happening around them than they are able to express. People do respond to the fact that you are paying them attention and do react to expressions of warmth and friendliness.

Activities may have to be tailored especially to bring about interaction with you, the practitioner, and group interaction may be very difficult to achieve, if it is possible at all. You may have to continually draw someone's attention to what you are doing and you may find people will only respond while you are directly relating to them; when you turn to someone else, the first person will lose interest.

I have found that some of the most appropriate activities in these difficult situations are ones that could be considered to be directly sensory as opposed to cognitive. You may find that, for example, you observe a more immediate response to activities such as music, dancing, eating, that involve immediate gratification of the senses and direct stimulation. Bear in mind that toleration of sensory stimulation varies from person to person and may be affected by a medical condition. If you find things are too much for someone, reduce the intensity or frequency of stimulation until you reach a level that is appropriate. Some activities cause animation, whilst others are calming and soothing. This should be taken into account when deciding what is suitable. Stimuli need to be clear and unambiguous and may have to be repeated. During reminiscence sessions you may need to focus on very early memories while providing continual reassurance and demonstrating acceptance of confused or repetitive replies.

As has been discussed, the atmosphere can have a very direct effect on behaviour. If staff generally feel harassed and stressed this can be passed on and make clients disturbed or withdrawn. You may not consider you are in a position to do anything about this, but you have a responsibility to aim to create an atmosphere that is conducive to the well-being of those in your care. Encourage staff to sit with the patients, talk to them and if appropriate hold their hands. Help visitors to feel at ease and create comfortable opportunities for their involvement.

Activities may have to be simplified or broken into short sessions, but you should always remember that you are working with mature, experienced people and you must treat people as adults if you want to stimulate their enthusiasm and co-operation, although equipment and materials may have to be adapted to suit someone's capacity to succeed. Activities will be more successful when organized in very small groups with a high proportion of staff to patients, in many cases one-to-one. I stress that the main value of arts and reminiscence-based activity in high dependency contexts is the opportunity it creates for people to interact emotionally.

Examples of possible projects include the following:

listening to music together: all kinds for all moods,
singalongs,
gardening, being in the garden,
trips out to places that stimulate the aesthetic senses,
life and times reminiscence, possibly involving relatives,
handling old objects,
nature study,
clay modelling,
choosing photographs for an album,
making and looking at scrapbooks,
dancing,
making music,
religious observance, and
events involving children and animals.

Project ideas
1   Collect, from everyone you can think of, a variety of photographs of all kinds of subjects: pets, flowers, scenes, children and so on. Choose with your group which ones are to be enlarged, framed and used to decorate the room.
2   Try to find out the places that people can identify with, such as local churches, parks and schools; other aspects of interest such as sport or animals; events and occasions that they recall; then find pictures of these things or that suggest these things. Mount and

frame these to go in someone's room or near someone's 'place' to stress their individuality.

3   Either make or reproduce a good-sized map of the area, the country or the world. Identify on this where people were born, where they lived, went to school, went to work and went to church.

4   Make boards containing information about people's favoured colours, foods, animals, musicians, film stars and so on.

5   Find a spare wall and cover it with newspaper cuttings, photographs, articles, information and reminiscences, enlarged if required. Make sure this is a living display, continually developing and changing.

6   Bring in articles of natural beauty and interest — flowers, shells, wood, art, sculpture — things to touch, smell and play with.

7   Use the newspaper; read it together, following a story through; look at crosswords and horoscopes; discuss sport; enjoy cartoons; bring local, national and international events to people's attention. Look for human interest and stories that show older people involved in positive events.

Have fun; act positively and with warmth. Acknowledge people, talk to them, smile at them, sing to them. Cultivate an expressed emotional regard for people. Avoid confrontation, establish stable routines and retain a sense of humour.

I wish to mention here, although hardly doing them justice, two forms of valuable therapeutic approach often used in tandem with reminiscence work: reality orientation and validation therapy.

Reality Orientation

Reality Orientation (RO) is probably the most common therapeutic principle applied by those working with people suffering from confusion. It is a technique that aims to stimulate awareness of the here and now on a consistent basis and help a disoriented person to understand and act appropriately in response to the circumstances they are in.

Staff will be encouraged to repeat gently and confirm basic information that will help people relearn things about themselves and their environment. This process is often supplemented by orientation boards that show what day and date it is, the current weather and special events such as birthdays and holidays. If we lived in a world where each day is largely indistinguishable from another, where we cannot read newspapers and have no appointments to keep, all of us would be likely to become disoriented, so the passage of days and weeks may also be marked by regular and special activities. For example, seasonal themes and events can help people to have an awareness of the time of year or an activity session may be called the 'Tuesday Club'.

RO is sometimes considered contradictory to reminiscence work, the implication being that awareness and consideration of past experience is somehow going to impair awareness of the present. This view demonstrates a misunderstanding of both reminiscence work and RO, considering them distinct when in fact they are complementary techniques that can help a person orient themselves in both time and place while encouraging feelings of worth and self-esteem. RO, like reminiscence, has sometimes been considered of little worth after being seized upon enthusiastically in situations where solutions are few and applied indiscriminately. This can cause dissatisfaction amongst practitioners that then leads to dismissal of the whole concept of RO as something that does not work.

It is important, as with any other approach, that RO is used sensitively. To correct slavishly every factual error made by someone with dementia can be intensely frustrating for everyone concerned, possibly leading to distress as people are set up to fail. It may even be that retreating into the past or into fantasy — a form of involuntary, or even voluntary, disengagement — provides a defence against painful realizations of the present, of grief or awareness of deterioration. Thoughtless and indiscriminate use of RO techniques may cause distress if it repeatedly draws attention to unresolved and unhappy realities.

Used considerately and appropriately, RO, like reminiscence, is a valuable and useful technique if it encourages security and confidence, the use of conversational skills, participation and co-operation in social activities and an interest in the world around us. That we can orient ourselves to present concerns while drawing on past coping mechanisms and understanding in a context of interpersonal communication and support is not contradictory — most of us do this all the time.

Validation Therapy

Validation Therapy technique is, to paraphrase and oversimplify Naomi Feil's approach, a process of making contact with confused people by validating or respecting their feelings and concerns and responding to the emotional content of an inner reality, whether or not it appears to correspond to 'our' reality

The goal of validation is to allow meaningful communication that empathizes with the reality of the client, in order, amongst other things, to increase self-worth and ease distress. In practice, this can mean responding to the emotional, and possibly the symbolic, content within an interaction rather than challenging or correcting a delusion. For example, if a hospital patient is continually waiting for her mother to arrive, a common response would be to demonstrate to her that, as she is 85, her mother could not possibly be alive. This could initiate a process of grieving and, if continually applied, cause someone repeatedly to experience grief and pain as they discover for the first time about the death of their parent. A validation approach may be not to challenge but to regard this as an emotional need and respond with maternal reassurance. Another common example is repre-sented by the person who is 'waiting for a bus': perhaps they are telling us, symbolically, that they are unhappy and wish to leave.

Sometimes apparently bizarre behaviour will mime activity related to previous employment or tasks, as illustrated by a person who is continually making 'dusting' actions. I tentatively suggest that, in a context of validation, perhaps we should consider allowing the dementia sufferer to develop the fantasy/memory and explore the characters, events, thoughts and feelings which emerge.

Responding to the emotional content of an interaction is not the same thing as perpetuating a delusion and I would use as a bad example that of the nurse who, with great mirth, encouraged one of her patients to tell visitors she had a parrot on her shoulder. This is very distressing when it is obvious that many dementing people are aware of their confused state, can become very embarrassed and then compensate with aggression, withdrawal or compliance.

There is a need to broaden the general understanding of all the therapeutic techniques available to us. RO, reminiscence and validation all have a role to play in certain situations and are not mutually exclusive. They overlap and are interactive. All three techniques may be used together and they should be regarded as useful tools for those seeking to make meaningful contact with people suffering from severe confusional states.

"Can you tell me the name of the Prime Minister?" is one of a number of questions used in the UK to establish the degree of disorientation being expressed by a sufferer. Questions like this are asked to aid assessment of confusional states by identifying how aware someone is of the world around them, but they do not always take into account an individual's overall circumstances and their cultural background, or are not always asked in a meaningful context.

A comparable event in reminiscence work might be — and this happens — suddenly walking up to an unsuspecting person with, for example, a flat iron and saying loudly, "Do you remember this, Doris?" What is meant by 'Remember this'? This is not Doris's flat iron; why should she remember it? Is she supposed to have seen it yesterday? She has not thought about her ironing since coming to this strange place. Poor old Doris, who was thinking about her family or her lunch, becomes disoriented, cannot remember, is wrong all over again and feels bemused or confused. It does not really matter if Doris does or does not 'remember this'. If you are prepared to sit down quietly and communicate gently, using an object simply as something to talk about, and eventually Doris makes a little ironing movement (or not: perhaps she hums you a tune) and you respond positively ("How nice it is to spend some time with you, Doris") perhaps, just perhaps, you will have stimulated a flicker of awareness that is buried deep inside Doris because she is frightened and lonely. Perhaps, just perhaps, next time she sees the iron, or you, she will experience the pleasant feeling she had when someone was sitting with her and expressing warmth and reassurance.

Coda

You try so hard to get through to that person who sits in the corner so tightly and sadly. They turn away when you walk near, they lash out if you get too close. That person who feels they are wasting away, their strength ebbing. That person who is dragged out of bed and put to bed who used to be in charge. The woman with the ill-fitting false teeth whose child died before her. The man who saw his friends blown to pieces one Saturday in France. Those people the staff don't like too much: they are not very co-operative, so they do not really get much said to them. Those that do not ask for much, tired or spent, they do not really get much said to them either. No-one can explain what is happening: "Why am I here, where am I, when am I going home? Why am I here?"

They all wait patiently, or less than patiently. The general who has to have his bum wiped cannot understand why, every time he gets up to take a stroll, he is gently, or roughly, pushed back into his chair — a plastic chair that is painful; the eight-year-old who is 80-years-old does not know why her mother does not come to take her home; the man who is usually so fastidious about his appearance — a carefully trimmed beard and neatly tied tie — sits with shaving rash, his pyjama flies pulled slightly open; the fashion-conscious woman, always the belle of the ball, wearing what are surely someone else's nylon knickers (she would always have chosen cotton, since she got older), wonders why she is dressed in green; she hates green, it does not suit her complexion.

Someone enters the room — initially she looked up, but they never spoke to her — and she heard them say the other day, or was it years ago, that she wasn't all there. They are doctors, they must be right. He, missing his dog, couldn't remember the name of the prime minister — but he knew all the names of Manchester United.

Themes

IT CAN HELP YOU AND GROUP participants to focus, during a single session or for more elaborate projects, if you work to a theme. A theme needs to be interesting and to offer potential for exploration — subjects that have qualities that are likely to be associated with memorable activity. Usually, instead of concentrating narrowly on a specific idea, you will try to use a theme to create various opportunities for contributions. So, for example, if you are talking about occupations, you will not only discuss the nature of work but also ask about how people travelled to their workplace, pay and conditions, what time they got up, what they had for dinner and who made it, what they wore and suchlike. You may decide to talk about someone's education, career and responsibilities. A theme acts as a channel for an exploration that brings the past into the light of the present. It needs to be broad enough to have relevance to everyone in the group and at the same time specific enough to create a framework that encourages focused discussion and activity.

When using themes in sessions it is perfectly acceptable, in fact it is part of the process, to drift from a chosen theme or to change tack altogether. You can always bring attention back to the original subject if you feel the scope of what you are discussing has become too dissipated. It is also an element of the process deliberately to compare differences in people's experiences, to compare views of how things are now with how they were in the past and, if appropriate, how they were in this country with the way they were in another country. Reminiscence by its nature rises and falls, meanders and explores, moving from the past to the present and back again as one association leads to another. It is important to guide this motion, rather than try to control it. Themes simply provide a loose and common structure for discussion and activity, helping people to focus their recall on comparable and possibly previously unexplored areas of interest. They act as a starting point for all kinds of endeavour and help you seek out related resources in a disciplined way.

You may choose a wide-ranging theme, such as our town, rural life or schooldays, that allows for contributions about a variety of aspects of life from all kinds of people, including the opportunity for comparison with the way things are now. A very specific theme might be associated with traditional celebrations or anniversaries and dates. You could, for example, concentrate on the lighter aspects of romance and courting as Saint Valentine's Day approaches. The anniversary of Beethoven's birth might be an occasion to listen to some classical music, or Burns Night to listen to some Scottish poetry. There is a variety of local and national traditional festivals and anniversaries, sometimes no longer generally acknowledged, that can act as a framework for an event and an exploration of interest.

Triggers

Talking about the flat iron made Bill think about the Flat Iron pub and sparked off reminiscences of going out drinking with his friends. (Anne Braithwaite, student)

If you ever reminisce yourself, you are likely to find you have been prompted by a trigger, whether you are conscious of this at the time or not. Once a chain of associations have been precipitated you may find yourself remembering all kinds of things you had not thought of for many years and experience an almost irresistible impulse to describe and explore these. You savour the essence of a moment or a feeling from another time and place. Experience of this wellspring of emotional recall can be very enjoyable.

Sometimes memories may be crystal-clear, almost breathtaking in their clarity. Names, facts and figures are at your fingertips, details will be sharp and distinct. Other memories will be vaguely impressionistic and hard to grasp, suggestive of a flavour, a texture, a sensation or emotion from a single occasion or from a season of your life.

A trigger may be a chance thought or emotion that reminds you of something else; something you see, hear, smell, touch or taste; something that is said to you or asked of you; an experience you have that is reminiscent of another. The effective use of resources is deliberately to introduce potentially meaningful triggers into someone's awareness.

You do not need to be a fund of information about the past — the experts are there in your group — but a few meaningful references here and there can help reminiscence flow a bit better. For example, if you ask someone, "Who was your favourite singer?" you may well get the answer, "I can't remember." If you have a snippet of information, in this case a name or two to act as triggers, this — embedded in an open question — is more likely to elicit an answer. Instead of the above, you might ask something like "What did you think of Hoagy Carmichael?" and the answer might be, "Now he was quite good." You can now begin to weave a conversation. (Of course, if the answer is "I've never heard of him," you have to try again …)

It will take time and experience, especially if you are relatively young, but you will eventually get to a stage where you can talk with people about times gone by almost as if you can remember them yourself — except that you cannot ever in reality, and do not need to strive to. Most aspects of the past seamlessly blend into the present and, despite the pace of change, we can look back to our parents to see many connections with the way our grandparents lived. Some knowledge of past events and characters merely helps you to have a coherent conversation with mutually recognized reference points which can ease things along.

This brings to mind the story, probably apocryphal, of the enthusiastic young student working in rural Wales. The group consisted of very elderly women who had spent their lives toiling in isolated farming communities. Dutifully following instructions, the student passed round a picture of Wembley Football Stadium in London. None of the ladies had ever been further than 20 miles from home and memories of London were not a great talking point. (But I suppose they might have been, so no harm was done. In fact, a negative response to a trigger can provide you with indications about where to go next.)

Brainstorming

A useful way of creatively stimulating ideas and associations is by brainstorming. A brainstorm is a very simple technique that helps you to see a subject or a problem from a wide variety of perspectives and opens your mind to possibilities that might not have occurred to you.

All you have to do is list, spontaneously, all the words, thoughts and ideas you can associate with a subject, whether they seem to make any sense or not. It is crucial that no-one censors, judges or discusses the merits of anything as they come up. You make associations quickly and make sure that every contribution is written down. With a group it is helpful to write on a large sheet of paper so everyone can see the lists. Do this for ten minutes or so or until it is clear you have run out of ideas. You can then sort them into categories and discard ideas that do not have potential.

The advantage of doing this in groups is that one contribution sparks another and you often generate a variety of surprisingly different perspectives on the same subject. It is very important not to reject or discuss the subjects as they are being brainstormed and you must make it clear that contributions do not have to be clearly thought through ideas but just associations and spontaneous thoughts, however bizarre or disconnected they might at first appear. Brainstorming is an excellent technique to use when staff are preparing an event, activity or project at any point during the planning process. It can help get things going again when you are stuck for ideas and, if you let it, free your mind from considering a problem or task from a rigid perspective.

An example of the use of a brainstormed theme was the choice of *Fishing* as the context for a project in Fleetwood, Lancashire, England. Fleetwood, being a fishing port, has an industrial heritage, which meant that:

- some people would almost certainly have worked in the fishing industry or in trades allied to fishing;
- many people would have had friends and colleagues associated with the fishing industry;

- local people have an affinity with the fishing industry;
- depending on the perspective the participants take, it could have relevance to both men and women;
- there was potential for obtaining support and resources via local libraries and museums;
- the theme does not exclude those who were not directly involved, as everyone would be likely to have some kind of awareness of fish and fishing;
- the images and associations with fishing are interesting and colourful and a 'brainstorm' opens the imagination to other associated subjects:

fish — catching them, cooking them, eating them, keeping them;
fishmarkets — smells, sounds, ambience, products and prices;
seaside — beaches, seafront, seagulls and employment;
the sea — from paddling in it to sailing round the world;
the sea — its very nature, powerful, meaningful, dangerous and romantic;
boats — fishing, sailing, steam, rowing, big and small; rigging, nets, masts, funnels, the *Queen Mary*;
sailors, fishermen, fishwives;
the decline of an historic industry;
conservation issues;
shells;
goldfish;
angling;
the smell of fish.

You will probably find that, if your clients come from the same area and background, they will get down to discussing some very detailed specifics, such as fares on buses, grumpy shopkeepers and local characters. Be aware though, that is becoming progressively less likely you will find yourself working with a group who were all born and have lived in the same locality.

Try not to become so specific that the reminiscing alienates or excludes people who do not have experience of that particular place or event.

During our sessions we were focusing on Belle Vue, the North West of England's favourite playground of bygone years. It was a good subject; everyone seemed to have some experience of the place — the zoological gardens, the fun fair, the sports events — as a child or as a parent; a few had even worked there. But one lady never said a word, turned away when I tried to involve her and fell asleep much of the time. Finally, one day, and I should have done this much sooner, I sat alone with Agnes and asked her again whether she had ever been to Belle Vue. "Never 'eard of it," she said. I asked her where she was from. "Basingstoke" (250 miles to the south). And she had moved to Manchester? "Two years ago."

Consideration of the accessibility of themes you choose to discuss may have special importance when a group is made up of different nationalities. You need to choose themes that provide opportunities for all to make a contribution. Everyone has their story to tell. The following recollection could have arisen in a session about 'Where we have lived' or 'Home life', but has the potential for stimulating discussion about Africa, travel, immigration, emigration, leaving home, poverty, rented accommodation, racial discrimination, cooking, the Second World War, the street, lamplighters and thence on to other 'street' descriptions:

When I first came to England from Africa I didn't live in Moss Side, it was too posh. Later I rented a room on the top floor of a house there but they wouldn't allow me in the kitchen; I had to use a Primus stove in my room. It was about 1944 and all around you'd hear the sound of clogs on the pavements — they were flagstones not tarmac then. We had a lamplighter in the district. He used to come round lighting up the street lamps, carrying a long pole with a metal container on top. It was filled with acetylene and it took a lot of blowing out.

(George Nicol, *Those Were Dream Days*)

This next story reveals a person with experience of upheaval and travel, illustrated beautifully through descriptions of childhood toys:

> I don't remember having many toys but I had a doll when we were in Persia. Mother bought it in Tehran — the only doll in camp. Everyone wanted to play with her. They had to make a dress for her, then they could. She had evening dresses, sports dresses, everything. In India I had a little doll with a porcelain face. She had black hair that I could plait. Again she was the only doll in camp. In Italy father bought me a large doll but she got broken so she was kept in a cupboard. Then I had a black doll but I wasn't allowed to take her to school; the nuns didn't like to see me with her. (Eugene Karspinska, *Those Were Dream Days*)

Some themes, such as transport, washday and fashion, are relatively emotionally neutral. They are eminently suitable for light, enjoyable discussion and as contexts for social events. Other subjects, and this is very important, such as wartime, marriage, childbirth and the rearing of a family touch much deeper levels of feeling and are loaded with emotional triggers. *The potential for deep emotional stimulation inherent in certain topics can make them a context for intimate and profound interaction amongst the group and with the group leaders, but they require care and sensitivity in their use. Treat them with appropriate seriousness.*

We turned, laughing, as Joyce related an amusing story about her attempts to fend off fumbling adolescent advances in the air-raid shelter, to see that Harry, who had fought in the Far East during the Second World War and been rejected by his childhood sweetheart, was wreathed in tears and suffering great emotional pain. This was not a sensitive way to help Harry explore his past experiences. I am not suggesting we avoid emotionally loaded themes, and the example above could have happened in any session, but I do think we might have been a little more careful.

Some people will wisely block your attempts to lead them into 'difficult' emotional territory if the context is not right for them, and we must respect this. Just be sensibly cautious and aware of the effects of what you are doing and saying. When considering development of a theme, you will need to take into account the background of participants, the culture of participants, the gender of participants and the age of participants.

I am sure I must have made it clear by now that 'old' people are not all the same age. Consider the following facts about two 'old' people.

One 'old' person:

born in 1915, during the First World War;
aged ten when the Chicago Department of Health announced that the new craze of crosswords was good for our health and happiness and the federal government in Australia promised loans to state governments totalling £34 million, primarily for an estimated 450,000 British settlers;
aged 15 when nylon was invented;
aged 21 when the *Queen Mary* made her maiden voyage from Southampton to New York, the Spanish Civil War started and 20,000 Monopoly sets a week were being sold in the USA, 7,000 people queued up in London to see the first ever talking pictures on television, the Jarrow marchers walked to London and Jesse Owens was the (almost) undisputed star of the Berlin Olympic Games;
aged 24 when the Second World War started and 30 when it ended;
aged 40 when commercial television started in the UK, James Dean and Albert Einstein died, Marilyn Monroe starred in *The Seven Year Itch* and *Lolita* was published;
aged 42 when Bill Haley came to London, Elvis was drafted and when Russia was first into space.

Another 'old' person:

born in 1930, the year the first pea was frozen;
aged nine when the Second World War started;
aged 18 when the NHS was founded in the UK, Gandhi was assassinated, the Berlin Airlift began, Donald Bradman played his last cricket Test Match, Harry S Truman was elected president of the USA, and Alfred Kinsey reported that 56 per cent of American men had been unfaithful to their wives;
aged 24 when rationing ended in Britain, Queen Elizabeth visited Australia, Roger Bannister and John Landy ran a mile in less than four minutes and Ava Gardner was the 'Barefoot Contessa';

aged 32 when the Beatles recorded *Love Me Do* and 39 when the first man landed on the moon;

aged 40 when the Beatles split up and Germaine Greer wrote *The Female Eunuch*.

You can play this game by using data from one of the increasingly available books that record the events of the last 100 years. I used *Chronicle of the 20th Century*, published by Longman Chronicle Communications, London.

Themes and topics of conversation

This book is based mainly on personal observations and is being written at this time in this place. I am aware that the triggers and ideas that I associate with themes generally relate to the experience of working people brought up in the United Kingdom between the two world wars. I have tried to universalize references somewhat without losing the 'flavour' I am trying to intimate. Examples are vignettes from the time of writing to get you thinking and must not be assumed to have particular meaning for any individual, generation or cultural group. And, of course, we are all getting older. Try not to make stereotypical assumptions.

To obtain information that will help you prompt your group, you should talk to them (and listen to them), talk with other people of similar age, culture and background, and read collections of reminiscences and books based on oral history.

Childhood

Childhood represents the broadest possible theme, incorporating within it many other aspects of life in times gone by. It is the one great topic that can include contributions from everybody because we all have experience of it, even if our experiences were very different. It creates a context where people can be successful with their reminiscences as, even if short-term memory is impaired, long-term memory can be crystal clear. Unless something traumatic occurred, and care should be taken with initial exploration, consideration of childhood will usually be the basis for pleasant and enjoyable recall. You may also find people able to associate this area of interest with the experience of bringing up their own children.

With a childhood games session (courtesy of Jane Bourne, Hospital Arts Reminiscence Project), you begin by discussing the games we played when we were children. You might start by enquiring about the kinds of games that did not require any equipment. You can prompt by suggesting a few, such as tag or tig, hide and seek, relievio, and so on. (Relievio is similar to hide and seek, but people who are caught can be freed from the den by a shout of 'relievio!' or 'rallio!') Games often have local names and you will want to identify these.

A game that originates from England is 'Oranges and Lemons'. Two people stand facing each other with their hands joined and held in the air, making a bridge. Everyone else makes a line and goes under the bridge, singing:

Oranges and Lemons say the Bells of St Clement's
You owe me five farthings say the Bells of St Martin's
When will you pay me?, say the Bells of Old Bailey
When I get rich, say the Bells of Shoreditch
When will that be?, say the Bells of Stepney
I do not know, says the great Bell of Bow

Here comes the candle to light you to bed
Here comes the chopper to chop off your head!

The two people bring their joined hands down in a chopping action to catch someone. They then ask, "Oranges or lemons?" The captive chooses and stands in the correct row until there are two long lines of people. The game is sometimes ended with a tug of war.

How were people chosen to be 'it'? In one example, everyone held out their hands as a fist of 'spuds'. The count went round the fists in a chant:

One potato, two potato, three potato, four
Five potato, six potato, seven potato, MORE!

That person put their 'potato' behind their back. This continued until one person was left with a potato and they were 'it'.

You can then go on to games that need 'equipment'; remember that most of this 'equipment' was found or made. Examples include hopscotch, skipping, whip and top and diablo. If you have toys to play with, allow members of the group to demonstrate or show you how to do it. It is all right if people get a bit excited and things may get rather chaotic as people suggest all kinds of other games and variations. Just make sure you do not lose control completely and try to ensure that everyone's contribution gets acknowledged.

You can have a lot of fun remembering skipping songs:

> On a mountain stands a lady
> Who she is I do not know.
> All she wants is gold and silver
> All she wants is a nice young man.
> So come in my pretty maid.

And you call in your very best friend and you skip together. Or this:

> All in together girls,
> Never mind the weather girls.
> When I count twenty the rope must be empty.
> Five, ten, fifteen, twenty!

You and your group will probably be able to think of many of these kinds of games which go back into the mists of time and have local and national variations. It can be interesting to find out which are still sung and played today and what changes have been made. You can search your own memory for examples. These traditional games and songs seem to get passed down through generations of children and there are remarkable connections to be made through time and across different cultures.

Make a box of childhood, containing a variety of children's toys such as marbles and yo-yos.

Invite a group of children in to discuss games and songs. Which are still used by children today? Ask the children to bring in some of their own favourite games. See if your group will teach the children some of the games they used to play.

Discuss with your group 'a day at school' and invite children in to interview your group and compare experiences. Questions might include the following: Was there a school uniform? What were the teachers like — were they strict? What were people good at and did they ever get punished? What was the nature of punishment when they were at school? What time did school start and finish? (You will probably find that people got up much earlier.) What was it like in the classroom? How were the desks arranged; what was on the walls? (Modern schooldays are very informal compared with in the past.)

> School was terribly strict. On sums [math] I was not very good, not in those days, and I used to get the cane for not having the sum right. They'd think nothing of caning you. 'Larking about' I was, so I was told. I didn't like sums but I tried to learn them. (Phyllis Line, *Westminster Tales*)

A reminiscence project involving children can include question and answer sessions, interviews or discussion groups and sets up a dialogue between generations. It offers fascinating insight into the similarities between children now and in the past as well as the sometimes striking contrasts. It can awaken the 'child' that is inside all of us, encouraging playfulness and vitality.

The following reminiscence contains a great deal of interesting factual information about childhood in the UK between the wars:

> When I was a boy everything was different. I'm not saying better or worse but a street was a street once; you could knock on anybody's door for help ... The first thing that comes to mind is the different seasons we as children used to have. There were weeks when we used to run ourselves silly with a toy called a garth or a hoop — the girls used to have a garth which was a circle made out of wood and they used to run along hitting it with a stick. Now the boys used to have a hoop which was a circle made out of rod iron, and to drive it along we used a stick made out of rod iron with a hook on the end. The next thing that was the craze was whip and top. The top was made of wood with a metal tip in the bottom and each child would get coloured chalk and make a

design on the top so that when it was spinning it looked pretty.

Then there was the season for marbles for boys. We would take them to school in our pockets and on our way home we would play against our mates to see how many more marbles we could win or lose. Then when we arrived home we would get told off for not coming straight home. Another game with marbles was when we would get a piece of wood and cut holes into it with the holes having numbers painted over them and see who could make the highest score. This was called an alley board — alley was our name for marbles. Another thing we used to do was collect cigarette cards until we had a set, then we sent for an album and put them in. Some would be about footballers, some about different regiments of soldiers or about trees, plants or flowers ...

You could make extra money on Saturday mornings when you had finished running errands. You'd go round collecting empty jam jars and taking them to the shops and getting a ha'penny on each. People would nearly always say, "You can keep the money for taking them back."

By Saturday afternoon our parents were getting fed up with us and in order that they could go shopping in peace they would gladly give us tuppence in old money to let us go to Saturday afternoon cinema. There would be a cartoon on called 'Felix the Cat' or 'Mutt and Geoff'; usually a cowboy film with Tom Mix as the star; then a Laurel and Hardy comedy. After the interval we would have a singsong with the words on the screen and a ball bouncing over each word as we came to it. In the end we would be singing that loud we would have no voice when we got home but we had really enjoyed ourselves.

(Norman Worrall, *Those Were Dream Days*)

Topics for discussion include the following:

- Sweets/candy: bull's-eyes, gobstoppers, root liquorice, troach sticks (UK); lifesavers, tootsie rolls, jelly beans (USA).
- Naughty games: knocking on doors and running away; scrumping for apples; tying a purse to a piece of string.

- Telephones made from cocoa tins; The League of Ovaltines.
- What to do on a rainy day? The comics that were read, the indoor games played, the radio programmes enjoyed.
- How much control and discipline was there in the home?
- Did boys and girls play together? Where and what did they play?
- How did teenagers (if there was such a thing) entertain themselves? What did you wear? When did you first shave/wear make up; get your first smart pair of trousers; put on your first pair of high heels? Did your parents approve of your clothes?

Home life

Home life was obviously very different for people, according to their class, status and income and whether they lived in a rural or urban area, in one country or another. Where experiences are similar, you can use one person's memory to encourage another's; when different, compare. For some, discussion may be about how many shared a bed while the outside toilet froze down at the bottom of the yard. For others, it may be about books they read, the cars they drove and the pets they loved.

We were always taught [to work] from the very beginning. Every child had its own job. One would fetch sticks, one would get water for the day because there was no water laid on in your home, you had to get it from a well or a pump. Another would get the coals, another would do something else. Every child had its job, one would wash up, one would dry, one would perhaps tie the baby's shoes. And you did it. There was no squabbling, you did it in big families. We were taught to do things, to know how to do things and to be responsible.

(Dorothy Eales, *Westminster Tales*)

Try lighting and heating, coal fires and the hearth, sanitary facilities (bathing and washing), washday, cooking and cleaning, decorating and decor, shopping and street vendors.

There was always plenty do to at home for my mother. I remember washday with the posser and the dolly tub and dolly blue.* She used to do all her own baking, no going to the cake shop. She did bread too; she'd have it in a big bowl, rising. She used to make bread and butter pudding, spotted dick, pies and all of that. We had all my mother's baking. Today they don't seem to know how to bake.

(Louise Broomhead, *Those Were Dream Days*)

Project ideas

1   Focus on the home that people lived in when they were little; draw it, make it with clay or describe it in as much detail as you can. How many rooms, what was in these rooms? What was outside the front door? Was there a garden, a tree? Build a complete visual or word image of a place that people remember fondly.

2   What would be in the home that is unlikely to be there now? Washing equipment: flat irons, dollies, mangles, rubbing boards, possers, washing blues, dolly blues*; gas mantles; radio accumulators; fire bellows; blacklead polish; whitewash; distemper.

3   Describe and compare typical purchases. A 'shopping basket' might include carbolic soap, washing soda, potatoes, gravy browning, flour and dubbin. A 'plastic bag' might contain washing-up liquid, pasta, mineral water, 'cook in' sauce, chips and deodorant. You could seek out some of the older products that are still available, many of which, such as butter, lard, tea and sugar, would have been purchased unpackaged. Some products today are relatively unchanged and you could try approaching some well established companies. You can purchase posters showing old advertisements.

It is important not to be judgemental. It is not up to you to express opinions on the 'quality' of someone's background.

---

*Posser — a metal plunger with a handle for agitating washing; dolly tub — a large metal tub used for doing the washing; dolly blue bag — used for whitening the wash.

Food and recipes

Unlike our modern fast food culture, with its instant exoticism and all-year-round supply, earlier generations had to be much more careful how they used and kept food that was often only seasonably available. Living through times sometimes of great poverty and often of shortages, a family mother (as it usually was) would have to feed a hungry man home from a hard day's work or job seeking and a variety of young mouths. For many it was a struggle to make ends meet and mothers would have to find creative ways to stretch meagre rations and supplies and ways of using almost every-thing in some way or other — nothing would go to waste. Until recently, refrigerators were a luxury for the affluent few and food had to be prepared and used as soon as possible or preserved by pickling, salting or drying. Methods of preserving food is a good subject for discussion.

My mother used to get bacon pieces when she could and make broths and stews with dumplings in. Sometimes, if she had any, she'd put a bit of sage and onion stuffing in the dumplings to make it extra tasty. We wouldn't have it all together though, we could-n't afford that. We'd have a plainish broth made from the stock she'd cooked the bacon bits in and save the bacon itself for anoth-er meal. You'd get as many meals as you could from one bag of bacon bits.

(*A Little Bit of Bacon, Ladywell Lives*)

Ideas of good nutrition were not so developed, with an emphasis more on 'clearing your plate' than on a balanced diet. Food, of course, was not usually highly refined and not generally packaged, being scooped up and weighed (not always accurately) by the grocer. And then there are prices to consider.

As a project, make a recipe book. Most people will have their own recipes, perhaps for a traditional dish or a wartime tummy filler, such as the following:

Wartime Recipe for Bread Pudding
Ingredients:
1lb stale bread
8oz mixed dried fruit
3oz chopped suet
¼ level tsp salt
2oz chopped mixed peel
1 level tsp ground cinnamon
½ level tsp ground nutmeg
3oz soft brown sugar
1 large egg (or reconstituted)
a little milk

Reduce the bread to small pieces and cover with cold water and steep for 30–40 minutes. Squeeze the bread as dry as possible and place in a large bowl. Beat the remaining ingredients and mix well. Put the mixture into a large greased baking tin and smooth the top. Bake in a moderate oven for 2–2½ hours until the top is crisp and golden. When cold, sprinkle with castor sugar, cut into squares and serve. If desired, serve hot with custard. (Serves 3–4)
(*A Little Bit of Bacon, Ladywell Lives*)

Have a reminiscence 'feast'. There will be favourite foods that have not been tasted for some time. There are the drinks and the sweets of yesteryear, some of which are still available, such as ginger beer, peardrops and jelly (jello). What about making some home-made toffee?

Try Food from Around the World, including exotic fruits, cheeses, saltfish, aubergines, okra, fried plantains, samosas and noodles. Only produce a small quantity to taste. If you find something is popular, you can always provide it again another time. You do not want to make everyone feel sick!

Do not hold these sessions just after a meal or you will probably not get as much interest as you are hoping for — I know this from experience! The menu consisted of old-fashioned food chosen during reminiscence sessions and was served by 'waitresses' (nurses and occupational therapists) dressed in mob-caps and black dresses with white aprons. The choices included tripe. When it came to it, no one wanted it except one lady who ate three bowls and promptly felt rather ill!

Hungry people enjoy their food
The hospital ward was on a trip to Blackpool. Mrs S, who always had her food mashed and fed to her, sat in a café and slowly but with great relish polished off, without any help, a whole plate of fish and chips.

During an American event, we brought in hot dogs and hamburgers. Everyone had some and some people had a lot, with relish and onions.

Transport
Everybody would have been involved with travel and transport in some way or another, even if they usually walked everywhere. It is the universality of the subject and the fascinating differences between how it was then compared with how it is now that make it a good subject for discussion.

There was tram [street car] lines along there, along that road to get to Armstrong-Siddley and that's where I fell down, in the tramlines. I was riding my bike, which I always did, and I was late. It was Saturday morning and I knew there was a lot of work to do. And of course I was racing along the road there hoping to get there in time and get on with my job and I skidded in the tram-lines. A man was sauntering along with a horse and cart and I fell down under his blessed wheels and a cartwheel nearly went over my shoulder. (Phyllis Line, *Westminster Tales*)

Back streets were usually empty of traffic but main urban streets could be a chaotic bustle of motorized and horsedrawn vehicles. How was traffic controlled before traffic lights and complex markings. Were there speed limits?

What were the common modes of travel? Horses, carts; trams, charabancs, streetcars, trolley buses; canals, boats and ships; steam trains; bicycles, tandems, motorcycles and sidecars; aeroplanes, balloons, airships and gliders; tractors and agricultural machinery.

Visit museums, especially those directly associated with transport. Arrange visits by someone with a vintage car or arrange a trip out on a vintage bus. Talk to your local bus company; they may have ticket machines, uniforms and so on that they will let you borrow. Go on a familiar journey again. For example, retrace the journey from home to factory, country to town. (*Be very careful if trying out this kind of activity, which can put exceptional emotional demands on the older person and is only to be endeavoured by secure individuals with adequate support.*)

The theme of transport naturally incorporates that of travel. Travel round the world or round the country. Every day for a week, or over a longer period of time, focus on a different country or part of the country. Contact tourist boards for posters and information and look for music suggesting different cultures or different places. Art projects can include the enjoyable task of making relevant decorations, such as palm trees, mountain ranges and rivers, as well as maps. Try food from these places: a taste will do. The route can be determined by finding out where people were born, lived, worked and took their holidays. Help those who have been there to explain and guide those who have not.

Make a map of the country or the world and mark all the places people have been to or come from.

High days and holidays

For working people, holidays as we understand them now, implying a stay away from home, were a rare commodity. Usually, payment was not made for time not spent working and the idea of 'annual leave' was not common for working people.

> When I started work we'd get a week's holiday at Whit Week but got no pay that week. We couldn't afford a day out. We could only go dancing on a Saturday night.
> (*A Little Bit of Bacon, Ladywell Lives*)

Days off work were often bound to traditional and religious events and festivals: Wakes Week, May Day, Rose Queens, galas and church processions, amongst others. These 'high days' or 'holydays' can be a valuable topic, especially if people have common experiences, because they will usually evoke pleasurable memories that tend to stick in people's minds. Sometimes whole communities would go off on a charabanc trip to the seaside or into the country, often organized by employers, local businesses or trade unions.

Try discussing picnics, cycling, fruit picking, brass bands, parades, galas and sports days.

In the late 1940s and 1950s, the custom of having a paid annual holiday became more widely conventional. Many villages and towns had their factory fortnight for everyone at the same time, so that industrial production was disrupted as little as possible. Crowds would steam off to the seaside or beach with their buckets and spades. Try the following subjects: boarding houses (and their landladies), steam trains, ice cream and candy floss (cotton candy), lemonade, pier entertainment, shells and courting.

Of course, later, the era of the package holiday arrived, providing an hitherto inconceivable opportunity for many people who had never been far, except perhaps during the war, to travel further afield.

Work
There was rarely much choice of employment and the occupational horizons of most were determined by where they lived, their family background and class. A great proportion of the population expected little more than to leave school as early as possible and, if lucky, go straight into the factory, into service or onto the farm. For most, expectations were low and choices limited: "I polished curtain rings and stair rods at the Works and got ten shillings a week." (*A Little Bit of Bacon, Ladywell Lives*)

The identity of men, particularly, was often inextricably wound up with their jobs. The unemployment of the Depression in the 1930s was a devastating experience for everyone, not only financially, but in terms of undermining male self-respect and dignity. To be unemployed was to be ashamed. Many women went to work — in the factories and mills, in domestic service and in shops — while at the same time having to cope with running the family home and keeping it spotless. Children were often working before they left school.

> Conditions in general were poor and work difficult. People were not expected to complain but to be grateful that there was work available. Much was often made of the strong community life and the sharing of hardships during this period. Mutual support was indeed a factor of everyday life. But with long hours, poor pay and conditions that were frequently appalling, people were worn and wasted at an early age.
> (Joan Poulson, *Ladywell Lives*)

Try discussing wages and hours of work, availability of work, conditions, 'alf timers (UK), trade unions, the boss, the workforce, getting to work and what was for lunch.

With the advent of the Second World War, as most young men went to fight, women took over occupations traditionally done by men. They worked in industry, in agriculture as land army girls (UK), on public transport and so on, in almost every situation apart from 'reserved occupations' such as mining, the docks and other heavy industry. Women doing jobs previously held by men were sometimes resented by the wives of men who were in the forces.

There was role conflict in family life upon the return of men from the war and women were expected to revert to domesticity, to hearth and home, and make way for the traditional breadwinners. If you look at women's magazines from the 1950s you will notice a very strong re-emphasis on women fulfilling the traditional role of wife and mother.

Public occupations are familiar to most people, although details will differ: the postman, the milkman, the coalman, the bread boy, the butcher's boy, the greengrocer, the pawnbroker, the doctor, the rag 'n' bone man, the lamplighter and the mobile shopkeeper.

Healthcare
Traditionally in the context of the extended family, older people have been the transmitters of advice and wisdom to the young. Nowhere is this more evident than in the realms of healthcare and the relief of sickness. Brought up at a time when there was, in the UK, no National Health Service and little available health insurance, older people today can recall when the danger of serious illness was associated with the dread of being unable to work (no work, no money, no food) and

being unable to meet the costs of calling out the doctor. Many illnesses that today are regarded as relatively trivial such as measles, scarlet fever and bronchitis, were life-threatening. Birth was usually given in the home and child mortality and death in childbirth was high, although not as high as in previous generations.

> We lived in a house that had three steps going up to it. I was always falling down them because my eyes had been bad from when I got measles when I was a year old. In those days measles weren't dealt with like they are today, I was very ill, pneumonia and all sorts of things. They almost lost me.
> (Dorothy Eales, *Westminster Tales*)

As healthcare could not be afforded, the everyday complaints of child and adult had to be dealt with at home with many cures coming out of the kitchen cabinet or from the chemist (drugstore):

> Your mother would have everything for basic needs in the cupboard. Things like powdered borax which was used for your mouth ulcers and camphor which she would stitch into little bags and you would wear one round your neck as protection against bad chests etc. You had a dose of liquorice powder every week and held your nose as you were given it.
> (Norman Worrall, *Those Were Dream Days*)

Try discussing childhood illnesses; home, traditional and herbal remedies: goose lard and brown paper, bread poultices, bacon rind for warts, cod liver oil and orange juice, bicarbonate of soda, Syrup of Figs, Bile Beans; looking after children; the district nurse and the doctor. (*Take care, as someone may have lost a child, close family members or friends through illness.*)

The Second World War
If introducing discussion about the Second World War, especially if considering using it as a theme for an event, *it is important to remember that people will have suffered great pain and distress.*
Feelings about the Second World War, indeed any war, are likely to

be complex and not particularly welcome. Reports of increased depression and stress associated with commemoration events around the fiftieth anniversary of VE Day and VJ Day highlighted this. It is right that, in debate, the issues surrounding the war be discussed sensitively, and in a serious context they should not be avoided. It is important, though, that we do not trivialize the experience. For those who lived through the war, it will have had a profound effect and have great significance. Many people, perhaps most, wish to forget and may resent and resist efforts to bring up the subject and almost certainly will not want to turn their memories into a social occasion. Remember that, however much our perceptions have been influenced by the films of Robert Mitchum or George Formby, this was a *real* war and people did not know how long it would last and how it would end. Spare a thought for those parents who were separated from their children, for those who, in combat, witnessed and participated in terrible acts of death and destruction, and for those who lost friends, family and loved ones.

Men returning from the Front sometimes had great difficulty in coping at home, perhaps finding their families had become strangers, and equally being strangers to their families. Fathers had missed their offspring's childhood, family units that had functioned well were disrupted, women and children were expected to surrender control. The survivors, and those who had a 'good war', often felt great guilt. Those who were young during the war years, in their innocence, may have enjoyed much of the experience, whilst others who were old enough to be frightened, while putting on a brave face, may have had grimmer times.

I had a friend who had young children during the War, and every time they heard the planes going over she would tell the children to get under the kitchen table and sing hymns until everything was quiet. Years afterwards, one of the children said to her, "Why don't we ever get under the table and sing hymns anymore?" They thought it was a great game, you see, and their mother said that she hoped they would never have to do it again.
(Vera Maud Randle, *Westminster Tales*)

I am not suggesting we ignore or forget the Second World War, but that we treat the memories respectfully and seriously.

As regards projects, older people will sometimes find it easier to talk about the war to children and they can pass on a warning and dispel romanticized illusions. Liaise with your local school to set up some interviews.

The music from the war can be extremely evocative but also may cause distress. Songs like *We'll Meet Again* and *White Cliffs of Dover* may bring back a profound sadness. The music of Glen Miller and the Andrews Sisters is particularly evocative of wartime.

Sometimes, a private, intimate talk about wartime experiences may be appropriate if it is initiated by the older person. You may be the first one they have told, but if you find you are getting into the realm of personal counselling I suggest, unless you are trained to deal with deep emotional issues, that you do not dig too deep. Let your clients control the degree of discussion associated with wartime.

Most subjects can be addressed in other themes. Try subjects, such as those below, predominantly associated with the home front and make sure people who saw active service are willing to be involved. Take great care.

- dancing: the Jitterbug, the Palais Glide;
- rationing, recipes, 'Make Do and Mend';
- Dig for Victory (UK);
- Churchill/Eisenhower;
- The Home Guard, Air Raid Wardens, blackout regulations, Land Army (UK);
- Propaganda: Keep Mum, Walls Have Ears;
- ITMA, *Music While You Work, Workers' Playtime* (UK).

The age and experiences of the participants will determine their attitude to talking about the war. Everyone had their own private experience of the war, as well as the 'official' version represented by myth and the media.

Cinema
From the 1930s on into the 1950s, the cinema played a large part in the lives of, particularly, town and city dwellers. Often, even for those living in rural areas, the draughty hall with its rattling projector would provide a major source of entertainment and recreation. The atmos-

phere of luxury in the big old cinemas with their art deco interiors, musty smell, the padded seats and warm, secure darkness is very evocative. (After the talkies became widespread, the tradition of starting the show with an organist continued, epitomized in the UK by the style of Reginald Dixon.)

When the Hippodrome moved to Ardwick [Manchester] they showed films there and there used to be an orchestra, Sam Brough's, at the back of the stage when the curtain went up. Then the whole stage slid forward and the orchestra played. Then there'd be the film. I remember *Maytime* with Jeanette MacDonald. Earlier than that, though, when I was younger, I saw Bing Crosby at the pictures, before he became popular. The words he was singing used to come up on the screen so that you could join in. We used to go on Saturdays and sing our heads off.
(Norman Worrall, *Those Were Dream Days*)

Unlike the calm often experienced in cinemas more recently, the 'pictures' was often packed to capacity and the audience would be noisy and excited, shouting in response to the film, cheering the heroes and booing the villains, never doubting, but not totally sure, that good would eventually triumph over evil, that the handsome prince would win the beautiful girl, that Pearl White would be saved from a speeding train. Film stars, like pop stars for later generations, were icons to adore. Styles were copied and attitudes emulated. From Alan Ladd to Boris Karloff, you will find names that bring back a glimmer of excitement from the heyday of the Silver Screen.

A brainstorm of film stars might include the following: Anna Neagle, Ingrid Bergman, Dirk Bogarde, Humphrey Bogart, Charles Boyer, Jimmy Cagney, Marlene Dietrich, Diana Dors, Kirk Douglas, Alice Faye, Douglas Fairbanks, Douglas Fairbanks Junior, Henry Fonda, Gary Cooper, Fred Astaire and Ginger Rogers, Tyrone Power, Mary Pickford, Dick Powell, George Raft, Ralph Richardson, Flora Robson, Mickey Rooney, Margaret Rutherford, Moira Shearer, Jean Simmons, Alastair Sim, Barbara Stanwyck, Robert Taylor, Spencer Tracy, Rudolph Valentino, Jack Warner, Mae West, Greta Garbo, Richard Todd, Clark Gable, Judy Garland, Greer Garson, Betty Grable, Sydney Greenstreet,

Katherine Hepburn, Leslie Howard, Betty Hutton, Gene Kelly, Frank Sinatra, Alan Ladd, Peter Lorre, Dorothy Lamour, Margaret Lockwood, Jeannette MacDonald, Frederic March, Tom Mix, Victor Mature, Laurence Olivier, Pat O'Brien.

A cinema day would make a good project. Ideally, but probably with difficulty, you might find someone with a film projector. If not, hire or borrow a large-screen video and set up your own day at the cinema. Do not just watch a film but try and create the ambience of going to the pictures. Try having an usherette to show people to their places, typical cinema music, tickets to tear in half, a travelogue or similar, a newsreel and a big feature such as *City Lights, The African Queen, The Blue Lamp, Lassie, Mrs Miniver, Red Shoes, Night at the Opera, Snow White and the Seven Dwarves, Stagedoor Canteen, Wicked Lady, Cavalcade, Wuthering Heights, Seven Brides for Seven Brothers, The Sound of Music, Paint Your Wagon*. A blockbuster such as *Gone with the Wind* could be watched over a number of sessions. Do not forget the ice cream and popcorn.

The 'reminiscence' aspect lies in the process of going to the pictures as well as in the act of watching the film.

Entertainers

Live entertainment, although inevitably on the decline with the advent of the cinema and, later, television, was a popular and widespread leisure activity. Variety theatres flourished. Stars were popular and well loved. Like today, the pop stars of the past were perceived as friends and role models. Sales of 78 records soared. The all-pervasive presence of the wireless made household names of personalities, singers, band-leaders, musicians and comics, such as the following.

In the UK: Arthur Askey, Peter Brough and Archie Andrews, Elsie and Doris Waters (Gert and Daisy), Tommy Trinder, Wee Georgie Wood, Rob Wilton, Max Miller, Tommy Handley, George Formby, Wilfred Pickles, Tessie O'Shea (Two Ton Tessie), Nellie Wallace, Sandy Powell, Norman Wisdom, Bud Flanagan and Chesney Allen, Leslie Sarony, Larry Adler, Lupino Lane, Norman Long, Ralph Reader, Cavan O'Connor, Sam Browne, Gracie Fields, Vera Lynn, Issy Bonn, Ann Shelton, Al Bowlly, Mario Lanza, Nat Gonella, Teddy Brown, Josef

Locke, John McCormack, Charlie Kunz, Winifred Attwell, Adelaide Hall (the Singing Blackbird), Reggie Goff, Yehudi Menuhin, Ambrose, Roy Fox, Henry Hall, Joe Loss, Ivy Benson, Billy Cotton and Victor Sylvester; and in the USA: the Andrews Sisters, George Burns, Bob Hope, Bing Crosby, Frank Sinatra, Dean Martin, Jerry Lewis, Sammy Davis Jnr, the Dorsey Brothers, Benny Goodman, Duke Ellington, Glenn Miller, Paul Robeson, Jimmy Durante, Ethel Barrymore, Sophie Tucker, Eddie Cantor, Helen Traubel, Peter Lawford, Al Jolson, Judy Garland, Doris Day, Connie Francis, Patti Page, Harry Belafonte, the Mills Brothers, Red Foley, Mitch Miller, Rosemary Clooney, The Weavers, Perry Como, The Platters, Johnnie Ray, Louis Armstrong, Tony Bennett, Maurice Chevalier, Trini Lopez, Nat King Cole, Mickey Rooney, Ethel Merman, Carmen Miranda and Danny Kaye.

Weddings
Weddings, marriage and relationships is one of those subjects you must treat with care, although in serious discussion, if sensitively dealt with, it can be a valuable topic, touching on some of the things that truly matter to people.

As well as those who had or have a happy relationship, there are those who never married and regret it, those who married and regret it and those who miss their companion badly. There are many women who lost their husbands during the Second World War before they had the chance to have children and who never considered marrying again, spending the rest of their lives living alone. There are those whose sexuality was unable to find expression and who were trapped by the conventional morality of the time in inappropriate relationships. And there are those who simply made the wrong choice.

There is, though, something timeless in the beauty of a bridal gown, the bouquets and the tradition. The excitement and glamour of a wedding can be shared in the real sense. A member of staff in the days leading up to a wedding can get an opinion on his or her outfit, share their anticipation and excitement and, nicest of all, invite residents to the wedding itself. I remember with great fondness the couple who called into the hospital ward with a flush of excitement on the way to their honeymoon.

I met my husband at the cinema in Altrincham. I went there one evening on my own and just happened to be sat next to him. We were courting for 15 months before we got married. That was at St Alban's church, Broadheath on April 15, 1915. It was Easter Saturday. In those days a lot of people got married in the standard holidays because they couldn't afford to take time off work. I was working up to the night before. I wore a long white satin wedding dress with a long train. I cut that off because I didn't care for it. It was a quiet wedding. My husband's brother was best man and my sister's husband gave me away. My sister was bridesmaid. She wore a blue dress and white hat. A friend made the wedding cake and we enjoyed a small wedding and reception. Later I made a christening gown out of my wedding dress for my son.
(A Little Bit of Bacon, Ladywell Lives)

Try asking about cardboard wedding cakes and icing made from chalk.

Fashion and style
This topic is interesting to almost everyone. The clothes we choose to wear and the way we do our hair are significant components of our daily lives and a statement about our individuality and our generational identity. For some people it can be a good opportunity to show off their knowledge. Listen to the detail in this:

I was one of the Denton Mad Hatters. We always used to say, "Don't walk or talk with anyone who doesn't wear a hat!" There used to be fifteen or sixteen hat shops in Denton; now there is none. When Manchester United won the cup about thirty or forty years ago our firm gave them all a hat each. They all came in the dye shop. I had blue clogs on and there I were playing football with them. They had a look around and picked which hat they wanted. They all picked French velour and snap brims except Jack Rowley the goalie. He picked a navy blue Anthony Eden.
(Minnie Dutton, *Those Were Dream Days*)

After about three months meeting weekly, the reminiscence group were discussing Saturday Night Out and were talking about being dressed in blue. A quiet voice, a voice that had not spoken in all the sessions, asked, "Have you got Evening in Paris?* You must have Evening in Paris." We eventually got hold of an old bottle and the lady ... sessions.

... les, shingling, curling ... nderwear, dressmak- ..., Brylcreem, chenille, ... Discuss utility clothes: ... ere were limits put on ... coats, sleeve buttons

... tographs and articles ... lude period clothes — ... and accessories, such ... ir slides and compan-

... nd satins, ribbons and ... ashionable and when. ... erent materials? Make

... the event of the year. ... ines, about three feet ... ifferent decades, right ... The group were very ... n as the blue lady and ... ncreasingly concerned ... nd was relieved when ... she reminded the staff

... o was in charge of the ... quite respectable past. ... ned us that there must be a crinoline lady. The figurines were unveiled, and staff, dressed in a variety of past fashions and styles, promenaded the ward, which was

*Evening in Paris and Californian Poppy were inexpensive and extremely popular perfumes in Britain.

packed with visitors, accompanied by music from the different decades. The staff nurse with the lovely speaking voice was persuaded to announce each model.

A project like this takes a lot of planning and preparation, but it is important to remind yourself that the preparation is as important as the event itself, if not more so. The event which was enjoyable and quite a spectacle, was the climax of many months' activity.

Sport
An interest in sport was, and is, always popular. Many men, particularly, retain their interest in and awareness of sport well into their later years. Of course, before television, live events, newspapers and the wireless were the source of information and excitement.

Royalty
Most, but not all, people in Britain were customarily royalist. When the National Anthem was played at the cinema, people would stand in respect, sometimes even in their own home when it was played on the wireless! The Royal Family were well loved. Try discussing royal visits, the abdication of Edward VIII in 1936, Queen Elizabeth the Queen Mother and the Coronation in 1953.

Weather and the seasons
Ask about memories of hottest days, great storms, fog, snow, ice, the winter of 1947 (UK); unusual weather, keeping warm, keeping cool and keeping dry. Talk about trees and flowers, food, seasonal activities, clothes, beautiful scenery; the harvest, Christmas, May Day and summer holidays.

Talk about *the street*: shops, street entertainers, deliveries, transport, steps and doorways, windows, lampposts and traffic; and about *bars and public houses*: games, traditions, the first beer, breweries, entertainers and characters. *Romance and courting* is a fruitful topic: discuss the 'monkey run', first dates, dancing and relationships.

Farming, Hunting, Hobbies, Worship, Smoking, Pets, Books, Radio Programmes, Jokes and Pranks, Saturday Night Out, Danger and Taking Risks — there is no shortage of potential topics.

Then and now

In reminiscence sessions you will encounter, and desire to encourage, much reference back and forth between what things were like then and what it is like now. It can be a fascinating and thought-provoking exercise to make these comparisons. Until the social upheaval caused by the Second World War, although much had changed since the turn of the century, for most people life altered slowly when compared to changes that have been seen in the last 50 years. This pace of change is one of the reasons for the popularity of, and to some extent the necessity for, reminiscence work.

One of the greatest differences between now and earlier decades of the twentieth century must be the volume of instantaneous information that is available to us from an enormous variety of sources. We take for granted easy access to information, to ideas and to each other via a profusion of newspapers, books, next-day-delivery letters, radio stations, television channels, computer networks, fax machines and telephone services. Information is bounced across the world in seconds. News of tragedy and war is on our screens as it happens, in full colour. We see how others live and are constantly exhorted to change our own lives through the acquisition of material goods. It seems to be a different world from the one when information would take days, if not weeks, to reach home and crackly signals received on a home-made crystal set or 'cat's whisker', even a telephone call, were causes for excitement.

Cinema and theatre, which so enthralled previous generations, are now enjoyed in our own homes. Our families, with a television in each room perhaps, have access to a previously unimaginable choice of sources of entertainment. We do not sing along, we do not participate, although we may interact. Entertainment is increasingly (but not exclusively) presented to us from highly sophisticated sources intending to persuade us to part with money in our millions. Spending money itself has changed: we pay with cards, we pay electronically; we pay with money that we do not yet have. Rather than simply being a means to an end, albeit a sociable one, shopping has increasingly become a major leisure activity. Shoppers are consumers with extensive choices to make and most of us take this totally for granted.

Another almost inconceivable development, of course, has been the escalating and overpowering cultural dominance of the motor car. This has dramatically altered both the environment we inhabit and the way we experience it. In the 1930s, the average distance travelled by car in the UK was about the same as that travelled by bicycle. In 1993, the distance travelled by car was 12 times greater. We are able to travel considerable distances at high speed easily and relatively cheaply, but we find our children can no longer play safely in streets which have become inhospitable and polluted. The extended family we used to turn to when we were sick, who watched our children and who 'guarded' our moral well-being, is increasingly fragmented.

Sunday, in many places, has all but disappeared as distinctive day and family structures are, apparently, less durable. We are a wasteful society, throwing away good clothes, food and products with a naïveté that would have shocked our ancestors and will no doubt horrify our descendants. We do not conserve and repair but discard and replace. We no longer know those who live around us — there are so many of us that most people are strangers — leaving us unsure who is safe and who is dangerous and so trusting each other less. We lock our doors and have alarms on our houses and on our cars.

Public morals and attitudes to 'difference' appear to have changed, or at least discussion of issues to do with race, sexuality, gender, mental illness, disability and age is more open. We are, in our private worlds, more superficially tolerant of variants of dress, custom and belief. Yet there is still strife, racism and violence, public standards are increasingly suspect and there are beggars on the streets. There are certainly fewer horses around. Has society fundamentally changed or do we just know a little more about how people really are? Perhaps we have the same old mix of personalities there has always been: those who look back with longing and those who look back with relief; those who look forward with trepidation and those who look forward with optimism.

Differences between generations are interesting and significant but when it comes down to it we make most contact with each other via the common denominators that are *shared* across the generations. We are all of the same human family with hopes and fears, with needs, interests and aspirations that make us all more alike that we sometimes will admit. We have much to learn from each other if only we will take the time to listen.

In those days it was helping, caring, giving. "Have you got any milk?" someone would say and you would give some milk. You would think, "Well, that little old lady, Miss Jane didn't get herself milk", so you would make sure she had some. There was more love and unity. What I have I give you and what you have you give me. We had some mean old folk too. There was a lady with a citrus yard, about two acres, and most of the fruits I knew that woman, Miss Kate, had — even some I didn't know. But she wouldn't let anyone take any.

When we were children we didn't think about food when we were out in the day, we could go anywhere and say, "Uncle, could I have a cane, a few oranges?" and he'd say, "Boy, go pick some." It's different for children here than it was in Jamaica because we were not bound by this or that. When I say bound, I mean everybody lived in unity. It's part of children's growth to pick and name fruit — sugar cane, coconut meat, coconut milk. Children now don't have much fun, much freedom. They don't have anything that gets them together. In our days we'd have a little party in the bush and get some people to help us and supervise. They might take us on the sea beach. At fifteen we were still playing. Now children are just locked up.

(Lucille Morgan, *Those Were Dream Days*)

Some concluding thoughts

The memories and experiences of older people, however frail the memory or the person, represent a foundation for the formation of all kinds of interactive and imaginative relationships that can help illuminate understanding of the very nature of care itself. Reminiscence work, itself an unwieldy and not very comprehensive description of a range of possibilities, does not replace or contradict elements of good practice inherent to other disciplines, but rather brings them together in a context that is essentially social rather than clinical. It is not about the past, but about the present: the direct experience *now* of old age and the caring process.

It is always difficult to justify putting resources into aspects of care that are not always considered essential because we are talking of intangible concepts such as well-being and quality of life, but if we are not to allow our society cynically to 'warehouse' those who are in need of help then it is important that attention is given not only to alleviating physical pain and discomfort but also to creating situations that allow people to experience a sense of personal meaning and a sense of being valued for themselves.

Anyone trying to establish reminiscence practice will experience resistance from those whose perceptions are defined by low regard for older people, whether these be managers, colleagues or older people themselves. No enlightened approach to care has been easily established without hostility and setbacks and we must try to do what we can in the circumstances we are in. In many situations a new way of doing things initially regarded with some scepticism will become a normal and even essential component of day-to-day living. Nursing Auxiliary Hilda Ellis, when asked to sum up the progress made with reminiscence sessions, explained how she felt closer to the patients, had more understanding of them and that they had 'become her friends'.

Working *with* older people is a two-way process requiring their help and co-operation and we can only secure that help if we have a good working relationship with them. That relationship can only be established over time and with thoughtful effort. *The quality of care of elderly people lies with the process.*

Good luck!

Appendix

Further reading

Bender M, Norris A & Baukham P, *Groupwork with the Elderly*, Speechmark, Bicester, 1987.

Bornat J (ed), *Reminiscence Reviewed: evaluation, achievements and perspectives*, Open University Press, Buckingham, 1994.

Bulman B, *Music and the older generation*, EMSA Publications, Birmingham, 1995.

Butler RN, 'The Life Review: an interpretation of reminiscence in the aged,' *Psychiatry* 26, pp 65–76, 1963.

Butler RN, *Why Survive?*, Harper & Row, New York, 1975.

Chia SH (ed), *Activities Digest*, Speechmark, Bicester, 1986 (no longer published).

Chronicle of the 20th Century, Longman/Chronicle Communications, London, 1988 (no longer published).

Coleman P, *Ageing and Reminiscence Processes*, Wiley, Chichester, 1986.

Day in Day Out, Memories of North Manchester from Women in Monsall Hospital, GateHouse Books, Manchester, 1988.

Feil N, *Validation — The Feil Method*, Edward Feil Productions, Cleveland, 1982.

Gibson F, *Using Reminiscence: A Training Pack*, Help the Aged, London, 1989.

Gibson F, *Reminiscence and Recall: A Guide to Good Practice*, Age Concern England, London, 1994.

Gillies C & James A, *Reminiscence Work with Old People*, Chapman & Hall, London, 1994.

Memory Joggers, Speechmark, Bicester, 1996 (no longer published).

Norris A, *Reminiscence with Elderly People*, Speechmark Bicester, 1986 (no longer published).

Not Only Bingo, Counsel and Care, London, 1993 (no longer published).

Osborn C, *The Reminiscence Handbook: Ideas for creative activities with older people*, Age Exchange, London, 1993.

Poulson J, 'Ladywell Lives' (1996) and 'Window on Winwick' (1994), stories and reminiscences from hospital, Manchester Reminiscence Project, Hospital Arts.

Recall Users Handbook, Help the Aged, London, 1981.

Rimmer L, Reality Orientation — Principles and Practice, Speechmark, Bicester, 1982 (no longer published).

Schweitzer P, *Age Exchanges: Reminiscence projects for children and older people*, Age Exchange, London, 1993.

Senior P & Croall J, *Helping to Heal, The Arts in Health Care*, Calouste Gulbenkian Foundation, London, 1993.

Sutton C, Psychology for Social Workers and Counsellors, Routledge & Kegan Paul, London, 1979.

Thornton S & Brotchie J, 'Reminiscence, a critical review of the empirical literature', *British Journal of Clinical Psychology* 26, pp93–111, 1987.

Walsh D, *Groupwork Activities*, Speechmark, Bicester, 1993.

Useful Contacts

Age Exchange
11 Blackheath Village
London SE3 9LA
United Kingdom
www.age-exchange.org.uk
Leading reminiscence
organization, training sessions,
publications (including a
magazine) and reminiscence
theatre company.

Arts for Health
St Augustine Building
Manchester Metropolitain
University
All Saints Building
All Saints
Manchester M15 6BH
United Kingdom
www.artsforhealth.org
National advocates for the arts in
healthcare, advice and consultation.

Bi-Folkal Productions Inc
809 Williamson Street
Madison
WI 53703
United States of America
www.bifolkal.com
Multi-media, multisensory kits to
stimulate remembering, other
reminiscence tools.

Certain Curtain Theatre Company
Unit 128
Oyston Mill
Strand Road
Preston PR1 8UR
United Kingdom
www.cctheatre.co.uk
Theatre company with expertise
in reminiscence and community
theatre.

Charles Press, Publishers
PO Box 15715
Philadelphia
PA 19103
United States of America
www.charlespresspub.com
A Loving Voice: A Caregiver's Book
of Read-Aloud Stories for the
Elderly.

Directory of Social Change
24 Stephenson Way
London NW1 2DP
United Kingdom
www.dsc.org.uk
Training in fund-raising and
management issues for small

organizations, publications listing
trusts and companies that donate
money to good causes.

Flaghouse Inc
601 Flaghouse Drive
Hasbrouck Heights
NJ 07604-3116
United States of America
www.flaghouse.com
Recreation equipment and family
fun activities.

Geriatric Resources
11636 N Dona Ana Road
Las Cruces
NM 88007
United States of America
www.geriatric-resources.com

The Hammond Care Group
Level 2
447 Kent Street
Sydney
NSW 2000
Australia
www.hammond.com.au

LIME (formerly Hospital Arts)
St Mary's Hospital
Hathersage Road
Manchester M13 0JH
United Kingdom
www.limeart.org
Leading arts practitioners in
healthcare, founders of
Manchester Reminiscence Project.

Museum One, Inc
7823 Yorktown Drive
Alexandria
VA 22308
United States of America
Slide programmes containing
artistic and human interest
questions to elicit responses.

National Council on Aging
1901 L Street, NW
4th floor
Washington DC 20036
United States of America
www.ncoa.org
Large print publications for sale or
rent, such as Discovery Through
the Humanities Series.

Nottingham Rehab Supplies
Findel House
Excelsior Road
Ashby-de-la-Zouch LE65 1NG
United Kingdom
www.nrs-uk.co.uk

The Oral History Society
c/o Department of History
University of Essex
Colchester CO4 3SQ
United Kingdom
www.oralhistory.org.uk
Research and development in
reminiscence work, oral history.

Pro-Ed
8700 Shoal Creek Boulevard
Austin
TX 78757-6897
United States of America
www.proedinc.com

Psycan Corporation
12–120 West Beaver Creek Road
Richmond Hill
Ontario L4B 1L2
Canada
www.psycan.com

Relpar Pty Ltd
Unit 2/39 Laser Drive
Rowville
Victoria 3178
Australia

Rompa/Winslow
Goyt Side Road
Chesterfield
Derbyshire S41 0SW
United Kingdom
www.rompa.com

S & S Worldwide
PO Box 513
75 Mill Street
Colchester
CT 06415
United States of America
www.ssww.com

Sea Bay Game Company
77 Cliffwood Avenue
Suite 1D
Cliffwood
NJ 07721
United States of America
www.seabaygame.com

SHAPE, London
London Voluntary Sector Resource
Centre
356 Holloway Road
London N7 6PA
United Kingdom
www.shapearts.org.uk
Disability arts organization.
SHAPE is a regionally based
federation with offices in various
parts of the UK

Speech Bin, Inc
1965 Twenty-Fifth Avenue
Vero Beach
FL 32960
United States of America
www.speechbin.com

Super Duper Publications
PO Box 24997
Greenville
SC 29616
United States of America
www.superduperinc.com

The Third Age Press
6 Parkside Gardens
London
SW19 5EY
United Kingdom
www.thirdagepress.co.uk
Large-print books and booklets to
inspire remembrance.

Willowgreen
10351 Dawson's Creek Boulevard
Suite B
Fort Wayne
IN 46825
United States of America
www.willowgreen.com
Videos with inspirational words
set to nature photography to ease
grief and loss.

Speechmark Publishing Ltd
70 Alston Drive
Bradwell Abbey
Milton Keynes
MK13 9HG
United Kingdom
www.speechmark.net
Publishers and distributors of
reminiscence materials, training
resources, activity handbooks and
ColorCards®.

Words

The words we utter are a pale echo of ourselves
but if we are lucky,
they may last a little longer than us.

Like a thread catching the light.

(Roger Sim, *Ladywell Lives*)

Also available from Speechmark

Speechmark publishes and distributes a wide range of creative resources providing exciting and appealing ideas for countless group activities. Listed below are just a few of these products – a full catalogue is available on request.

Reminiscence Quiz Book

Mike Sherman

An enduringly popular, informative and unusual quiz book for use in reminiscence work. Covering the years 1930–1969, it draws on memories and experiences of daily life and recalls major events and celebrities.

The Reminiscence Puzzle Book

Robin Dynes

Spanning the years 1930 to 1989, this is a highly practical and enjoyable puzzle book produced in a photocopiable format. It covers events, people, entertainment and everyday life and is designed to encourage group participants to recall and discuss their own personal experiences.

Winslow Quiz Book

A well organized resource that contains more than 2,000 questions categorized into 40 stimulating subjects.

Musical Quiz on CD

Listen to the first few bars of each song and then – Name that Tune! This game, guaranteed to stretch the mind and bring back many memories, contains 80 different melodies on two CDs.

Creative Games in Groupwork

Robin Dynes

Offering the opportunity to create a balanced programme, this well-organized and easy-to-use book contains scores of ideas for both indoor and outdoor games. Ideas include: Introduction & mixing exercises; Games using gentle movement; Exuberant games; Puzzles & brain-teasers; Verbal games; Pen & paper games and many, many more.

Musical Bingo

Add variety to your bingo sessions with this musical version. This boxed set contains 20 different game cards, a CD with songs, counters and instructions. Songs include *Silent Night, Jerusalem, Loch Lomond, Blue Danube, Wedding March, Que Sera Sera* and *We'll Meet Again*

For further information or to obtain a free copy of the Speechmark catalogue, please contact us.